Why Public Schools?
Whose Public Schools?

WHY PUBLIC SCHOOLS? WHOSE PUBLIC SCHOOLS?

WHAT EARLY COMMUNITIES HAVE TO TELL US

DAVID MATHEWS

NewSouth Books

Montgomery

NewSouth Books
P.O. Box 1588
Montgomery, AL 36102

Library of Congress Cataloging-in-Publication Data

ISBN 1-58838-110-2

Design by Randall Williams

Printed in the United States of America

TO

DAVID CHAPMAN MATHEWS

AND

LAWRENCE ARTHUR CREMIN,

MY INSTRUCTORS IN HISTORY.

I HAVE NO WAY OF KNOWING IF EITHER WOULD THINK
THAT THIS IS THE BOOK I SHOULD HAVE WRITTEN. YET I
AM CERTAIN IT IS ONE I COULD NEVER HAVE WRITTEN
WITHOUT THEIR INSPIRATION.

CONTENTS

Acknowledgments

I AM INDEBTED to far more people than I can recognize here, particularly to the research assistants at the Kettering Foundation. Though most had never been to Alabama, they cheerfully combed through mountains of census records, legislative journals, and local histories. No one was more helpful than my administrative assistant, Angel George Cross, who produced endless drafts and created the review copy of this book. Judy Suratt, my friend and editor for more years than either of us will tell, was the principal editor, ably assisted by Melinda Gilmore, who was also responsible for preparing footnotes and double-checking facts.

Wayne Flynt at Auburn University, Hardy Jackson at Jacksonville State University, and Bob McKenzie of the University of Alabama were generous with advice about state history. Jay Higginbotham (who better?) at the Mobile Municipal Archives was my authority on Mobile history. Winston Groom, whose roots go back to the earliest settlers of south Alabama, called my attention to some excellent sources. Attorney and scholar David Bagwell, one of my former students, tutored me in legal history.

The always helpful staff in the reference section of the Alabama Department of Archives and History (ADAH) supplied reams of documents. Many were located by Ken Barr, a very diligent researcher.

I am especially grateful to Superintendent Gerald Stephens and Julia Ann Deas for making the Clarke County records available. Harold Dodge and Colette Martinez opened the Mobile school board minutes, and Penny Dendy tracked down obscure references in them.

When the manuscript was approaching final form, more than fifty prospective readers, along with my wife, Mary Mathews, reviewed the draft and made helpful suggestions. I can't thank them enough for their time and care. I am equally indebted to those who supplied details of county history and to my colleagues at the Kettering Foundation who helped analyze the quantitative data and read early drafts. I recognized their contributions in the footnotes.

In the early 1800s, people would have seen their world in sketches like those in *Harper's Weekly*. Adapting the same style, Dick Simms made sketches of the people and places mentioned in this book. He drew on illustrations from *Harper's,* portraits, photographs, and other sources. In a few cases, he had to imagine a scene using written accounts and photographs of similar settings. His contribution enlivens the pages that follow, for which I am grateful.

Finally, as we were deciding on a publisher, I was pleased to hear from Suzanne La Rosa and Randall Williams of NewSouth Books, whose enthusiasm for producing works that contribute to a new and a better South is unmatched. I admire what they are doing and count myself fortunate that the book attracted their interest.

Introduction

DESPITE EVIDENCE that parents like their local schools, many Americans are convinced that the public school system is failing in its most basic responsibility—to provide good instruction for all. And that perception is prompting reforms ranging from standardized tests to vouchers, changes that some believe are crucial to saving the schools and others worry will undermine public education.

Even worse for the long term, many schools may be losing their ties to a citizenry willing to consider the well-being of common education as a common responsibility. A few years ago, Kettering Foundation research found a number of people who don't equivocate in saying that the public schools are not their schools. Maybe that attitude tells us something about the public as well as the schools. For example, some without children enrolled may argue that schools are the parents' responsibility. Parents, on the other hand, may see the schools as tax-paid utilities, somewhat like the companies that provide gas and electricity. As consumers, their job is to watch educators the way they would watch a cashier counting change. Their children sometimes develop the same attitude and think they should help their parents "keep the teachers in line." This way of thinking reflects people's frustration; it shows the extremes they feel they have to go to in order to influence the schools.[1]

Who Is the Public?

How did we get to this point? Whose schools are the public schools, and who is ultimately responsible for them? How did we come to have the schools we call public and why? No one responds to questions like these without some prior assumptions. Mine are that the public schools are the public's schools and that the public wanted them because it can't do its work effectively without them.

But who or what is "the public"? I'm worried about the partial and limited answers I hear—that the public is just a body of voters or taxpayers. Though important, voting and paying taxes aren't all that it takes to make this country work as it should, and they certainly aren't enough to sustain a system of schools that has to be both open to all and beneficial to all. I worry even more about the tendency to treat the public as merely a body of consumers.

My definition of the public begins with citizens—specifically citizens deciding and acting together to promote their common well-being—people actively exercising these collective capacities. In plain English, our collective capacity is the ability to get things done by joining forces with others. One assumption I *would not* make is that such a public is always out there waiting to be engaged. We have a capacity to be a public but that potential has to be turned into a reality.

What are we capable of when we join forces, and what does it look like when we act together? While there are any number of places to search for illustrations, I decided to study how some of the first schools were established in hopes of finding examples of people exercising their powers as citizens. That is, I looked at the origins of the first schools in order to learn about the characteristics of the first public. Schools have to have places where teachers can teach, so I asked, "Who built the buildings?" Raising a new generation also involves making difficult choices about who should be educated at the expense of the community as well as what level and type of instruction children should have. Who made those decisions, and how? The textbooks students read, even how they were examined, I thought, might say something about what the public was like.

I drew heavily on the grainy details of local history to try to make "acting collectively" less abstract. That's important. Today, people have difficulty imagining themselves in the public, and when the public is invisible to itself, citizens lose faith in their ability to do something about the problems that frustrate them. I also wanted to experiment with taking some notions about the public found in political philosophy and see if I could put a human face on them.[2]

You might think of this book as a travelogue of a search for examples of the historical public in action. I didn't set out to marshal proof that there was indeed a public but rather to use people and events from the past to illustrate the collective capabilities we have as citizens, to show how those were used to provide education, and to describe the kind of relationship between communities and schools that developed as a result. Since the objective wasn't to write a history of either a particular period and place or of schools, I didn't deal extensively with many of the issues of interpretation that properly concern scholars. That said, I did propose a few hypotheses that historians might find interesting to explore, and I left a trail of notes.[3]

STORIES FROM EARLY ALABAMA

As a setting for the search, I chose Alabama between the last years of the eighteenth century and the middle of the nineteenth century—concentrating on six counties in the lower southwestern part of the state. I grew up in that area and have been browsing through its history for a long time. Every now and again, I stray over county lines or go beyond the time frame for a particularly good story. Or I use an account of what was happening in the state at large in order to give a sense of what was probably happening in the southwest. Still, most of the stories in the book come from the six counties, especially Mobile, which has the most comprehensive records of its schools. While I had to restrict myself to a specific place and time to keep the search from going on forever, I think that what I found in Alabama could have implications for other states and citizens.[4]

Since some readers may be interested in local history and others concerned with concepts, I've put additional historical information and more commentary on concepts of the public in side text like this.

In case you haven't been there, let me introduce southwestern Alabama, an area that is fixed in literature between *To Kill a Mockingbird* and *Forrest Gump*. On a map it extends about a hundred or so miles north of Mobile Bay. The six counties there—Clarke, Mobile, Baldwin, and Washington, along with their neighbors, Choctaw to the west and Monroe to the east—have a distinctive geography and a shared history. These are primarily Piney Woods counties, enriched by the economy and Creole traditions of the Gulf Coast. (Creoles,

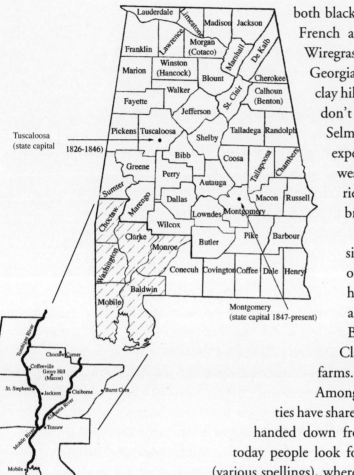

*Southwestern
Alabama*

both black and white, were descendents of the French and Spanish colonists.) Unlike the Wiregrass area on the eastern border with Georgia, these counties are covered with red clay hills that flow into sandy flats. And they don't enjoy the dark, fertile soil of the Selma Chalk or Black Belt region. The experiences of the people in the southwest have been, to some extent, the experiences that their fragile, sandy loam has brought them.[5]

As most who live there know, the six counties are far from carbon copies of each other. They never were. Mobile has always been different because it has a large city. Monroe, Washington, and Baldwin had the larger plantations; Clarke and Choctaw had more small farms.

Among the most important things the counties have shared are legends of their origins—stories handed down from generation to generation. Even today people look for the lost city of Maubila/Mauvila (various spellings), where Hernando de Soto defeated a large body of Native Americans led by Chief Tuscaluza/Tuscaloosa in 1540. School children learn about battles with the Creek Nation during the War of 1812. Rather than accounts of defeating the British or of the rise of General Andrew Jackson to prominence in national history, these are tales of personal courage and cowardice, of compassion and hatred, of cunning and stupidity. They are morality plays like the story of the runaway slave who gave his name to Hal's Lake, where he founded a community before being cruelly betrayed. The stories—as much as the geography—define southwestern Alabama.[6]

The years before 1860 are ideal for studying the first public and the first schools because the state was just being formed. Most of the southwest was still undeveloped, although European colonization dates back to French settlements in the early 1700s. Squatters began to farm there before the federal government had the legal mechanisms in place for selling land. The law was slow in taking hold, and the first people to arrive weren't always the noblest of God's creatures; crime was widespread. Outside the city of Mobile, most homes were primitive; the dress of the day was rustic. Don't imagine *Gone with the Wind;* the setting was more like a Clint Eastwood western.

Naturally, conditions changed as the decades went by. A territory was becoming a state; settlers were becoming citizens. Self-government took hold and flourished all across the American frontier, Alabama included.

After clearing land and building cabins, settlers turned to what might be called "community-building," which not only involved the physical construction of shops and streets but also the creation of a way of life to reflect the settlers' highest values. That is the reason people built churches and schools and—in case those didn't do the job—courthouses and jails.

Pioneers founded schools almost as soon as they arrived, and the Alabama legislature incorporated them into a state system in 1854. Common schooling was but one of many social movements sweeping the United States in the first half of the nineteenth century. Reformers championed a range of causes, including better treatment of the mentally ill, expanded legal rights for women, fewer saloons for alcoholics and, most controversial of all, the abolition of slavery. This was a time of "freedom's ferment," as Alice Tyler writes in her history.

Twenty years ago, if you had asked me about the public and the early schools, I would probably have said that I hadn't given them much thought. Reading the first histories of American education, which concentrate on the school laws, gave me the impression that state assemblies, inspired by great educators like Horace Mann of Massachusetts, created the public schools. But a serious problem with this interpretation is that most of these schools were *already* operating *before* the legislatures acted. So if not the legislators, who saw to it that future generations had access to instruction?

In southwestern Alabama, I found citizens in community after community who spurred other citizens to build, finance, staff, and operate many of the first schools, which were public in the sense that the public created them for public purposes. While legislators justified their laws on education with the most compelling rhetoric since the Revolution (stirring words about the need for a general diffusion of knowledge to complete the great work of independence), communities had more immediate and practical reasons. They needed schools for their survival, and their schools needed them. Community expectations gave schools what amounted to a "charter" with a number of mandates to carry out (in conjunction with other educating institutions like families).

You will notice that people in the nineteenth century had a number of ways of describing the schools that served their communities—so many that I don't think anyone could say categorically what made a school public. Schools and education were called "common," "popular," "universal," and "free," as well as "public." These were usually different names for the same institutions; each adjective emphasized a particular characteristic. When schools were called "free," it typically meant that they didn't charge tuition, that they waived it in some cases, or that the intent was to lower fees gradually until they disappeared. (Those unable to pay were assisted with various kinds of scholarships.) In other cases, "free" referred to schools *exclusively* for the poor. Adjectives like "universal" suggested an education that was "available to everyone," reflecting egalitarian notions that all citizens should have access to instruction and that resources should be distributed fairly. "Common" or "popular" might have meant "for the common people," and "common" was sometimes a code word for the conviction that cities or counties needed a common culture and that schools were to promote good relationships among different economic classes.

Although I find the nineteenth century helpful in understanding the public, some may not think it relevant because it was a long time ago and conditions were different. While the point is well taken, I believe the differences between then and now, as well as some similarities, put today's educational issues in a context that provides us with an expanded perspective on our potential as citizens.

I don't mean to imply that antebellum Alabamians created a golden age of education. They would be the last to say that. Despite their best efforts, the results were disappointing. Although not that different from other frontier states, nearly half of Alabama's white children weren't in classes. Worse, illiteracy among slaves was estimated at 95 percent, even though free blacks had literacy rates equal to or slightly higher than whites.

While circumstances are quite different today, experiences from the formative years of public education speak to many of the issues we worry about now. Take local control, which is now called "home rule." In the beginning, control was almost exclusively local; most schools had their own trustees, usually at least three. (Significantly, the combined membership of all of these boards resulted in a much larger percentage of citizens directly connected to public education than is the case these days.) Yet if local control didn't mean public or community control, it could be unacceptable. In Mobile, citizens overthrew a self-perpetuating school board because they didn't think it represented the community. A collection of able people, even with a progressive plan, didn't necessarily make for a good board—certainly not for a public one. Today, when some argue that local trustees have outlived their usefulness, the experiences of the first boards are highly relevant.[7]

Public control may also have been at issue in an experiment with what we now call faith-based organizations. Sound policy or not, having churches take on public responsibilities is nothing new. Alabama churches once received tax funds to operate nonsectarian public schools. Although it was a short-lived experiment, why it ended is instructive. (More about that later.)

Accountability is another issue that has been around since the 1800s. People in those days, as now, wanted to know what was going on in the classroom and whether students were getting a good education. Nineteenth-century teachers had the equivalent of a standardized test, an exercise in which pupils repeated back, word for word, what was in the textbook. Teachers were the judges of good instruction. But I also found examples of a more open form of examining students through public demonstrations of their abilities. Communities could see firsthand how their schools were doing and judge for themselves.

Differences between then and now can be as revealing as similarities. For instance, few communities today have the same relationship with their schools that they originally had. State and federal governments now play a much larger role. Why the change? Was it some failure of the communities or did other considerations promote this centralization? For instance, conventional wisdom holds that local control is the mortal enemy of equity. Was it? Or, perhaps local officials were "soft" on the need for excellence in education?

Were they? Did instruction have to become professionalized in order to be good?

Another striking difference is the absence of an educational bureaucracy. The first schools were freestanding institutions directed by the citizens of a community. Today, everyone—parents, students, teachers, school board members, would-be reformers, even bureaucrats—complains about bureaucratic control, which seems to be spreading faster than kudzu. Regulations of every kind and from every source combine to entangle schools. Individual rules may be reasonable, and yet when added together, they often immobilize, frustrate, and inhibit. This trend isn't a product of modern society; it dates back to at least the mid-1800s, when the public's schools were absorbed into state systems designed to produce what reformers called a "public school." State officials reordered instruction and management to conform to supposedly infallible scientific principles.

The School at Tensaw

Hard as it may be to believe, bureaucratic centralization was once a reform. Notwithstanding recent "site-based management" efforts to give schools more control, we have long been consolidating authority on the assumption that it would improve the quality of instruction. Still, Americans today aren't convinced that public education is what it should be or that they have the means to correct what needs correcting. One of the questions raised in this book is whether quality might have something to do with the relationship between communities and their schools.

This study looks into the beginnings of school administration and, particularly, the relationship of the first administrators to the public. It's an important chapter because the people's ability to act together effectively is often challenged by forces from outside their communities. When that happens, as it did in Alabama, it has to be included in the illustrations of the experiences of the public.

The 1850s saw tremendous growth in the number of classrooms and students as a result of community initiatives. Yet the decade also marks the beginning of the eclipse of the community as the leading force in education. In the name of excellence, reform-minded educators made changes that had a host of unintended consequences, which still affect us. Citizens and the schools began to drift apart as the public's role in education diminished.

The stories in this book begin in 1799. That was the year when the boundary with Spain was located, showing that most of the southwest belonged to the United States. The history of Alabama schools dates back to that same year, when John Pierce opened what appears to have been the state's first American school on Lake Tensaw, or Boatyard Lake, which is just off the Alabama River.

The year 1799 might have been to Alabama education what 1776 is to American independence—a time of celebration and reflection. Sad to say, the two hundredth anniversary passed without being recognized. The fact that it went unnoticed suggests something about how schools today understand the public—and how the public has come to understand its relationship to the schools.

NOTES TO INTRODUCTION

[1] The Kettering research on the perception that the public schools aren't the public's schools is in a report I wrote, titled *Is There a Public for Public Schools?* (Dayton, Ohio: Kettering Foundation Press, 1996). The attitude of parents as consumers is described in a study done for the Kettering Foundation by Doble Research Associates, *A Consumer Mentality: The Prevailing Mind-Set in American Public Education* in March 1999, pp. 2, 9-10.

[2] Along with the works cited in the text, those that have influenced the concepts of the public found in this book include Amy Gutmann and Dennis Thompson's *Democracy and Disagreement* (Cambridge: Harvard University Press, 1996); James S. Fishkin's *Democracy and Deliberation: New Directions for Democratic Reform* (New Haven: Yale University Press, 1991); Carmen Sirianni and Lewis Friedland's *Civic Innovation in America: Community Empowerment, Public Policy, and the Movement for Civic Renewal* (Berkeley: University of California Press, 2001); Peter Levine's *The New Progressive Era: Toward a Fair and Deliberative Democracy* (Lanham, Md.: Rowman and Littlefield, 2000); Noëlle McAfee's *Habermas, Kristeva, and Citizenship* (Ithaca, N.Y.: Cornell University Press, 2000); and John Gastil's *By Popular Demand: Revitalizing Representative Democracy through Deliberative Elections* (Berkeley: University of California Press, 2000). I also drew on the writings of Michael J. Sandel, Giovanni Sartori, and John Dewey. Kettering research is summed up in a report I wrote, *Politics for People: Finding a Responsible Public Voice*, 2d ed. (Urbana: University of Illinois Press, 1999).

[3] While I didn't deal with many of the issues of educational historiography, for those who want a brief overview of the major controversies, I would recommend a review of the literature by Diane Ravitch, *The Revisionists Revised: Studies in the Historiography of American Education* ([Stanford, Calif.]: National Academy of Education, 1977). She later expanded this essay into a book-length discussion in *The Revisionists Revised: A Critique of the Radical Attack on the Schools* (New York: Basic Books, 1978).

[4] Although concentrating on Alabama, I looked into the origins of the public schools in other states to see if what I was finding was unique to just one area of the country. For reference, I chose three states with populations comparable to Alabama's: Maryland, Michigan, and New Jersey. Jon Perdue, a Kettering researcher, located sources such as Malvina Hauk Abonyi, "The Role of Ethnic Church Schools in the History of Education in the United States: The Detroit Experience, 1850-1920" (Ph.D. diss., Wayne State University, 1987); Charles O. Hoyt and R. Clyde Ford, *John D. Pierce, Founder of the Michigan School System: A Study of Education in the Northwest* (Ypsilanti, Mich.: Scharf Tag, Label, and Box, 1905); Michigan House of Representatives, *Report of the Board of Education of the City of Detroit*, no. 14 (n.p., 1843); Leo Joseph McCormick, *Church-State Relationships in Education in Maryland* (Washington, D.C.: Catholic University of America Press, 1942); Arthur B. Moehlman, *Public Education in Detroit* (Bloomington, Ill.: Public School Publishing Company, 1925); David Murray, *History of Education in New Jersey* (Washington, D.C.: Government Printing Office, 1899); *Report of the Committee on Common School System* (Trenton, N.J.: Joseph Justice and Son, 1837); Mary Rosalita, *Education in Detroit Prior to 1850* (Lansing: Michigan Historical Commission, 1928); Bernard C. Steiner, *History of Education in Maryland*, Contributions to American Educational History, no. 19 (Washington, D.C.: Government Printing Office, 1894); and Vernon S. Vavrina, *The History of Public Education in the City of Baltimore, 1829-1956* (Washington, D.C.: Catholic University of America Press, 1958).

[5] The descriptions of the six counties came from Neal G. Lineback, ed., *Atlas of Alabama* (University: University of Alabama Press, 1973) and Lewy Dorman, *Party Politics in Alabama from 1850 through 1860* (1935; reprint, Tuscaloosa: University of Alabama Press, 1995).

[6] The most recent account of Hernando de Soto's expedition in southwestern Alabama is an interesting book by the director of the Mobile Municipal Archives, Jay Higginbotham, *Mauvila* (Mobile: A. B. Bahr, 2000). Heroes of the southwest include William Weatherford, the Creek chief who led a massacre at Fort Mims and later returned to live among the survivors, and an African-American known only as "Caesar," who paddled the small canoe that Captain Sam Dale and his companions from a Clarke County militia used to attack a large war party in the middle of the Alabama River. Because he and his wife Helen, who assisted him, are from the area, David Strode Akens tells the stories the way I heard them told in his master's thesis "Clarke County to 1860" (University of Alabama, 1956), pages 17, 23-24, 82-83.

[7] Jay Mathews, "Are School Boards Really Necessary?" *Washington Post*, 10 April 2001, A19.

Why Public Schools?
Whose Public Schools?

Chapter 1

Are the Public Schools
the Public's Schools?

ALTHOUGH MORE THAN two centuries have passed since John Pierce's classroom welcomed its students, Alabama's system of public education faces a less certain future than might be expected after those years of school building.

Not too long ago, an Alabamian who has spent his career teaching told me that the state's public schools won't last another ten years because they are losing the confidence of the public. Not intending to exaggerate, he spoke matter-of-factly, the way a television meteorologist announces the likelihood of rain. Maybe he was only thinking of inner-city schools that have predominantly minority students from low-income families, but my friend in Alabama seemed to have in mind a more pervasive problem. He didn't mean that there wouldn't be any schools financed by tax revenue. He meant that there would be few schools attractive to all, supported as a community responsibility, and legitimized by a valid charter from the citizenry at large to act as the community's agent. What he said suggests that public schools in many communities could eventually be seen as the equivalent of "welfare," understood as a refuge for those who have nowhere else to go. That will surely happen if people no longer believe the public schools are *their* schools.[1]

Some don't think this grim prediction will ever be realized; they say their schools are still embraced by the public, and I have no basis for doubting them.

Some believe that it could, but must not, happen. Others aren't alarmed; they've already written off public education.

These Aren't Our Schools!

I take the warning to heart. The perception that the schools are no longer community agents is more serious than an occasional failure to pass a bond issue. Today's public schools often mean little other than schools paid for by tax revenue; but if that is all they are, they may mean far less in the future than they have in the past. To elaborate on what I wrote in the Introduction, people pay taxes but don't think they own the schools. That doesn't mean they don't care; it often means they don't think they can do anything to act on their concerns. "Control" is too strong a word for what they are looking for; it is more the collective ability to contribute to and influence schooling. Absent that sense, people are less inclined to think they are accountable for what happens in the educational system ("It's the teachers' or the parents' job"), or they may withdraw in frustration from schools that don't appear to give "outsiders" (sometimes including parents) a meaningful role. That's the gist of the Kettering Foundation report already cited. It is based on more than ten years of research on the deteriorating relationship between the schools and the public. These findings aren't the Foundation's alone; they are reflected in many reforms these days: vouchers, charter schools, stricter standards, more accountability, home schooling. They are all about regaining "control."[2]

Equally ominous, even though Americans still cling to the idea that we should have schools open to all, the broad mandate that once tied these institutions to this and other social, economic, and political objectives may be losing its power to inspire broad commitment.

What Public Does Public Engagement Engage?

Increasingly sensitive to alienated citizens, educators have tried to regain support through public engagement campaigns. The American Federation of Teachers, the Annenberg Institute for School Reform at Brown University, the George Gund Foundation, the National School Boards Association, and the United States Department of Education funded a study of engagement by Public Agenda, a nonpartisan research organization. The report shows that the relatively new term is used by people who believe "that the relationship between the public schools and the public is fraying." Parents who think their schools are doing poorly are particularly interested in being more engaged personally, but citizens with strong democratic values want the schools to have closer ties to their community as well. Traditional channels for improving communication and building relationships seem to be blocked, however. Superintendents, teachers, and citizens alike single out school board meetings as "the least satisfying, least productive" setting for reaching the community. Hearings aren't just unproductive, they are often counterproductive. And people's irritation easily turns to frustration because the board meetings are "the only game in town."[3]

Engagement campaigns are welcome efforts to break through this sort of blockage. Yet their strategies have various notions of the public implicit in them—and these have quite different implications for restoring ownership and accountability. For instance, imagine a campaign based on the assumption that America is a nation of shoppers who will be reengaged if the schools promise better service and if educators become more attentive to complaints. That would be treating the citizenry as a body of consumers, which is a far cry from a public defined by its collective ability. Other campaigns might put all of their emphasis on "educating the public," which would suggest that the citizenry is like an audience, already assembled but passive, waiting to be told what to do.

I confess that I may have contributed to what I am warning against. The title I gave a book reporting on citizens' attitudes toward schools (*Is There a Public for Public Schools?*) might give the false impression that the public is no more than a political constituency *for* schools. That would be putting the cart before the horse: public schools exist to serve the public, not the other way around.

While parents will surely appreciate better service and greater responsiveness—and two-way communication is a big plus—these improvements will not get at all the problems that separate too many schools from their communities. Not only are parents of school-age children in the minority in most towns, but also treating the public as a collection of consumers slights citizens who don't have children enrolled but want a partnership with the schools. These are people who want to strengthen their towns as well as educate young people. To make matters worse, campaigns that emphasize satisfying consumers could diminish the sense of shared responsibility that schools need to be effective. Consumerism invites equating classrooms with TV repair shops. Parents as customers might say to teachers, "I brought my children in at 8 A.M., and I want them 'fixed' by 3 P.M. If they aren't, it's your fault."

Community Renewal and School Improvement

If customer dissatisfaction, poor communication, or even a sense of alienation were the only difficulties to overcome, many engagement campaigns would succeed. Schools could, unilaterally, change their way of dealing with people. But, historically, engagement was first citizen to citizen—and *then* citizens to schools. That suggests educators alone can't rebuild the web of relationships needed to connect communities to schools and schools to communities. Only a community as a whole can do that. So I believe there isn't likely to be a public in our educational system unless there is a public in our communities. *Before we can have the schools we want, we must have the public we need.*

Curiously, the public in communities isn't always a major player in matters of education. Recently, a group of reformers, reflecting on what they had learned, said it had been a mistake to assume that for schooling to be improved, the *only* people who would have to change were educators. Why aren't citizens and communities taken into consideration in education when studies have shown that a "society of citizens" can have a powerful influence on everything from economic productivity to government effectiveness? Isn't it reasonable to think that the quality of education is also affected by what the citizenry of a community does or doesn't do?[4]

Doubts about Citizens

While I am convinced that school reform has to begin in or with the public, others question whether the public ever "owned" the schools or should. That never happened, according to one of the people interviewed in the Kettering study of how Americans understand public education. "Oh, maybe some deep thinkers thought it happened," one woman responded, "but it didn't." Others have said it is hopelessly idealistic to think that the public in a community could be a major factor in what they see as the professional province of educators.

This skepticism goes beyond doubts about the role of the public in the schools. Some Americans believe the public has never been a political force in anything—that it is just a political myth. Uncertainty about the public and its power lies deep in our political culture. Although our Constitution says that "We, the People" are the ultimate authority, we wonder whether that's only rhetoric. A real sovereign decides and acts. Do we? People suspect that money rules, not citizens. Maybe the public really isn't any more than a phantom of our imagination, as Walter Lippmann once insisted.

If the public is real, where can we see it? Do citizens actually do anything other than elect a government to represent them, and if so, how? A democratic public not only has to believe in its collective right to govern itself but also has to have confidence in its collective power to act. Americans aren't certain they have that power—even in election years.

OUR COLLECTIVE CAPACITIES

There are examples of the citizenry acting beyond the ballot box, and these give us insight into the nature of the public—*if we can only recognize it for what it is*. The first half of the nineteenth century is a good time to get a sense of the public because, according to Robert Wiebe's excellent history, it was an age of democratic self-rule, a time when thousands of people were inciting thousands of others to act. Andrew Jackson, accurately or not, is often used as a symbol for this era of popular sovereignty. In this period, I found a basis for a broader and richer notion of the public than a body of consumers or clients and a definition that includes but goes beyond the familiar "law-abiding voters and taxpayers." I saw a citizenry in motion, people doing things with other people, not still but dynamic. The motion defines the public; in a sense, it is the public. Think of electricity rather than a light bulb. That is one way of appreciating how much the public is a force, not just an object, like an audience or a market.[5]

The historical public didn't live only in ballot boxes; it lived in the interactions of citizens with citizens. People were joined in common action to address common problems and got their hands dirty doing "public work." The problems that first prompted them to act together were those that stopped them from doing what they had to do. If a road or a bridge washed out, settlers couldn't travel. If warring bands of Indians attacked a nearby family, a fort had to be put up—and quickly.

Public work was usually done in and for communities, and while I recognize that "public" doesn't mean the same as some definitions of "community," the public I am talking about is much like the community as a body politic or a political entity. We see this definition in headlines such as "Community Saves Post Office." In order to show this, I use terms like "community-based public." A concept of the public divorced from community strikes me as too divorced from reality to be useful.

Nineteenth-century Americans impress me as pragmatic—see a problem, solve it, move on. Sooner or later, however, even practical people have to think about where they *ought* to be moving. They need a guiding sense of purpose and direction. And those require collective decisions. The public comes alive in the *struggle to make sound choices when things that are deeply valuable to people pull them in different directions* (freedom and security, for example). Citizens do physical work, and they also do "choice work," particularly on long-term, never-ending responsibilities like educating new generations.

Choice work, or public decision-making, is done best by a form of talking and reasoning together called "deliberation." While the term may be unfamiliar, deliberation goes on all around us. We deliberate in private within ourselves and among our friends when we have difficult decisions to make about marriage or a career. We deliberate in public in jury rooms. And we should see deliberation in our legislative bodies. Deliberation is simply weighing (fairly) the pros and cons of various options against what is truly important to us as a people.

A public that decides and acts on both long-term challenges and more immediate physical tasks isn't a phantom; it produces things everyone can see—roads, schools, a way of life.

PUBLIC TERMS

All of us who talk about or try to relate to "the public" might be more self-conscious about what we mean, not because some definitions are right and others aren't, but because they all have profound political implications. I'll try to take my own suggestion.

Clearly, I don't consider "the public" simply everybody or society at large. I think "voters" and "taxpayers" are too limited as definitions and believe "consumers" is way off the mark in a democracy. As I've said, I associate the public in its most basic form with citizens joined in exercising their collective capacities. Groups of people acting collectively in the nineteenth century are what I refer to as a "historical" or "first" public—without meaning to imply that the examples I cite prove that there was a fully developed public active everywhere in southwestern Alabama or in the cause of education. And I am not suggesting there wasn't an American public before 1800.

Citizens exercise their collective capacities in many ways, and I looked at two in particular: people doing common work (usually to build things) and making choices that set the directions for long-term tasks like educating young people. These efforts suggest a shared sense of responsibility or ownership, which is a prerequisite for self-government.

When people work together over time, they form relationships that may evolve into a "society of citizens," a "civil society," or a "citizenry." These terms for "the public," though not always synonymous, emphasize continuity in collective action as well as a form of political association that is longer lasting than an ad hoc gathering.

Because I found that citizens often exercised their collective capacities in and for their communities, I use phrases such as "community-based public" to capture that connection. That is sometimes shortened to "community" even though "community" can also refer to a common feeling among people or to feelings of solidarity. I don't use these definitions.

In many instances, "the public" is a noun—a collection of people doing concrete things. The word is also used as an adjective with other meanings. A "public meeting" is simply an open one; a "public life" is the life we share with others. Nineteenth-century legislators frequently used "public" as an adjective. They didn't have in mind people exercising their collective abilities. In fact, they were often contemptuous of that citizenry. Except as "consenting voters," the elite's "public" was more ideal than actual; it was a society in the abstract. The word referred to what was best for all, as in phrases like "the public interest" or "the public good."[6]

Notes to Chapter 1

[1] I reported on the feeling that the public schools, as we know them, may not last in *Is There a Public for Public Schools?* (Dayton, Ohio: Kettering Foundation Press, 1996).

[2] Ibid.

[3] Public Agenda's *Just Waiting to Be Asked? A Fresh Look at Attitudes on Public Engagement* (New York: Public Agenda, 2001). In addition to page 7, see Chapter 6.

[4] The influence of a "civil society" or society of citizens has been described by Robert D. Putnam in *Bowling Alone: The Collapse and Revival of American Community* (New York: Simon and Schuster, 2000).

[5] Robert H. Wiebe, *Self-Rule: A Cultural History of American Democracy* (Chicago: University of Chicago Press, 1995).

[6] You may have noticed that the book always refers to "the public" in the singular rather than, as is customary, to "publics" in the plural. The reason is to reintroduce a sense of ourselves as a citizenry, which has been obscured by today's understandable attention to the differences among groups of people. Another way to think of the public is as a political realm or estate distinct from other centers of power, which originally were the monarchy, the aristocracy (lords), and the church. (We retain this notion nowadays when we describe the media as the "fourth estate.") Members of an estate shared interests. The public estate consisted of common people who had, despite many differences, a collective identity as citizens. (That history is reflected in the name of the lower chamber in the British parliament, the House of Commons.) People still have interests they share as citizens. For example, members of the American public estate have an interest in self-determination and their freedom as citizens (which originally meant freedom from coercion by any of the other centers of power). Gordon S. Wood's *The Creation of the American Republic, 1776-1787* (Chapel Hill: University of North Carolina Press, 1998) prompted me to compare the modern notion of a society of citizens with the eighteenth-century concept of a public estate.

It is useful to revive the notion of a public estate because it opens the door to the idea that the public schools have a common, unifying core or identity and that they are more than institutions beholden to a wide variety of "publics" (actually constituent groups) and nothing else.

John Dewey provided an exhaustive discussion of the public in *The Public and Its Problems* (Chicago: Swallow Press, 1954). Dewey agrees that the American democratic polity formed in communities. But he saw the public as inchoate until represented by the officials of government. Such a public can only agree or disagree with its representatives. The public, as I see it, expresses itself directly in informal associations and collective action as well as in elections. It has a larger role as a producer of public goods like universal education.

Chapter 2

The Historical Public in Early Alabama

I T IS IMPOSSIBLE to appreciate fully how frontier Alabama came to have public schools without real-life illustrations of how the public formed. Counties in the southwestern corner of the state were merely lines on a map until the people who lived in them began to see themselves as citizens connected by shared decisions and the work of implementing what they had decided.

Hardy Jackson illustrated how much had to be done on the frontier with his description of Claiborne, which went from a fort site to a community with two thousand people, thirty businesses, two schools for young women, and a grammar school all in a relatively short time. Making this progress even more remarkable, the town sat on a bluff three hundred feet above the Alabama River, which required constructing a wooden staircase of 365 steps so that visitors could reach Claiborne. The most daunting task that caused people to work together, however, was combating the vice and violence that came with rapid growth.[1]

The People: A Noah's Ark of Differences

The Alabamians who took on this work included planters with large tracts of land and numerous slaves; farmers with less land and few if any slaves; a small population of free black Alabamians; and poor whites living on land that had little agricultural value. They were joined by merchants, skilled artisans, and laborers, often from the North or foreign countries. These people not

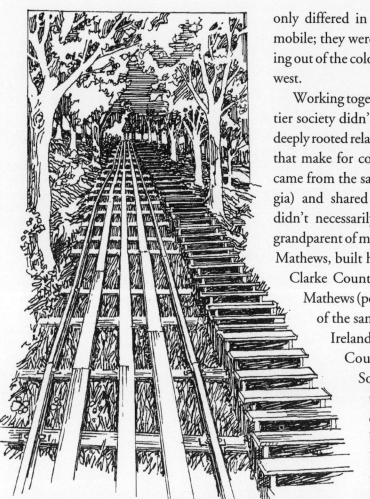

Stairs from the Alabama River to Claiborne

only differed in many ways, but also were highly mobile; they were part of a river of humanity sweeping out of the colonies and moving farther and farther west.

Working together didn't always come easily. Frontier society didn't have the accumulated reservoir of deeply rooted relationships and well-established norms that make for cooperation. Although many settlers came from the same states (the Carolinas and Georgia) and shared a common Celtic heritage, they didn't necessarily recognize these ties. A yeoman grandparent of mine in the nineteenth century, Josiah Mathews, built his cabin on a pine-covered ridge in Clarke County and tended his hogs. Joel Early Mathews (possibly a distant cousin from a branch of the same Welsh family that had moved to Ireland) constructed a mansion on a Dallas County plantation that represented Southern living at its grandest. The two Mathews didn't know each other and might not have cared to become acquainted, not necessarily because of class rivalry, but because they experienced different realities. Josiah probably measured his prosperity by the amount of meat in his smokehouse. For Joel and his immediate kin, such as his brother Thomas, also of Dallas County, success was measured by the quality of the fine furniture in their homes and the number of books in their libraries. Yet even the Dallas County brothers, though in the same economic class, were divided politically. Thomas was an ardent defender of the Union while Joel was a champion of secession. In the Mathews family and throughout Alabama, there were differences in similarities, and similarities in differences.[2]

Josiah Mathews's reality was the most common. John Massey of Choctaw County left a detailed account of the "simple rural life" of yeoman farmers in the 1840s and 1850s. "We raised everything in the way of provisions at home," he writes. "Cows furnished milk and butter, and beef occasionally. Hogs supplied bacon and lard, and spareribs and backbones at 'hog-killing time.' Sheep furnished mutton chops and wool for our winter clothing. Bees produced the honey for sweetening and wax for candles. The poultry yard supplied eggs and chickens

Above, Josiah Mathews's Cabin in Clarke County

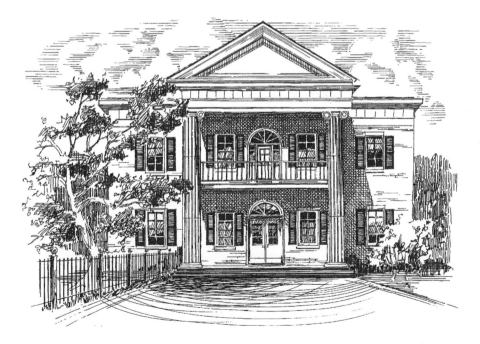

Left, a Mathews Home in Dallas County. While there is apparently no photograph of Joel Early's house, his brother Thomas's home in Cahawba reflects the family's wealth. This mansion was built by Henry Crocheron.

for frying and chicken pies. Deer furnished venison frequently."[3]

Later to become one of the state's leading educators, Massey received his first instruction at home. "Many a night I have read and studied by a 'lightwood' fire," he recalls, while his mother made the family's clothes using dyes of copperas, indigo, walnuts, and sumac berries. "I never wore a store-bought garment until I was quite a large boy." He also remembered that his first pair of shoes was made by his father, who was the "shoemaker, cooper, and blacksmith for the household." Study was a part of his world, but cash was not: "While we had plenty of all the necessaries of life, we had little money. I do not think I ever saw, all told, ten dollars in money until I was twelve or fourteen years old."

Self-reliance was surely one of the imperatives of Massey's society. People had to be responsible for themselves if they were to survive—there was no safety net to speak of. Lessons in self-sufficiency began when settlers stepped off their wagons. Benjamin Faneuil Porter, a city fellow from Charleston, was shocked when he arrived in Claiborne by conditions he calls "savage and wild." Though trained as a physician and lawyer, he had to learn new skills to make the furniture his family needed.[4]

Porter writes about his new vocation as a carpenter: "I went into the swamp, cut down a large poplar, split it into pieces, and carried it on my shoulders a fourth of a mile; and with a hatchet, saw, old plane, and a chisel, made a not contemptible bedstead, table, and arm chair; in the latter of which, my wife, son, and myself used to sit under the shade of a grove of cotton wood."

Pioneering families were the backbone of the state; they saw to their own well-being, and their solidarity made them a significant public force. No one captures their cohesion better than Frank L. Owsley. The whole family, he writes, "worked together, hunted together, went to church and parties together, and expected to be buried together and to come to judgment together on the Last Day."[5]

Another segment of Alabama society consisted of people called "poor whites" or, more derisively, "rednecks," "poor white trash," and "squatters." They were the advance guard for state-making—the people who came first. Short on funds, they saw thousands of acres of unclaimed land and "simply 'squatted' where they pleased." They rushed in as soon as the government acquired tribal holdings (and often before). And "upon finding an appealing tract of land, they would establish their claim by girdling a few trees and laying the first logs for a cabin."[6]

Historians disagree on exactly what these poor whites were like. They are sometimes described as the most independent, least publicly invested segment in the society—an uneducated rabble that disdained book learning. Clement Eaton showed, however, that the poor weren't a single, homogenous group; they ranged from stranded frontiersmen in the hills and valleys of the Appalachian chain to gaunt, yellow-skinned "crackers" in the coastal pine barrens. Highlanders lived Spartan lives and had economic interests and social attitudes distinct from those of the squatters who hunted and fished in the lowlands. Other historians have described these whites as nomadic herdsmen making use of a vast public domain and living among the Choctaws, Creeks (Muscogee), and other tribes. Many Alabamians who began poor eventually moved up the social and economic ladders.[7]

Black Alabamians, nearly half the population, obviously led different lives in a slave state. Yet there were also differences within the differences. Not all were slaves; free blacks numbered around three thousand in 1850. This group included an elite who lived comfortably in nice homes, had considerable property (sometimes including slaves), and enough capital to make loans to whites. They invested in educating their children. The majority had only modest homes but steady jobs and some education. The uneducated worked for low wages in seasonal jobs, though few were charity cases.[8]

While a handful of free blacks made their homes in small towns like Grove Hill, where Tom Brown operated the first hotel (which housed Governor Arthur Pendleton Bagby and others having business with the county court), the majority lived in larger towns like Mobile where they had greater economic opportunities.[9]

Despite all, however, black Alabamians had a hand in creating the state and its educational institutions—even before 1865. As W. E. B. DuBois demonstrated in his research, these often forgotten people contributed by virtue of the roles they played in the economy—as professionals, farmers, skilled artisans, and shopkeepers.[10]

Most people of African descent weren't free, but the quality of their lives also varied, as reflected in accounts of daily routines like the meals they ate. One former bondsman recalls that "The food eaten by the slaves usually consisted of cornbread, molasses, pig feet, pig ears, chittlings, hog head; dried peas in the winter and fresh vegetables in season, including watermelons. Game and fish were plentiful. The masters at Christmas allowed the slaves to have a barbecue and some were given a little whiskey. However, tobacco and snuff were luxuries."[11]

While this account suggests there may have been opportunities for a social if not public life, others tell of isolation and degradation:

> I was owned by Mr. Hardy Clements. I worked in the "Big House." Since freedom, my life has been a good one. I mind my own business and do not bother other people. I have a nice family who help look after me. I have been sick a whole lot since I turned ninety years old. When I was a young girl, my job in the big house was to pour the water at the table and fan the flies to keep them from the food while my master and his family ate. When the day was over, I would go back to the special quarters for us slaves who lived near the big house. We had to get up at four o'clock in the morning to get breakfast ready for Ol' Master and his family at seven in the morning. We would cook fat back, corn bread and serve milk and serp to the slave hands at five o'clock in the morning. They would eat out of wooden plates. At noon and supper, if any slaves had not worked as well as the "Overseer" thought, then their food would be served in the Hog Troughs and only then after the hogs had eaten. The meal for noon and supper was usually black eyed peas, fat back and corn bread. This was always a bad sight to see. I, even though very young, would pray to God to deliver us from this type of treatment.[12]

Slavery was at its worst when runaway slaves were captured or free blacks were treated as runaways, as John Hope Franklin and Loren Schweninger have documented. Physical mistreatment; the breakup of families when husbands, wives, and children were sold to different masters; fear of punishment; or simply the desire to be free prompted slaves to leave plantations, even though they knew they could face the cruelest retribution.[13]

JOINED IN COMMON WORK THROUGH CIVIC ASSOCIATIONS

In this diverse nineteenth-century society, "public relationships" developed as strangers became neighbors. As I explain in Chapter 1, public relationships are more inclusive than those among family members and friends; they are formed around interests that citizens share with other citizens. People may not necessarily like one another but recognize that they need each other. Without the attachments and routines of established communities, pioneers created substitutes; they formed ties with one another that were more civic than familiar.

People in southwest Alabama went about organizing themselves to exercise their collective capacity in the same ways Alexis de Tocqueville found other Americans doing. When citizens saw a problem that needed to be solved, they relied on each other, not just on the government, making them the most unusual people in the world, according to this French observer. When something needed to be done, he marveled, people would go across the street and discuss the matter with neighbors—not to the courthouse. Neighbors would then form a committee or deliberative body to deal with the problem. All of this was done by people on their own initiative. Impressed by what he saw, Tocqueville sensed that the health of a democratic society was determined by the number of things that citizens did for themselves.[14]

Although the French visitor said some uncomplimentary things about violence in frontier Alabama, citizens there were gathering, assembling, meeting, and associating as in other states. They went across the street (across a road or creek) for many reasons, and in the process, formed associations around everyday tasks and grand business ventures. People "of all conditions, minds, and ages," Tocqueville reports, "acquire a general taste for association, and grow accustomed to the use of it. There they meet together in large numbers,—they converse, they listen to each other, and they are mutually stimulated to all sorts of undertakings. They afterwards transfer to civil life the notions they have thus acquired, and make them subservient to a thousand purposes."

Tocqueville found the distinctive character of American politics in the way people used space *outside* the formal political system for political purposes. Gatherings after church, in wagon yards, and on front porches weren't political in the usual sense, yet they led to informal alliances and made connections that were useful later in governance. As a result, Americans expanded the meaning of politics, making it more than the work of elected officials. Now it included what neighbors did with neighbors in the interest of their common well-being.

Social events influenced public life indirectly but profoundly. People acquired a "taste for association" in the most ordinary occasions. Preserving meat for the winter was one of the tasks that often brought people together. Hog-killing day had to be "bracing" but not "bitter cold." Animals were "slaughtered, scalded, dressed," and then cut up for salting. To ensure that enough people would be on hand for the work, an "old-time party" would customarily be given the night before. The practice encouraged mutual assistance and a spirit of reciprocity.[15]

Frank Owsley provided additional examples of how people worked together: community members built houses for newlyweds, women sewed at quilting bees, men cleared land by logrolling and woodburning, people shucked corn to the sound of communal singing (work and play were often combined), and neighbors gathered the crops of those who were ill. All-day singings, weddings, and dinners on the ground (outdoor lunches in the North) generated connective tissue for the southwest's civic infrastructure.[16]

Other assemblies combined the atoms of family into larger civic molecules. For instance, camp meetings, often held on church grounds, served a number of community purposes. The campground at the Union Methodist church near McLeods Beat in Clarke County eventually became the site of soldiers' reunions. Although churches reflected denominational divisions, camp meetings brought together people from different communities and even from surrounding counties. Organizers enclosed "a grove of several acres" where frequent participants built "comfortable log cabins . . . around the border." In the center, a large roof-covered pavilion was erected and furnished with benches (preachers were given chairs). People moved entire households to the area, bringing "an abundance of bedding, all their best tableware, their kitchen utensils, etc.; their house servants and an ample supply of food." Settlers were eager to visit with friends from the states they had left and would travel as many as one hundred miles to renew acquaintances. The schedule of events followed a common pattern: "The mornings and evenings were set apart for religious services; the afternoons were devoted . . . to social enjoyment."[17]

Though we hesitate to mix politics and religion, the two were often joined in these settings. Campground revivals reflected the egalitarian spirit that permeated frontier politics. As Wayne Flynt showed in his study of Alabama Baptists, these gatherings affirmed the power and freedom of ordinary people and promoted a political consciousness that advanced public education and other causes.[18]

Curing meat and going to church together paved the way for other forms of cooperation and more explicitly political gatherings. Nearly every issue of a newspaper seems to have had a notice of a public meeting. People didn't just express opinions on what others should do; they made decisions about what *they* were going to do. The choices they made resulted in roads being built, businesses organized, agriculture improved, and armies raised. All were the products of people's collective power.

Military units formed in response to crises like the conflict with Mexico between 1845 and 1848. The War Department asked Alabama to have troops "in readiness to enter the service of the United States when called for," and "the excitement that prevailed at that time" produced a number of companies that assembled on their own initiative in Mobile. A regiment quickly formed and elected field officers. The enthusiasm was so great that six additional companies created a second regiment.[19]

Organizing collective action was often quite elaborate, as is shown in the records of an association formed in 1857 to build a railway between Jackson and Uniontown. The citizens of Jackson and the surrounding counties met on the 24th of October "at a large and enthusiastic Railroad Barbecue Meeting." On the motion of Isham Kimbell, Dr. F. L. Sewall was called to the chair, and seven vice presidents were appointed. At first glance, this seems like a lot of officers (only banks have that many vice presidents), but most of them were members of pioneer families in various parts of the country—the Duboses, Singletons, Dabneys, Smoots, and Chapmans. Appointing so many officers joined different communities in a collective undertaking. Maybe that is why the association selected two secretaries: J. B. Taylor and Isaac Grant. Public speeches (the movies of the time) were the main event, with the honors on this occasion going to James S. Dickinson and Dr. Neal Smith of Clarke, S. S. Houston of Washington, and Major J. E. J. Macon of Marengo. After what must have been hours of rhetoric, citizens adopted a resolution encouraging the proposed rail line and selected delegates for a similar meeting to be held at Choctaw Corner.[20]

Public meetings launched other business ventures. In 1853, a gathering took place in Suggsville to organize a joint-stock company to bring badly needed industry to an overwhelmingly agricultural economy. This was not a purely private matter; it was a patriotic cause, which speakers made clear. As a result, a committee formed to organize the Clarke County Manufacturing Company.

The need for roads linking one part of a county with another also spurred common work. Every able-bodied male (white and black, free and slave) was required by law to donate labor to clear and maintain roadways. Josiah Mathews, for example, was charged by the Clarke County Commissioners Court with organizing the work to keep up the road from Macon to McLanes (McLeans). Only ministers, students, and teachers were exempt from road duty, presumably because of the civic value of their regular work.[21]

Benjamin Porter, the new settler from South Carolina, recalls his experience with this almost democratic arrangement:

> I had some experience of the patriotism of working roads. I was summoned and, of course, went. I toiled for three days with slaves in the hot sun. The whites who were also summoned sat under the shade and talked and laughed. I was so young and foolish that it never occurred to me that one required to perform a public duty could neglect it. I injured my reputation very seriously by working, instead of sitting in the shade![22]

People not only gave their time and donated money but also lent their houses for public purposes. For instance, frontier counties had to create a legal system and needed places to hold court. With no courthouses available, justice was dispensed in Clarke County at the homes of John Laundrum and William Coate. Coate, best known as a pioneer who rolled his belongings to the county in a hogshead barrel, wasn't an attorney, and none of the others is listed as a lawyer. They were apparently just good citizens with larger or more centrally located homes.[23]

To be sure, a connected citizenry is not an unmixed blessing. We can be as wrong collectively as we can be individually, and some frontier gatherings brought out the worst in people, not the best. Take the case of one of the lesser sins, "barbecuism." Public gatherings typically ended in roasting a pig or side of beef; it was a long-standing practice, going back to the time when the Virginia gentry would entertain common folk on occasions like elections. In the 1820s, some communities saw these happy festivals turn rowdy, even violent. Crowds drank, gambled, and fought. In that atmosphere, politicians played to the baser instincts of their constituents. These excesses eventually prompted an antibarbecuism movement, which was linked to the temperance crusade.[24]

Other accounts suggest that Alabama had no real public life—only a fondness for socializing. Tocqueville was dismayed to find Alabamians, even lawyers, who had no respect for the law. He didn't write about civic associations in the state; he was more impressed (and distressed) by a lawyer who believed in returning violence with violence rather than settling disputes in court. Harriet Martineau, another foreign visitor, found slavery so appalling that she believed a valued way of life or moral order was impossible. She wrote that Alabamians were brutal and crassly materialistic: their main, indeed sole, object in life was to grow cotton, and they had "few but money-getting qualifications." Martineau thought the absence of refinement was particularly evident in an almost total disregard for education. Planters made millions by cultivating a fine grade of cotton, yet their children, she reported, could scarcely read or write. They were "'gawks' . . . unable to learn, or even to remain in the

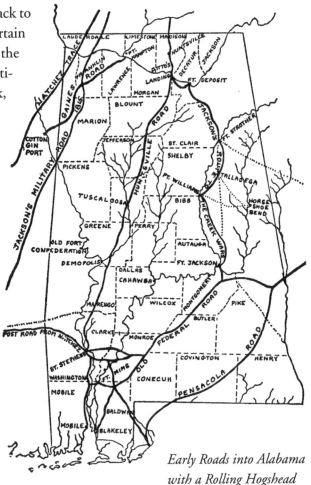

Early Roads into Alabama with a Rolling Hogshead

society of others who were learning." In her eyes, there was nothing remotely resembling a public in the state, much less a public concerned about the future of the next generation.[25]

I don't doubt that Tocqueville saw lawyers who preferred to settle personal disputes personally or that Martineau met materialistic planters. Still, many documents from this period suggest that in white society a public life, based on shared responsibility for collective well-being, was gradually taking shape in Alabama—in response to the conditions that the critics observed.

Were quilting bees and the like truly *public* events? They certainly aren't political in the sense that a campaign rally is. In fact, most of what I have just described could be written off as purely social or charitable—no more than examples of individuals helping one another. There is a legitimate distinction between what we do to enjoy ourselves or to assist those in need, on the one hand, and what we do to deal with the problems facing our communities, on the other. But it is a philosophical distinction. In day-to-day living, the social so easily blends into the political that it is not only difficult to draw a line between them but also counterproductive. Recently, scholars have demonstrated that the political vitality of a community is correlated with its social structures and practices. In other words, the number of hog killings make a difference.[26]

BUSY IN COMMUNITY-BUILDING

People got things done by acting through their communities. And, because communities were so important, Alabamians invested a good deal of effort in developing them. That work was partly physical and partly normative. A piece of real estate becomes a community only when it creates a way of living that reflects and promotes the things people care about and want to share.

The same is true today when people work together to build playgrounds, clean up cemeteries, and patrol neighborhoods. The objectives aren't simply structural; they are to create a community that embodies what citizens value. In organizing neighborhood watches, people don't want only to keep their streets safe, they want to instill a respect for law. In cleaning cemeteries, they want to perpetuate their heritage as well as remove weeds from tombstones. In building playgrounds, they want to encourage people to care for the younger generation as well as provide places where children can play.

Community-building is critical. People can't live well or long in places where there isn't a good measure of lawfulness, fair dealing, and mutual assistance. Interviewed in a 1999 study, a man from Richmond said that communities (referring to neighborhoods) are the natural way that people survive. After all, he reasoned, "wolves have packs, the whales have pods, fish have schools." I suspect this man's observation wasn't just a latter-day insight. In searching for interest in community-building in the first six decades of the nineteenth century, I inferred motives from the way people spent their time and money. Everywhere they were busy creating the institutions that define community—churches, libraries, hospitals, and schools.[27]

Mobile is particularly rich in examples of the practices and institutions needed to sustain a community even though it had the southwest's most diverse population. The people were black/white, Protestant/Catholic, American-born/foreign-born, Northern/Southern, laborer/merchant.

Mobile evolved from a French fort built in the early 1700s, which served traders and a colonial government. On the surface, very little of what happened at the fort seems to have been community-building; traders came and went while soldiers manned their posts and probably dreamed of going home. But this may be a limited view of fort life. Merchants like Panton, Leslie, and Company soon established stores, and developers divided land into lots to attract residents. Businesses created a port and put up warehouses. The Catholic Church, followed by a host of Protestant denominations, erected houses of worship—evidence that the purpose of community life was not just economic. One of Mobile's first collective efforts went into projects like opening streets—Joachim, Dauphin, Royal.[28]

In 1819, the city received a charter and organized legislative bodies (the Board of Aldermen and the Common Council). Individual settlers and, more important, families—the building blocks of a community—began to arrive. People organized associations to do everything from battling fires to developing a literary culture. Those who came to seek their fortunes as doctors, lawyers, and teachers took on civic identities as aldermen. Collective experiences created a collective memory, which was kept alive in organizations such as the Can't-Get-Away Club. Other institutions like the Protestant Orphanage and the Samaritan Society suggest a sense of shared responsibility.

Mobile was developing both a distinctive physical structure and a distinctive way of life. It was becoming a genuine community, not just a location for intermittent contact among individuals pursuing their own private interests. Generations of work went into producing things citizens could share—from sewers that drained the lowlands to Mardi Gras, which refueled the spirits.

I n addition to schools, literary societies were important educational institutions in the antebellum period. The Franklin Society, founded in 1835, was described as "the cultural center" of the community. It had a library, reading room, and even a small archeological collection. Franklin offered lectures by visiting authors and scholars. Another organization of this type, the Mobile Literary Society, begun in 1855, catered to young businessmen who might otherwise be absorbed by their mercantile pursuits without speeches and debates to stimulate their minds.[29]

The same thing was happening on a lesser scale in the smaller towns of the southwest such as St. Stephens, Claiborne, and Blakeley. Community-building was a major industry.

Despite its importance, however, people weren't necessarily self-conscious about community-building nor did they even use the phrase. If Alabamians had been asked why they went to the trouble of building libraries and churches, I imagine they would have given practical explanations. They might have simply said they wanted places to worship and read. A scholar who studies societies of citizens today found choral groups among the institutions that contribute to a community's way of life. Yet he reported that their members didn't think of themselves as strengthening their community; they joined because they liked to sing.[30]

COMMITTED TO SELF-RULE

In addition to valuing mutual assistance and self-reliance, settlers in the southwest were committed to self-rule, which was another defining imperative of the period. Though surely creating one of the great contradictions in history in this state where slavery was common, citizens were determined to govern themselves and not have their liberty compromised by any form of privilege or external power. In fact, their freedom was defined by its antithesis, slavery—the total domination by others. And the safeguard of their freedom was autonomy, which translated into local control.

Alabama inherited the political legacy of a country that had begun to move away from the political system of the constitutional era, a system that had relied heavily on a central government. People had given a good deal of their "power of attorney" to their federal representatives. They were left with only the power to consent, and even that influence was restricted by requirements for voting, like having to own property. (That condition wasn't without reason, however; odd as it seems today, it was to ensure that those who voted would be responsible because they had a stake in law and social order.)[31]

Robert Wiebe reported that about half of the colonists were legally bound in some form of servitude and that farmland was difficult to get. As late as 1800, one out of every three settlers as far out as the Shenandoah Valley had no land. But when the victory in the War of 1812 opened vast tracts to settlement and the system of indentured servitude collapsed, the meaning of both work and citizenship began to change. That war was particularly significant for the southwestern counties of Alabama because it brought waves of new settlers to the area after Andrew Jackson's defeat of Britain's ally, the Creek Nation, at the battle of Horseshoe Bend in 1814.

Those settlers were property owners, not indentured servants. Any white man engaged in self-directed work was a citizen, and he carried that citizenship with him wherever he went. Wiebe believed that as more people started working for themselves—as work changed from other-directed to self-directed—the political system began to change in response. Restrictions on the right to vote fell away, and more issues were decided at the polls as shown by the frequency with which citizens cast ballots in local elections. Nearly everyone who could vote did and on every conceivable issue.

If owning property wasn't going to be used to ensure a responsible electorate in this age of popular sovereignty, what was? The answer was the education of all citizens; and as more and more people acquired the right to vote, the more emphatic that answer became. Only a virtuous citizenry could govern itself, and virtues were both moral and rational. Knowledge increased virtue, and education increased knowledge. That logic dominated the political rhetoric throughout nineteenth-century America, giving schools a decidedly political mandate.

Old centers of authority disintegrated, and power was redistributed under a wave of egalitarianism (no favoritism to anyone, especially the rich). In Alabama, the elite Georgia, or "royal," party lost control after 1823, and a new generation of politicians based their careers on championing popular causes.

Egalitarian principles were so appealing that both political parties at the time pledged allegiance to them.[32]

These parties were also vehicles for self-rule—up to a point. Unlike today's scripted party conventions, where political messages come indirectly through television, the early parties used meetings, rallies, and parades to reach citizens directly. Yet it isn't clear whether these organizations were more interested in helping elites gain political power or in aiding citizens in setting their own agenda. Not fully established until the 1830s, Alabama parties usually came in pairs, first Democrats and Whigs, then Democrats and Know-Nothings (a name for the American Party), and finally States' Righters and Union Democrats. Every party had its own newspaper whose editor was an influential leader because the print media and party conventions were the principal means of rallying citizens.

Whigs tended to champion state-aided internal improvements and commerce. That is why Mobile, with a cash economy, usually supported them. Democrats, on the other hand, opposed the concentration of power, particularly in the state government, and railed against moneyed interests in hopes of solidifying their hold on yeoman farmers. Both parties endorsed self-rule and popular sovereignty—at least in principle. As the Whig Party's influence began to decline in the mid-1850s, some members (along with certain Democrats) embraced the Know-Nothing Party, which tried to build a political base by promoting fear of foreigners and non-Protestants.

The primary "driving force behind nineteenth-century democracy," however—the impulse that sent people to the ballot box and to public work— didn't come as much from parties as from citizens themselves, which prompted Wiebe to describe the public as thousands spurring other thousands to civic action. Public life was boisterous and deferential; people could and did enter it without anyone's permission. They simply acted as though they belonged, which is the original meaning of "participation."[33]

Surely, it is not a coincidence that during the years when democracy meant self-rule, the cause of public education flourished.

NOTES TO CHAPTER 2

[1] To read about communities along Alabama's rivers, read Harvey H. Jackson III's *Rivers of History: Life on the Coosa, Tallapoosa, Cahaba, and Alabama* (Tuscaloosa: University of Alabama Press, 1995). The description of Claiborne is on pp. 47, 66.

[2] Grady McWhiney's account of the influence of Celtic culture is in *Cracker Culture: Celtic Ways in the Old South* (Tuscaloosa: University of Alabama Press, 1988). For the details on differences within families, compare Anna M. Gayle Fry's *Memories of Old Cahaba* (Nashville: Publishing House of the M. E. Church, South, 1908), pp. 53-54 with David Mathews's "Children's Stories" (Clarke County Historical Society, Grove Hill, Alabama, 1999, photocopy), p. 5.

[3] All quotations from John Massey are in *Reminiscences: Giving Sketches of Scenes through which the Author Has Passed and Pen Portraits of People Who Have Modified His Life* (Nashville: Publishing House of the M. E. Church, South, 1916), pp. 22-23.

[4] Benjamin F. Porter, *Reminiscences of Men and Things in Alabama,* ed. Sara Walls (Tuscaloosa: Portals Press, 1983), p. 30.

[5] Frank Lawrence Owsley, *Plain Folk of the Old South* (1949; reprint, Baton Rouge: Louisiana State University Press, 1982), p. 95.

[6] Wayne Flynt, *Poor but Proud: Alabama's Poor Whites* (Tuscaloosa: University of Alabama Press, 1989), p. 4.

[7] Clement Eaton, *The Growth of Southern Civilization, 1790-1860* (New York: Harper and Row, 1961), pp. 169-173 and Owsley, *Plain Folk,* pp. 28-37.

[8] Gary B. Mills, "Shades of Ambiguity: Comparing Antebellum Free People of Color in 'Anglo' and 'Latin' Louisiana," in *Plain Folk of the South Revisited,* ed. Samuel C. Hyde, Jr. (Baton Rouge: Louisiana State University Press, 1997), p. 181. There is a detailed account of the circumstances of a wealthy family of free black Southerners in Michael P. Johnson and James L. Roark's *Black Masters: A Free Family of Color in the Old South* (New York: Norton, 1984).

[9] Timothy H. Ball mentioned Tom Brown, the free black who operated a hotel in Grove Hill, in *A Glance into the Great South-East, or, Clarke County, Alabama, and Its Surroundings, from 1540 to 1877* (1879; reprint, Tuscaloosa: Willo Publishing Company, 1962), p. 195.

[10] African-Americans had the same disposition to create civic associations as whites according to W. E. B. DuBois's *The Philadelphia Negro: A Social Study* (1899; reprint, with an introduction by E. Digby Baltzell, New York: Schocken Books, 1967), pp. 19-20. DuBois uses examples like Philadelphia's Free African Society (1787) and the Negro Union of Newport, Rhode Island. Similar organizations probably existed in Mobile.

[11] Robert L. Glynn collected accounts of slavery in Alabama from the records of his church and published them in *"How Firm a Foundation": A History of the First Black Church in Tuscaloosa County, Alabama* (Tuscaloosa: Friends of the Hunter's Chapel African Methodist Episcopal Zion Church and the City of Tuscaloosa, Alabama Bicentennial Committee, 1976), p. 31.

[12] Glynn, *"How Firm a Foundation,"* pp. 31-32.

[13] John Hope Franklin and Loren Schweninger, *Runaway Slaves: Rebels on the Plantation* (New York: Oxford University Press, 1999).

[14] Alexis de Tocqueville's observations about neighbors crossing the streets to form a "deliberative body" are a very loose translation of what he wrote about political associations. See *Democracy in America* in the recent version prepared by Harvey C. Mansfield and Delba Winthrop (Chicago: University of Chicago Press, 2000), pp. 181-182. The direct quotations in the next paragraph are from *Democracy in America,* ed. Richard D. Heffner (New York: Penguin Books, 1984). See particularly p. 208.

[15] F. L. Cherry wrote about hog-killing in "The History of Opelika and Her Agricultural Tributary Territory," *Alabama Historical Quarterly* 15 (summer 1953): 229. Ray Oldenburg identified the modern equivalents of these gatherings in *The Great Good Place: Cafés, Coffee Shops, Community Centers, Beauty Parlors, General Stores, Bars, Hangouts and How They Get You through the Day* (New York: Paragon House, 1989).

[16] Owsley, *Plain Folk,* pp. 90-132.

[17] The description of the campground in Clarke County is from David Chapman Mathews's "Early Sketches," *South Alabamian,* 27 January 1966. The account of what happened at such places is based on a report of a Presbyterian camp meeting in Talladega County in 1839. Samuel Ster-

ling Sherman of Vermont visited this assembly on his way to Tuscaloosa to take a position at the state university. *Autobiography of Samuel Sterling Sherman 1815-1910* (Chicago: M. A. Donohue, 1910), pp. 32-33.

[18] Wayne Flynt, *Alabama Baptists: Southern Baptists in the Heart of Dixie* (Tuscaloosa: University of Alabama Press, 1998), p. 52.

[19] Alabama General Assembly, *House Journal,* 1st biennial sess., 1847-1848 (Montgomery: McCormick and Walshe, 1848), pp. 24-25.

[20] All of the reports on meetings in Clarke County are from Ball, *Glance into the Great South-East,* pp. 231-232, 244-245.

[21] Leonard Calvert Cooke commented on the "patriotism" of roadwork in "The Development of the Road System of Alabama" (master's thesis, The University of Alabama, 1935), pp. 71-74.

[22] Porter, *Reminiscences,* p. 31.

[23] Ball, *Glance into the Great South-East,* pp. 170, 211, 370.

[24] Daniel S. Dupre explained antibarbecuism in *Transforming the Cotton Frontier: Madison County, Alabama 1800-1840* (Baton Rouge: Louisiana State University Press, 1997), pp. 179-192. While the descriptions of these events may be accurate, the way reformers characterized them suggests they had a negative bias toward them.

[25] Alexis de Tocqueville, *Journey to America,* ed. J. P. Mayer (1957; reprint, Garden City, N.Y.: Doubleday, 1971), p. 103 and Harriet Martineau, *Society in America,* ed. Seymour Martin Lipset (1962; reprint, New Brunswick: Transaction Publishers, 1994), pp. 150-154.

[26] Robert D. Putnam documented the political effects of social life in *Making Democracy Work: Civic Traditions in Modern Italy* (Princeton: Princeton University Press, 1993), pp. 83-120. Vaughn L. Grisham, Jr., had a similar account

of public life in the American South: *Tupelo: The Evolution of a Community* (Dayton, Ohio: Kettering Foundation Press, 1999).

[27] Richard C. Harwood, "The Nation's Looking Glass," *Kettering Review* (spring 2000): 8.

[28] Of the numerous studies of antebellum Mobile, none is more exhaustive than Alan Smith Thompson's "Mobile, Alabama, 1850-1861: Economic, Political, Physical, and Population Characteristics" (Ph.D. diss., The University of Alabama, 1979). I found his second chapter very useful. Jay Higginbotham's *Old Mobile: Fort Louis de la Louisiane, 1702-1711* (1977; reprint, Tuscaloosa: University of Alabama Press, 1991) is a very readable account of the antecedents of nineteenth-century Mobile.

[29] Examples of Mobile's civic infrastructure came from Caldwell Delaney, ed., *Craighead's Mobile: Being the Fugitive Writings of Erwin S. Craighead and Frank Craighead* (Mobile: Haunted Bookshop, 1968), p. 49 and Harriet Amos, *Cotton City: Urban Development in Antebellum Mobile* (University: University of Alabama Press, 1985), p. 78.

[30] Putnam, *Making Democracy Work,* p. 90.

[31] I am particularly indebted to Robert H. Wiebe's *Self-Rule: A Cultural History of American Democracy* (Chicago: University of Chicago Press, 1995). I used the information in his book as the basis for my overview of nineteenth-century politics.

[32] The end of the influence of the "royal" party in Alabama and the democratic/egalitarian tenor of politics in the late 1820s is reported in the first chapter of J. Mills Thornton III's *Politics and Power in a Slave Society: Alabama, 1800-1860* (Baton Rouge: Louisiana State University Press, 1978). He explained the positions of the parties in Chapter 3.

[33] Wiebe, *Self-Rule,* p. 71.

Chapter 3

Public Schools from Public Work

LABAMIANS BUILT SCHOOLS much the same way that they built roads. Saying that these schools were "public" is like saying that roads built by citizens and open to all travelers were "public" roads—in contrast to those that landowners built for private use.

The Earliest Schooling

The public begins to form when a handful of people decide they have a problem and that something needs to be done about it. Often one or two people will start the ball rolling, and others will join in. Something like that may have happened in Tensaw in 1799, which encouraged John Pierce to found Alabama's first school.

When the British gained control of the region in 1763, Protestant missionaries took up the campaign to convert the native population to Christianity. And Parliament authorized a salary for a tutor, William Gordon, who may or may not have opened a school—definitive evidence is lacking. British rule ended in 1783, and the Spanish held the area until American soldiers evicted them in 1813. Their missionaries tried to inspire religious conversion through Christianity and taught the Native Americans farming so they could be absorbed into the agricultural economy. American missionaries, aided by Silas Dinsmoor (Dinsmore) who would later become a champion of public schools in Mobile, succeeded the Spanish. Dinsmoor was a federal agent appointed to deal with the Choctaws, and the church schools he encouraged include the renowned Mayhew Mission.

The year the Pierce school opened is significant because it was the same year surveyors established that Tensaw was, in fact, part of the United States rather than Spanish West Florida. Spain controlled everything south of the 31st parallel. Everything north of this latitude, which included the Pierce holdings, became ripe for development because the United States could grant or sell land with precise deeds calculated from a baseline named for the principal surveyor, Andrew Ellicott.

B efore the Pierces arrived and Tensaw became the largest of the first settlements in south Alabama (except for Mobile), the area had been home to various tribes of Native Americans including the Tensas, who left their name on the land before going back to Louisiana. Opening the Pierce school certainly wasn't the beginning of education in Alabama, but it was the start of institutions established by citizens to take over some of the instruction traditionally provided by families. Even then, the 1799 school was only "the first American" institution. Indians living in the area had long educated their children for survival through skill-building and for the perpetuation of their culture through stories, dances, and art. The French arrived in 1702 under the command of Jean Baptiste LeMoyne (Bienville) and brought missionaries who may have provided some instruction. France refused Bienville's request to begin a college in Mobile, but legend has it that his cousin, Madame Langlois (L'Anglois), taught seven of the colonists' children in her home in 1711.[1]

OBJECTIVES: MORAL AND POLITICAL VIRTUE

Whatever prompted John Pierce to start teaching, the reason the pioneers in the Tensaw country needed schooling is clear: to bring order to the frontier. Their intent was civic. The thick swamps at the confluence of the Alabama and Tombigbee Rivers had been an inviting sanctuary for robbers and outcasts, who were more of an obstacle to settlement than bears, alligators, or snakes.

Developers were quick to recognize that the Tensaw country was rich in farm and timber land, and Alexander McGillivray was one of the first to see its potential. He was an influential Creek (or Muscogee) chieftain whose father, Lachlan, was a Scottish merchant and Tory from Charleston. His mother was Sehoy Marchand of the powerful Wind clan. McGillivray encouraged British loyalists to migrate to the area when it was in British and, later, Spanish hands.[2]

McGillivray gave good advice: some settlers, such as John Linder, a native of Switzerland who had served with the British as a surveyor and later with the Spanish as a justice of the peace, became quite wealthy (although John Linder, Jr., was said to have joined the lawless

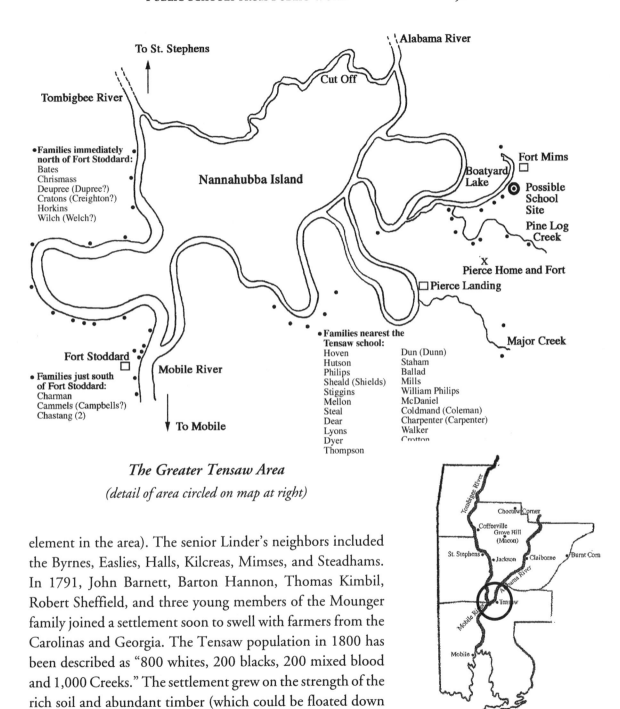

Alabama River

Cut Off

To St. Stephens

Tombigbee River

Nannahubba Island

Fort Mims

Boatyard Lake

Possible School Site

Pine Log Creek

• Families immediately north of Fort Stoddard:
Bates
Chrismass
Deupree (Dupree?)
Cratons (Creighton?)
Horkins
Wilch (Welch?)

X Pierce Home and Fort

☐ Pierce Landing

Major Creek

Fort Stoddard

Mobile River

• Families just south of Fort Stoddard:
Charman
Cammels (Campbells?)
Chastang (2)

↓ To Mobile

• Families nearest the Tensaw school:

Hoven	Dun (Dunn)
Hutson	Staham
Philips	Ballad
Sheald (Shields)	Mills
Stiggins	William Philips
Mellon	McDaniel
Steal	Coldmand (Coleman)
Dear	Charpenter (Carpenter)
Lyons	Walker
Dyer	Crotton
Thompson	

The Greater Tensaw Area
(detail of area circled on map at right)

Tombigbee River

Choctaw Corner

Coffeeville
Grove Hill
(Macon)

St. Stephens • • Jackson • Claiborne • Burnt Corn

Alabama River

Tensaw

Mobile River

Mobile •

element in the area). The senior Linder's neighbors included the Byrnes, Easlies, Halls, Kilcreas, Mimses, and Steadhams. In 1791, John Barnett, Barton Hannon, Thomas Kimbil, Robert Sheffield, and three young members of the Mounger family joined a settlement soon to swell with farmers from the Carolinas and Georgia. The Tensaw population in 1800 has been described as "800 whites, 200 blacks, 200 mixed blood and 1,000 Creeks." The settlement grew on the strength of the rich soil and abundant timber (which could be floated down "industries," such as brickyards, sawmills, and William Pierce's cotton gin (John's brother).[3]

Settlers wanted a civilized way of life, as is evidenced in the correspondence of Ephraim Kirby, Thomas Jefferson's land commissioner in the territory. Kirby complained vigorously about the lack of moral and political virtue in the settlements. The situation was critical, and people other than Kirby knew it. Judge Harry Toulmin described those in the neighboring Tombigbee River basin as "born amidst the clouds of ignorance" and likely to die in the same condition. These eyewitness accounts convinced James Doster that a good many in the Tensaw area were not only "ignorant, uncouth, and ungovernable" but also "violent and vicious, strangers to moral principles."[4]

No one knows the Tensaw area better than local historian Davida Hastie and Major Tunstall, who lives on the Pierce homesite. No trace exists of the first school, but they guess that it was located where it could have served two groups of settlers, one around Pine Log Creek to the south and the other just north and west of the lake in the vicinity of Sam Mims's home.[6]

Settlers surely recognized that they had to have the kind of institutions that would foster social responsibility and the rule of law. John Pierce, who had taught in Kentucky, where he stopped on his way to Alabama, responded. Four years after he arrived, he opened a school on the banks of what is now Boatyard Lake (previously Lake Tensaw or Lake Steadham).[5]

At the Boatyard school, reciting lengthy written texts was the principal method of instruction, and passersby unfamiliar with this pedagogical device called the institution a "blab school," probably because of the sounds coming from the classroom. The student body was an integrated collection of young people "mixed in blood" and with skin "of every hue," according to Alabama historian, A. J. Pickett. Some were of Creek ancestry—"the high-blood descendants of Lachlan McGillivray, the Taits, Weatherfords, and Durants." Others were children of "the aristocratic Linders, [and] the wealthy Mims's." According to one source, William Weatherford (or Red Eagle), a war leader of the Creek Nation, was one of Pierce's students.[7]

The school at Tensaw has been ignored in Alabama's educational history because it wasn't considered "public." Certainly it wasn't by today's definition. Still, I want to make the case that the Pierce school had public characteristics—if for no reason other than to question the prevailing assumptions about what makes a school public.

The most obvious reason for disqualifying this institution is because one person, John Pierce, opened it. But Pierce was more than an itinerant schoolmaster passing through the Tensaw community; he played a significant role in it as one of the key stakeholders. And many public projects are sparked by just one citizen; strong leadership is quite common in strong democracies. The litmus test is how many other people were allies in establishing the school. In this case, no one seems to know what the relationship was between Pierce and his neighbors or who else wanted to see a school established. We do have Pickett's list of families who sent their children and conceivably did more to sustain the institution. The most compelling reason for considering the school public is that it helped create a public life in the Tensaw settlement where order would replace violence and self-government would prevail over anarchy.

The Tensaw community met a tragic end in 1813 when a warring band of Creeks led by William Weatherford attacked the settlers gathered at Fort Mims. The assault wiped out a substantial portion of the population, including women and children; local sources claim about five hundred people died. A fort at the nearby Pierce home wasn't touched, however, and the Pierce brothers, unlike Sam Mims, escaped to safety there. If the school was still open in 1813, the massacre probably closed it.[8]

After teaching for seven years, John Pierce went into business with his brother and then served as postmaster from 1811 to 1818, when Tensaw reemerged as a new community away from the river and closer to a rail line. There is no evidence of a successor to the Pierce school, although there are accounts of schools nearby—one established in 1840 on Holly Creek and another founded by the Montgomery Hill Baptists in the early 1850s.

To insist that Pierce's was the first public school in Alabama would be claiming too much; to say that it has nothing to tell us about public education would be claiming too little.

FROM FAMILIES TO SETTLEMENTS

Most early settlements didn't have an experienced teacher like John Pierce on hand. The first schools were often started by parents, with the support of people living nearby. Self-reliant families created institutions that would, in time, take over some of their educational responsibilities. Just as courts began in private homes, so did schools.

Why families took the lead isn't difficult to imagine: parents cared about the education of their children. Some only employed their own tutors. Most did more: they opened their classes to relatives and neighbors because they cared about what their settlements would become. Typically, one family out of a small group of pioneers would use a room in its newly built cabin to teach children. Both men and women would take turns as instructors.

Southwestern Alabama followed the practice of the colonies, where parents, elders, or older brothers and sisters taught responsive and communal reading. Youngsters growing up in homes where no one was available to teach would be sent to a neighboring household. In time, some people became specialists in primary instruction. A New England woman who taught reading on a regular basis and charged a modest fee was said to be operating a "dame school." A Virginia family that had a servant (or tutor) teach its children and those of neighbors was said to be running a "petty school." Families were expected to provide a rudimentary education before sending a child to a formal classroom. Frontier states in the South had the same expectations.[9]

The first school in Clarke County seems to have been located in the home of Caleb Moncrief, one of a group of settlers who arrived in 1808 or 1809 and built houses near Bassett's Creek. Angeline Wilson, who had no small children of her own, devoted much of her time to teaching in the Moncrief home.[10]

The classes in the Moncrief home led directly to a community school. Eventually, neighbors joined forces to build a separate building for both a primary school and a Sunday school (supervised by Moncrief). Sometime later, the weekday school was relocated near Grove Hill and kept the name of its founder. This school served families in the area and helped make education an ongoing community responsibility. In 1824, Clarke County citizens built a more substantial schoolhouse for the Macon Male and Female Academy in the vicinity of the James S. Dickinson home in Grove Hill. It is said to have had its roots in Moncrief's school.

Every county had its Caleb Moncrief. At Burnt Corn, where Monroe and Conecuh Counties meet, John Green opened a school in his home around 1817. A local history reports that "Mr. Green came to this wilderness in 1816 and found it without any civilization. He was a self-educated man and realized the need of a school for the few settlers who were coming into this area."[11]

Green migrated from South Carolina to Georgia to Alabama, a common pattern. After practicing law, he settled down to farming and, two years before opening the school, married Nancy Betts Jones. Typical of young couples on the frontier, she was fifteen and he was twenty-five. With a family that grew to fourteen children, they had an obvious self-interest in education. Green himself taught for a number of years. The Green school served a neighborhood of families, all related, that lived along the old Federal Road. Among them were the O'Briens, whose father, Pat, had been educated for the Catholic priesthood in Ireland. By 1841, the Green school had become the Burnt Corn Academy. John Green was a trustee. Pat O'Brien, his wife, Nancy Clingman, and their daughter, Bettie Lanier, were all teachers.[12]

Schools were usually among the first institutions established in other settlements of the southwest. In Conecuh County, for instance, George Andrews opened a school in 1821 (near where the courthouse was built). In the same county, the town of Evergreen actually took its name from the high school—the Evergreen Male and Female Academy, founded in 1838—because the community grew up around it. As was true of the Burnt Corn and Macon schools, the Evergreen Academy evolved from a one-room institution. It was founded by Alexander B. Travis, a noted Baptist minister, who rallied the families living around "Cosey's Old Field" to build an academy. Instruction was available at a neighboring community, Sparta, but the people living in what was to become Evergreen (then a much smaller settlement of one hundred and fifty) wanted their own school.[13]

Moncrief, Green, Andrews, and Travis appear to have had similar motives: they acted in the interest both of their families and the settlements that hoped to grow into communities. Ultimately they did more than open a single school; they made education a tradition. When these founders died, others took up the responsibility for providing instruction. As one Alabamian said, successor generations always took care to see that there were schools.[14]

These founders left few records, but their reputations suggest they had strong civic interests and spent a good deal of their time in community-building. Moncrief, for instance, is remembered for his Jeffersonian

Top, John Green, Sr., and Nancy Betts Jones Green; above, Bettie Lanier O'Brien.

sympathies and for his participation in a range of social causes, including temperance.[15]

FROM SETTLEMENTS TO COMMUNITIES

Community-building was school-building. Though no one said so in these exact words, I got the strong impression from what I found in Alabama that the schools enjoyed broad support in communities because they were seen as extensions of the communities; they were the public organized to make learning available. Later, educational reformers would argue that local schools had actually been too responsive and that communities didn't require high enough standards. Their criticisms may have had some merit, although only a good school was a competitive advantage. And the school was a community's proudest symbol of public spirit.[16]

Settlements on their way to becoming village towns competed with one another for new arrivals and facilities like railroads. In order to be attractive, they believed they had to demonstrate the civic responsibility of their residents and the morality of their way of life. A school was evidence of both.

Newspaper accounts reflect the pride communities took in the willingness of citizens to support good schooling. While today's towns might boast of outlet malls, Grove Hill made quite a different case for itself in 1857 by calling attention to the pedagogical prowess of a teacher, Edward A. Scott, and the excellent instruction available at the local academy. After assuring readers that Scott was about as good an educator as could be found, the *Clarke County Democrat* went on to say:

> The citizens of Grove Hill seem determined to build up schools that shall not be surpassed by any in the South. They have now a flourishing Male School; but that of the Female, for want of a more commodious building, is small at present. A few days since the erection of a Female Academy, to suit the emergency, was presented to the citizens of the place, and every one to whom the subject was mentioned made a liberal donation, and in a short time an amount nearly sufficient to build such an institution was subscribed.
>
> The Town of Grove Hill has many advantages over almost any location in South Alabama, particularly from the fact of its being remarkably healthy, and of

strictly moral and good society—not even a grocery or ten pin alley disturbing the quietude of its citizens.[17]

New towns lost no time in making provisions for education. St. Stephens persuaded the territorial legislature to authorize a school in 1811, the year the town was incorporated. Capital of the Alabama Territory in 1817 and the first center of government in the area north of Mobile, the St. Stephens settlement dates back to a French encampment and a Spanish fort, San Esteban, built in 1789. It wasn't until the settlement became a community, however, that a group of citizens including James Caller, Thomas B. Creagh, and George Strother Gaines asked for and received a charter for the Washington Academy, which seems to have been known later as the St. Stephens Academy. Initial funding came from a five thousand dollar lottery.[18]

The St. Stephens fortification and trading post benefited from new settlers arriving after England lost the War of 1812. Visitors report that "the town of St. Stephens . . . is advancing with a rapidity beyond that of any place, perhaps in the western country. It has at this moment at least thirty new houses commenced: many of them would vie with those generally built in the United States." Among the main attractions pointed out by the press were a steamboat capable of reaching the ocean and "an academy, supported by the voluntary contributions of the citizens; with two teachers and sixty or seventy students, who have since their commencement, made progress highly honorable to the institution." In 1816, the legislature appropriated five hundred dollars for the school, in addition to voluntary contributions. D. H. Mayhew was the

Opening schools was just another facet of pioneering. And the pioneering spirit wasn't confined to more prominent settlers like these three leaders from St. Stephens: Caller, Creagh, and Gaines. Caller was a senior militia officer and territorial commissioner. Creagh was an educated British officer who stayed in America after the Revolution to become a wealthy planter. Gaines is the best known of the three because he left detailed reminiscences. Compare Gaines's contributions to those of Caleb Moncrief. While both were from North Carolina, they came to occupy different stations in Alabama. Gaines became far more famous, but Moncrief was no less a factor in education, maybe more. The two shared a Jeffersonian sense of civic duty; in fact, President Jefferson appointed Gaines as a federal agent for dealing with the Choctaws. Gaines also owned a trading business, served as postmaster in St. Stephens, and became a bank president in Mobile. And though avoiding partisan politics, he was elected a state senator. That office didn't seem as important to him, however, as experiences like organizing the citizenry in St. Stephens to defend themselves against the English and their Creek allies. While this conflict sent citizens to building fortifications, it didn't stop preparations for the school that Gaines and others founded.[19]

first teacher; the most notable student was Mingo, son of Choctaw chief Pushmataha.[20]

Tabitha Gordy, a settler who arrived in St. Stephens in 1812 or 1813, recalled that the Academy wasn't the only educational institution. There were schools in homes and one taught by a Mr. and Mrs. Duncan around 1830. Mrs. Gordy said the children used homemade pens made from goose feathers, which the teacher constantly sharpened until he introduced steel pens. "The country," she remembers, "was filled with young men looking for land, school teachers getting up schools." She describes D. H. Mayhew, who came from North Carolina, as "a splendid teacher and a good man."[21]

In other counties, school followed community as day follows night. Aside from the classes in the Moncrief's home, Clarke County's first formal school appears to have been in what is now Jackson in 1816. It shared space with a rather substantial church. By 1831, the Jackson Male Academy, taught by W. W. Alston, was advertising its courses as far away as Mobile.[22]

Rockville reputedly had the second oldest school in the county, an academy also dating back to the 1830s. Recall, however, that there was a school building in Grove Hill by 1824 near the home of James Dickinson. The town, eventually the site of the county government, was known as Macon at the time, as was the school. (Grove Hill had several names before 1851: Center, Magoffin's Store, Smithville, as well as Macon.) Timothy H. Ball said that a "Grove Hill Academy" opened in 1836. Since there was no Grove Hill then, he was probably referring to the Macon Male and Female Academy. It received a legislative charter in 1846 and Rufus H. Kilpatrich was named principal. In 1859, the Eclectic Academy, about four and a half miles east of town on the Claiborne Road, announced that it was ready for students, according to the Reverend Ball, who had been teaching at the Grove Hill Academy (successor to the Macon Academy).

Harvey and Elizabeth Jackson identified another early school, perhaps founded around 1830, which was located about two miles northeast of Grove Hill near the Methodist or Spinks Chapel. Elijah Gilmore served as minister and probably teacher both.[23]

Coffeeville, on the western edge of the county, opened the Pendleton Academy in 1833, followed or succeeded in 1859 by the West Bend Academy.

Suggsville, an older community to the east, was flooded with education: G. W. Creagh recruited students to attend the Franklin Academy in the *Mobile Commercial Register* in 1826. Around 1836, Mrs. McCary, wife of the *Clarke County Post* editor, opened the Suggsville Female Academy. Then, a year later, the Suggsville Institute (also for young ladies) began classes.[24]

The Lambard School was providing instruction in Gainestown in 1840. Choctaw Corner, site of the railroad meeting, had a Masonic Institute and a Rural Male and Female Academy in the late 1850s. Nearby Bashi opened a school in 1859, but even earlier (1829) Lewis Spinks taught a school in that vicinity. Morvin seems to have had a school run by Robert King, an "early settler," though little is known about it.

Pioneer schools didn't always survive. According to one source, twelve of the sixteen institutions founded in Clarke County before 1859 were still offering classes by the end of the decade. Local officials, however, reported to the state superintendent that there were forty-one schools of all types in the county in 1858; thirty-six were public, five were private. Instruction ranged from the primary to the intermediate to the advanced, or high school, level. The average term was five and a half months. A total of 1,200 students were registered out of 2,517 school-age children in the county. Only 128 were in the private schools and one academy.[25]

VARIETIES OF INSTITUTIONS

When the Green family and their neighbors or the citizens of Grove Hill built schools through their collective efforts as citizens, what did they look like? Apparently, they varied a great deal, reflecting their surrounding. Some were as primitive as the frontier; others were more substantial and mirrored the affluence of new communities.

OLD-FIELD SCHOOLS

Places of learning, located where they could serve widely dispersed families that weren't close to any particular community, were called "old-field schools." We would probably call them rural schools today. Unlike the private enterprises in England, these institutions usually grew out of Alexis de Tocqueville's associations. People would form themselves into a board of trustees, put up a building, and hire a teacher, with each family paying its proportionate share of the expenses. New settlers could enroll their children if they paid an equivalent amount in tuition.

Old-field schools were quite rustic. The Rockville school in Clarke County, for example, said to be a "true pioneer school," consisted of a large room built from logs and "heated by a fireplace taking up most of one end of the building. Seats were of the crudest kind—split logs without backs and held up by four pegs. If there was a blackboard at all, it was made of wide planks painted black."[26]

Instructors in the rural schools sometimes complained that they had to compete with the attractions of country life for the attention of young scholars. One teacher in Dallas County describes his students as "real young hunters, who handle the long rifle with more ease and dexterity than the goosequill, and who are incomparably more at home in 'twisting a rabbit,' or 'treeing a 'possum,' than in conjugating a verb."[27]

COMMON SCHOOLS

The typical school, often called "common," offered a primary education. Most had only one room, one teacher for students of all ages, and one session that might last for only three months, either June through August or December through February in farming country. (Agricultural demands were fewer then, so the choice was between being too hot or too cold.) Instructors had fairly free rein in what they taught as long as they covered the three Rs. There were no grades; students passed through the curriculum by mastering one text and then moving on to another. The "blab" method used at Tensaw was standard practice. Enrollments were small, usually fewer than twenty pupils.[28]

ACADEMIES

In the larger communities, citizens also founded schools called academies. These ranged from small institutions offering primary education and a smattering of secondary instruction to those with college preparatory curricula, which drew boarding students from the surrounding area. Numbering about two hundred in their heyday, academies cropped up across the state; most had a corporate charter from the legislature so they could carry on financial and legal transactions. Because they served the public, these schools often received various forms of state support.[29]

Presbyterians were particularly fond of this type of school and used their churches and pastors to establish them. This denomination wasn't alone in its enthusiasm for academies, however, as is evident in the long list of citizens who went to the legislature to secure charters.

A charter granted in 1820 to the Solemn Grove community in Monroe County illustrates both the reasons for establishing academies and their method of operation. Residents between Limestone and Flat Creeks petitioned the general assembly for a school that would be "productive of general utility, and conduce to the good order and happiness of society." That mandate couldn't have been clearer about the public purposes to be served. The Solemn Grove Academy, and the particular way in which it was incorporated, became the standard for hundreds of others created for similar reasons.[30]

Some accounts of education have made much of the difference between the academy and the common school on the grounds that one was private and the other public. Yet their similarities are striking: both were products of voluntary associations, both served public purposes, and both received encouragement along with direct assistance from the state. To be sure, common schools typically had more government support from federal land grants. But even historians such as Stephen B. Weeks, who liked to emphasize the differences, admitted that in many cases "public" institutions and "private" ones were virtually indistinguishable. This isn't to say, however, there weren't truly private schools that operated as businesses, with little public intent.[31]

PUBLIC MANDATES IN THE CURRICULUM

While a community's investment in schools was evident in everything from constructing classrooms to collecting funds to securing teachers, its relationship to these institutions wasn't limited to the physical and financial. Communities had an investment in what was taught. They didn't appear to interfere with teacher's prerogatives, and yet they provided an underlying intent for the curriculum. And that intent reflected the objectives that caused citizens to exercise their collective capacities in the first place. People wanted to create a way of life that would perpetuate what they valued, and communities established schools to help in that work, giving the schools a public mandate. That mandate influenced the tenor and spirit of the curriculum.

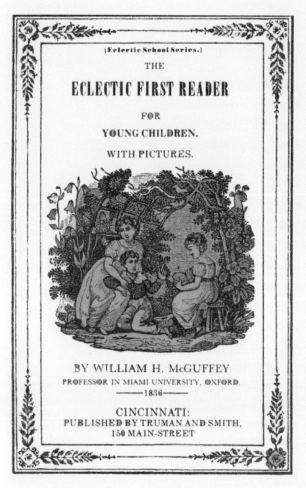

A McGuffey Reader

Teachers prepared students for public life through the textbooks they selected, the subjects they taught, and the expectations they had for their students. When the public built schools, it built doorways into the society that citizens hoped to create.

Hardly any subjects in the curriculum benefited students personally (perhaps hygiene), and only a few developed job-related skills (bookkeeping). The basics—reading, writing, and arithmetic—were just that: foundations for everything else. Some subjects explicitly prepared young people for citizenship: history (with an emphasis on the United States Constitution), geography, and declamation or public speaking. Interestingly, the curriculum of institutions that taught young women included these same public studies. Academies for women advertised courses in history, government, moral philosophy, and rhetoric. An introduction to the natural sciences rounded out the basic curriculum; art and music were also available.[32]

Much of the instruction conveyed precepts to guide the behavior of youngsters, and there were no better books for doing this than those for teaching reading, particularly William Holmes McGuffey's famed texts.

Students were fond of these books. John Massey of Choctaw County recalls, "My studies during the first summer session with Mr. James were spelling, reading, and writing . . . I have often wished to see those old readers again, but have not been able to find a single copy. . . . The next summer, . . . we used a new series of readers, just published, by Dr. W. H. McGuffey, of the University of Virginia. I was very much interested in grammar and reading, and everything moved on smoothly as far as I was concerned."[33]

The Mobile *Mercantile Advertiser* advertised other popular texts. Webster and Pickett had the leading spelling books; others include "Daboll's arithmetic, Morse's geography, Enfield's *Speaker*, the *Columbian Orator*, Goldsmith's *Rome*, Blair's *Lectures*, [and] Valpy's *Greek Grammar*." Parents were also encouraged to buy school supplies: "foolscap, paper, pencils, quills, ink powder, slates, . . . and sealing wax."[34]

As people tried to decide on the way of life they wanted to prevail in their communities, they had to confront two powerful imperatives that pulled them in different directions. The welfare of Alabama depended on having citizens with initiative, creativity, and the freedom to follow their instincts. Enterprise was considered the key to economic growth. Yet these same people had to have a sense of social responsibility and not be seduced by "money madness." Not willing to resolve that tension by favoring one purpose over another, the public charged the schools with giving entrepreneurship a social conscience. The curriculum showed that educators understood that mandate. Books used in upper-level courses included two very popular ones by Francis Wayland, president of Brown University: *The Elements of Moral Science* and *The Elements of Political Economy*. Wayland's criticisms of slavery probably weren't welcome in Alabama, although his views on moral science and political economy were. Wayland envisioned a society where individuals were free to pursue their notion of the good life but where self-direction resulted in the greater well-being of all, not simply personal fulfillment. He drew on one of the authorities on both morality and the economy, Scottish philosopher Adam Smith, who has said, "He is certainly not a good citizen who does not wish to promote, by every means in his power, the welfare of the whole society of his fellow-citizens."[35]

Given this charge, the curriculum emphasized character as well as intellectual development. It reflected the sentiments of a citizenry that had a great deal to say about "the habits, manners and morals of children," as in this letter in the *Linden Jeffersonian*. Fearing the lack of parental discipline, T. W. Price warned that the younger generation could degenerate into idleness and ruin. "I am inclined to think," he writes, "that we cannot, with safety, leave this government in the hands of those who are to follow us, unless there is a change of some kind in the education and discipline of youth." His intent was civic; schooling was a public matter. "This great work," he goes on, must begin in early childhood; if not, "little can be done on the part of teachers." Price was proposing standards not so much for the schools as for the community. He urged his fellow citizens to set high expectations for families. He was particularly concerned about wealthy parents who indulged their children with "fine clothes" and the diversions of "guns, dogs and horses."[36]

Accountability and Evaluation

The idea that community is accountable for the education of its children, and not just the schools, implies that the community is in a position to affect the quality of schooling. And in order to do that, the community has to know what is going on in the classrooms. In the early nineteenth-century, that knowledge appears to have come as much, or more, from direct observation as from test scores.

When the "standardized test" consisted of reciting back pages in textbooks, the judge was the schoolmaster. When schools had their students perform in public, as frequently happened, the community was the judge. Perhaps there wasn't a great demand for the skills developed by classroom recitations, and people wanted to see what else students could do. Whatever the reasons, public examinations sparked considerable interest. Large audiences turned out for up to three days of recitals, plays, and speeches by students in both male and female departments. Newspapers covered them fully, as in this account from the *Clarke County Democrat* of July 16, 1857:

> The annual Examination of the Male and Female Academies at Suggsville, came off Tuesday, Wednesday and Thursday of last week, before the largest audience that had ever assembled in that village to witness similar displays. The sister counties of Baldwin, Monroe, Washington and Choctaw were fully and respectfully represented . . . the exercises of the pupils of the Male Academy . . . reflected credit alike on teacher and pupils.[37]

While this report may have been overly generous, citizens could judge the quality of instruction directly. Naturally, the schools selected those they put on stage and influenced what they presented, yet there weren't any interme-

diaries between the students and the community. Schools apparently understood the value of having people see and judge for themselves because they
pointedly advertised annual "Public Examinations," where people could
witness "the proficiency" of the students. Only vestiges of this practice remain
today in events like band concerts and athletic contests.[38]

WHO PAID THE BILLS?

The public revealed itself in very tangible ways through school financing.
Community funding was the prevailing practice across the country, and
public support wasn't primarily tax support in states such as Alabama.

Communities had been responsible for providing instruction since colonial times. In Boston, forty-five citizens, including town officials, donated
money to found a grammar school. Nearby Dorchester leased Thompson's
Island and used the rental income for a school. Some colonial governments
made local responsibility a legal requirement. In 1647, the Massachusetts
general court passed legislation to ensure that communities provided schooling: every township of fifty households had to have a schoolmaster, to be paid
either by parents and masters of apprentices or by "the inhabitants in
general."[39]

Of the many ways of funding schools in southwestern Alabama, the most
common was probably subscription, a practice used widely in nineteenth-
century America. Subscriptions typically meant donations; people gave cash,
materials, and labor. But subscribers could become investors rather than just
donors. When schools were incorporated in some states, donors were given
membership in the corporation, along with voting rights.[40]

Subscriptions were also used to raise money for other purposes, such as the
capitalization of business ventures and towns. For example, developers would
secure a large tract of land and then generate revenue by selling shares in the
venture. A body of commissioners supervised the resulting fund, using it to
purchase and prepare the site. Developers then sold the lots and distributed
the income among subscribers according to the number of shares they owned.
In 1815, when the Pine Level Land Company in Clarke County planned Pine
Level (now Jackson), it hoped to sell lots to some fifteen hundred people in the
area. To attract subscribers, the company set aside land for a church and a

school—an indication that people saw these institutions as essential to community life.

Donations or subscriptions were not the only ways of funding education; tuition was another major source of income. Some schools also received county taxes, fees collected by local governments, and revenue from the sale of federal lands. The Alabama general assembly provided various kinds of support by exempting schools from taxation, making direct appropriations from the state treasury, and allowing trustees to raise additional money through lotteries. When the St. Stephens and Mobile banks were founded in 1818, their charters from the legislature stipulated that local academies share in their profits, which amounted to support from a designated tax.[41]

Baldwin County had community resources as well as license fees. The income funded schools outside the Tensaw area, which opened in a pattern similar to that in Clarke County. Tuition probably sustained a "petty school" in Bon Secour, where a governess taught the children of John Cook and his neighbors in 1840. In Montrose, tuition and donations were likely sources of revenue for the Sibley Academy, founded in 1859, where Ansel Lamson (a Harvard graduate) taught the boys and Louise L. Morse, the girls. The name of the school honored Cyrus Sibley, because he gave the land. "Public schools," which imply broad support, opened in Coburn, Plash, and Wenzel. Local histories also mention a "Creole School" as well as the Witt and Swift schools.[43]

In 1824, the legislature permitted Baldwin County to build ferries on several rivers and lease them to private operators, with the understanding that fees paid by the concessionaires would be used to support a local academy and a hospital. In other instances, schools such as the Pendleton Academy in Clarke County were given the federal land grants set aside for public education.[42]

From time to time, the state granted special privileges to schools as a means of support; for example, the legislature excused schoolmasters and students from military service (in 1825) and exempted some schools from taxation (after 1823). It also permitted literary institutions to deposit their funds in the state bank at 6 percent interest (in 1836), which was a means of both raising capital for the state and supporting education. In addition, the legislature asked Congress to grant auxiliary funds for schools like the Franklin Academy in Suggsville (in 1827).[44]

WHO RALLIED THE COMMUNITIES?

Raising funds, getting neighbors to help build a schoolhouse, and petitioning a committee to ask the legislature for a charter all required the kind of initiative that settlers like Caleb Moncrief and John Green exhibited. Each brought his community together to establish a school. When these pioneers were most effective, they worked through informal and formal associations. Organizations of women were among the most influential.

WOMEN'S ASSOCIATIONS

Although excluded from legal citizenship, women participated actively in the civic order, often motivated by their responsibilities in the domestic sphere for nurturing the young. They weren't voters, but women perfected the use of nonpolitical space for political purposes ("political" in the broadest sense). They took advantage of personal relationships and social settings to organize collective responses to collective problems. They drew on what we would call "networks" today.

Women in the Typical Dress of the 1840s

Wielding considerable influence in all of the benevolent enterprises of their time, women of the 1800s formed voluntary organizations to provide services, which were later administered by governments. Occasionally stereotyped as shrinking violets, the women of the southwestern counties were known to speak their minds about their role in society. When some "musty, good for nothing grey beard" was quoted in the Mobile press as saying "females have no influence," a dozen women shot back, "we have influence." And they proceeded to explain how they exercised it, with tongue in cheek.[45]

Ministers relied on fund-raising by women's groups to augment their salaries. Scottish clergyman George Lewis recalled that the ladies of one church collected a thousand dollars, a significant amount in those days, by organizing "fancy fairs and suppers." And their influence wasn't limited to raising money; in some denominations, they played a role in the governance of churches—for instance, by participating in the election of pastors.[46]

Women were especially active in education. Several years after the Macon

Male and Female Academy opened in Clarke County, citizens decided that a new building was needed for the female division. Three women—Mary Francis Dickinson, wife and first cousin of James S. Dickinson; Elizabeth Ball Woodard; and R. J. Underwood—organized the Grove Hill Sewing Circle to raise funds. Woodard served as architect and drew plans for the building; John A. Coate donated the necessary land, which was just west of his home. (Coate is an example of settlers who made investments in community-building. He was the son of the man who lent his home to the court. John carried on the tradition by serving the county in a variety of ways as justice of the peace, coroner, and sheriff.)[47]

The sewing circle's first sale of children's clothes and "fancy sewing" at the county courthouse netted two hundred dollars; the second, expanded into a fair, was actually held in the new school building (opened in 1857), which shows the drive was a success. (This was the fund drive praised in the local newspaper in April 1857.)

The sewing circle project illustrates what historian Albert B. Moore calls in his research "abundant evidence" of the importance attached to educating daughters as well as sons. Girls were reputed to be better students than boys; yet despite plans to open a "female institution" as a branch of the state university, Alabama did not instruct girls beyond the secondary level before 1860.[48]

Grove Hill's Sewing Circle was by no means an exception. The Ladies Education Society of Selma played a similar role and is credited with bringing public education to that town. In 1838, Dr. Uriah Grigsby, a prominent citizen, chaired a meeting to determine whether to build a female academy in connection with the local Episcopal church. When the people at the meeting decided to proceed, they were about to appoint a committee of men to raise the necessary money. A successful motion from the floor added an equal number of women—including Dr. Grigsby's wife, Leticia Ann Wood. The women appear to have been members of the Ladies Education Society.[49]

In 1839, the legislature, having earlier acknowledged the need for a female academy in every county, granted a charter to the Academy of the Ladies Education Society, which was rechartered in 1845 as the Dallas Male and Female Academy. It occupied a substantial two-story brick building located at the corner of Alabama and Donation (now Mabry) Streets. Was this academy the beginning of public education? Citizens of Selma think so. They recognize

1838, the year of the town meeting, as the date their public schools were founded.

Ad Hocracy: Neighbors Enlisting Neighbors

Other school builders didn't proceed in the grand style of the Ladies Education Society of Selma with fairs and suppers. Farm families were more likely to build schools the way they organized killing hogs or raising barns. This type of public work persisted into the early twentieth century.

Around 1900 in the Union community of Clarke County, Mima Morgan Bumpers, wife of a farmer and merchant named Stephen, was unhappy having their children walk several miles to the nearest school, which was in the Tompkins community. Temptations were around every bend in the path—creeks to splash in, large vines that made excellent swings. She became a driving force in organizing her neighbors (the Dukes, Fowlers, Pauls, and others) to construct their own school on land the Bumpers family donated. There was no doubt about who owned this school—the Union community did. The school wasn't only theirs; it was them. It was the community in another form. Citizens not only built the schoolhouse, but also selected the teachers, paid them (perhaps with some help from the state), and provided their lodging. One of the instructors, David Chapman Mathews, who had learned the art of teaching from his older siblings, boarded at the Bumperses' home, where he met and later married one of their daughters, Emma. He continued to teach and eventually became superintendent of the county system.[50]

Schoolhouses in communities like Union showed the schools' role in the community by the way the structure was used. It served as a social center, meetinghouse, and church before eventually becoming a tenant farmer's home. Though only the well remains under a chinaberry tree, the building was reported to have been a "step up" from those that housed the first rural schools.

Churches

Neighbors helping neighbors meant organizing churches, which later opened schools to serve the community. For example, Baptist churches in many areas of the state built log cabins to house schools, which, like other "free schools," charged tuition of one dollar but exempted students whose parents couldn't afford even this modest payment. Ministers who preached on Sunday frequently taught on weekdays in these institutions.[51]

A number of these church-based schools seem to have been responding to the concern of a democratic public. The major denominations, including the Baptists (whose constituency included some who regarded book learning as a threat to piety), argued, as Milo P. Jewett puts it, for educating "THE WHOLE PEOPLE." The objectives were to create what James Harvey DeVotie calls "mental capital" and to give "all classes an opportunity to rise from ignorance." This wasn't purely a social or political goal. Strange as it might seem for ministers to be making economic arguments, DeVotie was saying that prosperity depended on the collective intellect of the state's citizens; it was the primary source of wealth. No rhetorical flourish, this was the dominant economic theory of the time. The editors of the *South Western Baptist* elaborated: Just as education combated vice, it also combated indolence (presumed to be the chief cause of poverty). And it promoted the enterprise that led to prosperity. Educated farmers and mechanics would be far more productive than those not educated. Furthermore, they would have access to the new machinery that resulted from a society's storehouse of knowledge.[52]

In addition to churches, Sunday schools were another force in bringing communities together to promote learning. It wasn't uncommon for founders of neighboring schools, like Caleb Moncrief, to make sure that primary education was also available on Sundays. Sunday schools (often non- or multi-denominational) originated in England in the late eighteenth century, prompted by dismay over "the low tone of manners and sentiment" and what was considered a grievous neglect of education for the laboring classes. English schools were considered the beginning of popular education and the origin of that country's equivalent of our public schools. American Sunday schools had some of the same focus and effect.[53]

INDEPENDENT TEACHERS

Public-minded educators were another spark that roused communities to action and began what became public schools. Other schoolmasters, who put out their shingles much as doctors or lawyers did, conducted schools solely as business ventures. These usually closed when the proprietor moved because they weren't the product of public intent or encouragement. For instance, a Mr. and Mrs. Pilate opened the Suggsville Institute in 1837, which was primarily a music school, charging one hundred to one hundred twenty dollars a year. Harp lessons were the most expensive; foreign languages, drawing, and science (botany) were "extras," with tuition for those subjects ranging from twenty-four to forty dollars. Entrepreneurial schoolmasters moved around, and this may have been the same Mr. Pilate who had advertised his availability to teach French, drawing, and music in the May 18, 1836, edition of the *Mobile Commercial Register and Patriot*. He said he was from the University of France. The Pilates seem not to have had any lasting influence in either town.[54]

Rebuilt Gainestown School

Jesse A. Lambard, on the other hand, is a good example of the civic-minded teachers whose work led to public schools. He began to offer classes at the request of Gainestown planters to whom he was related by marriage (his wife, Sarah White, was the granddaughter of one of the town's founders). Community ownership of the Lambard School was evident when a storm destroyed the original building in 1911. The entire citizenry gathered on October 3 and 4 of 1919 and put up a new building out of old materials. That schoolhouse still stands on a foundation of hand-hewn floor joists made from the original pine logs; it is preserved as testimony to Gainestown's civic pride. The Lambards were probably among those who helped develop such a sense of collective responsibility.[55]

Timothy Ball, who taught first at the Grove Hill Academy, was another educator who appears to have been an active community organizer. He was instrumental in establishing several schools, including one in Rockville, which served the children of the Payne and Austill families as well as boarding students. Ball later opened the Eclectic Academy. Although an enterprising man who earned his living by teaching, he was also a missionary for community schools; his civic commitment is reflected in his histories of Clarke County.[56]

Ball wasn't alone. Other teachers in the Southwest appear less motivated by the desire to make money than by the sheer love of teaching. The Finches in Clarke County, for instance, are remembered for their work in education. Ball, who knew them well, wrote that they descended from Hight Finch, who was from a North Carolina family dedicated to books and learning. Finch apparently gave the land for the Gainestown School, which he acquired from the federal government in 1819. Perhaps this interest is genetic; it was passed along to three granddaughters and a grandson who moved to Texas and continued to teach.[57]

LOCAL GOVERNMENTS

Town councils were yet another organizing force; they had pressing reasons to promote public education because they were responsible for the welfare of their communities, specifically for what was referred to as "the rising generation." Mobile's municipal government, in collaboration with the citizenry, was particularly active in expanding access to instruction, so active that the story of what Mobilians did takes another chapter to tell. It is a story of what governments in this period did *with*, not just for, communities.

NOTES TO CHAPTER 3

[1] Tensaw was part of a larger area that extended south to Pensacola and Mobile and north to St. Stephens. Information on that territory and the education that went on before there were schools is from *Reminiscences of George Strother Gaines: Pioneer and Statesman of Early Alabama and Mississippi, 1805-1843*, ed. James P. Pate (Tuscaloosa: University of Alabama Press, 1998), pp. 47-48; Willis G. Clark, *History of Education in Alabama, 1702-1889*, Contributions to American Educational History, no. 8 (Washington, D.C.: Government Printing Office, 1889), pp. 25-26; and Alabama State Department of Education, *History of Education in Alabama* 7 (1975): 2-5.

For more details, I recommend Jacqueline Anderson Matte's *The History of Washington County: First County in Alabama* (Chatom, Ala.: Washington County Historical Society, 1982). I drew from pp. 15-16.

The reference to a Langlois (L'Anglois) dame school in 1711 is in a typescript note in the Oakleigh Collection of the Historic Mobile Preservation Society, Mobile, Alabama.

[2] Other sources used to reconstruct life in the Tensaw settlement include George Stiggins, *Creek Indian History: A Historical Narrative of the Genealogy, Traditions and Downfall of the Ispocoga or Creek Indian Tribe of Indians*, ed. Virginia Pounds Brown (Birmingham: Birmingham Public Library Press, 1989), p. 27; William Stokes Wyman, notes to *Creek Indian History*, p. 138; Albert James Pickett, *History of Alabama and Incidentally of Georgia and Mississippi, from the Earliest Period* (1851; reprint, Birmingham: Birmingham Book and Magazine, 1962), pp. 342-343, 416-417; Jack D. L. Holmes, "Alabama's Forgotten Settlers: Notes on the Spanish Mobile District, 1780-1813," *Alabama Historical Quarterly* 33 (summer 1971): 88-90; and Peter J. Hamilton, *Colonial Mobile: An Historical Study*, ed. Charles G. Summersell (1910; reprint, University: University of Alabama Press, 1976), p. 95.

[3] Charles E. Bryant characterized the population of Tensaw in *The Tensaw Country: North of the Ellicott Line, 1800-1860* (Bay Minette, Ala.: Lavender Press, 1998), p. 200, and Kay Nuzum commented on the economy in *A History of Baldwin County* (Fairhope, Ala.: Eastern Shore Publishing Company, 1971), pp. 52-53.

[4] The views of Ephraim Kirby and Harry Toulmin on the character of the first inhabitants of the Tensaw area are reported by James F. Doster in "Early Settlements on the Tombigbee and Tensaw Rivers," *Alabama Review* 12 (April 1959): 84-88.

[5] The history of the Pierce (Peirce) family has been collected by C. G. Breland and F. P. Peck in *John Peirce's Boatyard School, Boatyard Lake, Alabama and Forebears of John Peirce Founder of the School* (Huntsville: C. G. Breland and F. P. Peck, 1988), pp. 2.4, A.2.

[6] My colleagues and I are indebted to Davida Hastie of Stockton, Alabama, for taking us to the site of the Pierce home and the landing on Boatyard Lake. We also learned a great deal from Major Tunstall, who lives on the site and was our guide.

[7] Pickett, *History of Alabama*, p. 469, and L. J. Newcomb Comings and Martha M. Albers, *A Brief History of Baldwin County* (Fairhope, Ala.: Baldwin County Historical Society, 1928), p. 29.

[8] There are many accounts of the massacre at Fort Mims, and the number killed varies. The description in the text is from Pickett's *History of Alabama*, pp. 528-543. Also see Breland and Peck, *John Peirce's Boatyard School*, pp. 2.4-2.5, A.1-A.2, A.6.

[9] Lawrence A. Cremin, *American Education: The Colonial Experience, 1607-1783* (New York: Harper and Row, 1970), pp. 128-129.

[10] T. H. Ball told about pioneer families like the Moncriefs in Clarke County in *A Glance into the Great South-East, or, Clarke County, Alabama, and Its Surroundings, from 1540 to 1877* (1879; reprint, Tuscaloosa: Willo Publishing Company, 1962), pp. 387, 606. The long-term influence of schools established by pioneer families is documented in "History of the Public School System of Clarke County, Alabama," *Clarke County Historical Society Quarterly* 23 (fall 1998): 15-16. This monograph was first published by the Clarke County Alabama Board of Education in 1955. "Obituary of Caleb Moncrief," *Clarke County Historical Society Quarterly* 6 (winter 1982): 10-11 has more on Caleb Moncrief.

[11] Mary E. Brantley, *From Cabins to Mansions: Gleanings from Southwest Alabama* (Huntsville: Strode Publishers, 1981), p. 214 and John Harry Dey, Jr., "The History of Education in Conecuh County, Alabama: 1818-1938" (master's thesis, Alabama Polytechnic Institute, 1939), p. 15.

[12] Mary E. Brantley told the story of the John Green family and their neighbors in *Early Settlers along the Old Federal Road in Monroe and Conecuh Counties Alabama* (Baltimore: Gateway Press, 1976), pp. 116, 119, 189.

[13] Documents on Conecuh County's first schools are in the county files of the Alabama Department of Archives and History, Montgomery, Ala. Also see Members of Beta Club, "Present High School Was Once a Pioneer Academy," *Evergreen Courant,* 27 April 1939, special edition and Brantley, *From Cabins to Mansions,* pp. 82, 215-216.

[14] J. L. M. Curry made the observation about the importance of schools to communities, which can be found in "Reminiscences of Talladega," *Alabama Historical Quarterly* 8 (winter 1946): 360.

[15] "Obituary of Caleb Moncrief," p. 10.

I learned more about Moncrief from his great-great grandson, Raymond Tharpe. My wife, Mary, and I had lunch with him at Gloria's Café in Grove Hill just before Christmas, 2001. He told us the Moncriefs were French Huguenots, which was not uncommon in the country where other Huguenots such as the Daffins and Bumperses (Bompasses) eventually settled. Tharpe said Moncrief lived first in the vicinity of James and Bassett Creeks, then moved "up the hill," which could be where T. H. Ball placed the home on the southwestern edge of section 18. That or the earlier location could have been the site of the first classes in the county. The Moncriefs fled to Fort Sinquefield in 1813 with other settlers who probably were the patrons of the Moncrief school. See the account of this fort for the families there in H. S. Halbert and T. H. Ball's *The Creek War of 1813 and 1814.* This book was reprinted by University of Alabama Press, University, Alabama, in 1969 with an introduction and notes by Frank L. Owsley, Jr.

I was also pleased to hear from Regina Overton Parden, another great-great grandchild. In a letter to the editor that appeared in the *Clarke County Democrat* of September 6, 2001, she reported that Moncrief was born in North Carolina and married Sally Ann Short in Georgia in 1807, which was just before the young couple arrived in Alabama to raise a family of five sons and eight daughters.

[16] Nineteenth-century America's keen sense of responsibility for public schools—as well as the extent to which this feeling affected attitudes toward local government—was documented in the reports filed by an English observer, Francis Adams, in the latter part of the century. I imagine

Alabamians shared some of those feelings. Adams wrote:

That which impresses us most in regard to America is the grasp which the schools have upon the sympathy and intelligence of the people. Those of the cities are the lions of America. The intelligent foreigner, and also, as it would appear from some recent criticisms, the unintelligent foreigner who visits the States, into whatever town he goes, is taken to the schools as the first objects of interest. Amongst public questions education occupies the foremost place, and of all topics it is that upon which the American speaker is most ready and most willing to enlarge.... This widespread popular regard which constitutes the propelling power, appears to be chiefly due to two features—government by the people, and ownership by the people. It is a vast proprietary scheme, in which every citizen has a share. While it is undoubtedly true that all do not set the same value on school rights, it is also certain that their existence immensely stimulates public interest and diffuses a sense of responsibility through the entire community.

In one of Adams's most interesting observations—one especially relevant in Alabama today because of the concern about the absence of local or "home" rule—he found the argument that self-rule promotes an appreciation of public schools turned on its head. Americans valued local institutions of governance, he discovered, because of the control they gave citizens over their schools. Adams's report is included in David B. Tyack's *Turning Points in American Educational History* (Waltham, Mass.: Blaisdell Publishing Company, 1967), pp. 171-172.

[17] The article on the advantages of the Grove Hill schools by "H. A. J." appeared in the April 2, 1857, issue of the *Clarke County Democrat.*

[18] Jacqueline Matte wrote about St. Stephens and its academy in her *History of Washington County,* pp. 5, 8, 49-50, 52.

[19] Thomas McAdory Owen, *History of Alabama and Dictionary of Alabama Biography,* vol. 3 (Chicago: S. J. Clarke Publishing Company, 1921), pp. 291, 422, 628-629; *Reminiscences of George Strother Gaines,* pp. 55-69; and Matte, *History of Washington County,* p. 50.

[20] St. Stephens was featured in the *Alabama Republican*

(Huntsville), 30 September 1817. Also see Matte, *History of Washington County,* p. 50.

21 Mary Brantley quoted from a paper written in 1899 by Mary J. Welch on her grandmother, Tabitha Gordy, in *From Cabins to Mansions,* pp. 23, 44.

22 Clarke County schools are described in David Akens's "Clarke County to 1860" (master's thesis, University of Alabama, 1956), pp. 103, 108 and in an article by Mrs. Charles L. Pezent, "Rockville," in *Historical Sketches of Clarke County, Alabama,* ed. Clarke County Historical Society (Huntsville: Strode Publishers, 1977), p. 308. T. H. Ball's report on the early schools of Grove Hill is in *Glance into the Great South-East,* pp. 711-712.

Samuel T. Barnes, William Crawford, John G. Creagh, James H. Fitts, Isham Kimbell, and Joseph P. Portis signed an advertisement in the *Mobile Commercial Register* of July 27, 1831, for the Jackson Male Academy.

23 Harvey and Elizabeth Jackson, "Early Methodism in Clarke County," *Clarke County Historical Society Quarterly* 5 (spring 1981): 11-13.

24 Dates of other Clarke County schools came from "History of the Public School System," pp. 13, 16, 22; Ball, *Glance into the Great South-East,* pp. 186, 196-197, 244; Mrs. Gene Armistead, "Morvin," in *Historical Sketches of Clarke County,* p. 281; Mrs. W. I. Ingram, "Bashi," in *Historical Sketches of Clarke County,* p. 54; Louise M. Finlay, Jr., "Suggsville and Manila," in *Historical Sketches of Clarke County,* pp. 356-359; Philip E. Frank, "Barlow Bend— Choctaw Bluff—Gainestown," in *Historical Sketches of Clarke County,* p. 52; Annie Turner, "West Bend," in *Historical Sketches of Clarke County,* p. 395; and "Franklin Academy," *Mobile Commercial Register,* 5 December 1826.

25 Akens, "Clarke County to 1860," pp. 111-112 and *Report of Gabriel B. DuVal, Superintendent of Education, of the State of Alabama, Made to the Governor, for the Year 1858* (Montgomery: Shorter and Reid, 1859), p. 11.

26 David Chapman Mathews recalled what pioneer schools were like in "Early Sketches," *South Alabamian,* 27 January 1966.

27 Philip Henry Gosse left his impression of Alabama schoolboys in his *Letters from Alabama (U.S.), Chiefly Relating to Natural History* (1859; reprint, Mountain Brook, Ala.: Overbrook House, 1983), p. 44.

28 The account of antebellum schools is from Dey, "The

History of Education," pp. 20-25.

The blab method seems akin to what scholars call "simultaneous recitation." In "'Chanting Choristers': Simultaneous Recitation in Baltimore's Nineteenth-Century Primary Schools," which appeared in *History of Education Quarterly* 34 (spring 1994): 1-24, William R. Johnson said this instructional technique was thought both to provide information and stimulate learning. Repetition and memorization, according to the pedagogy of the time, taught children how to learn. For more on the history of teaching, see the works of Larry Cuban and Barbara Finkelstein.

29 Edgar W. Knight described academies in some detail in *Public Education in the South* (Boston: Ginn and Company, 1922), pp. 75-77, 82-83.

30 The Solemn Grove Academy charter is in Toulmin, *Digest of the Laws of the State of Alabama,* pp. 550-551. Academies are characterized in Dey, "The History of Education," p. 550.

31 Stephen B. Weeks, *History of Public School Education in Alabama,* U.S. Bureau of Education Bulletin, 1915, no. 12 (Washington, D.C.: Government Printing Office, 1915), p. 48.

32 Courses for young women are listed in the *Catalogue and Circular of the Metropolitan Female Institute, at Montgomery, Alabama, for the Year Ending July 15th, 1850; Together with the Conditions of Admittance* (Montgomery: Job Office of the Alabama Journal, 1850), pp. 3-4.

33 John Massey, *Reminiscences: Giving Sketches of Scenes through which the Author Has Passed and Pen Portraits of People Who Have Modified His Life* (Nashville: Publishing House of the M. E. Church, South, 1916), pp. 48-49.

34 Paul Wayne Taylor, "Mobile: 1818-1859 as Her Newspapers Pictured Her" (master's thesis, The University of Alabama, 1951), p. 60. He discussed some of the texts advertised in the *Mobile Mercantile Advertiser,* 24 December 1823.

35 Adam Smith explained his concept of social responsibility in *The Theory of Moral Sentiments* (1976; reprint, Indianapolis: Liberty Classics, 1982), p. 231. Lawrence Cremin commented on Francis Wayland's understanding of an ideal society as well as Adam Smith's influence in his book *American Education: The National Experience 1783-1876* (New York: Harper and Row, 1980), pp. 23-28, 128-133, 273-280. Minnie Clare Boyd said that Wayland's texts were,

in fact, used in the state in *Alabama in the Fifties: A Social Study* (New York: Columbia University Press, 1931), p. 137.

[36] T. W. Price, "Interesting Letter," *Linden Jeffersonian,* 12 January 1858, reprinted in the *Clarke County Democrat,* 25 February 1858.

[37] David Akens quotes the article from the *Clarke County Democrat* in "Clarke County to 1860," p. 110.

[38] Jackson Male Academy advertised that it would hold annual public examinations, particularly for the benefit of tuition-paying parents and guardians, in the *Mobile Commercial Register* on 27 July 1831.

[39] The source for comparing practices in frontier Alabama with those of the colonial period is, again, Cremin, *Colonial Experience,* pp. 180-181.

[40] Virginia E. and Robert W. McCormick discussed subscribers as investors in *New Englanders on the Ohio Frontier: The Migration and Settlement of Worthington, Ohio* (Kent, Ohio: Kent State University Press, 1998), pp. 98-100. The way subscriptions were used to develop a community was recorded in the 1816 Minute Book of Commissioners of the town of Pine Level, which is quoted by John Simpson Graham, *History of Clarke County* (1923; reprint, Greenville, S.C.: Southern Historical Press, 1994), pp. 91-108 and in "History of the Public School System," p. 22.

[41] Harry Toulmin, *Digest of the Laws of the State of Alabama: Containing Statutes and Resolutions in Force at the End of the General Assembly in January, 1823* (Cahawba: Ginn and Curtis, 1823), pp. 540, 543. Academies were also covered by Stephen B. Weeks in his *History of Public School Education,* p. 23.

[42] Legislation providing support for academies is in the following: Alabama General Assembly, *Acts,* 6th annual sess., 1824 (Cahawba: William B. Allen, 1825), pp. 125-126 and Alabama General Assembly, *Acts,* extra and annual sess., 1832 (Tuscaloosa: E. Walker, 1833), pp. 119-120.

[43] Kay Nuzum, *A History of Baldwin County,* p. 95 and Kay Nuzum, "Bon Secour," *Baldwin County Historical Society Quarterly* 1 (October 1973): 14.

[44] The statute setting the interest rate at 6 percent was in Alabama General Assembly, *Acts,* 5th annual sess., 1823, (Cahawba: William B. Allen, 1824), p. 4. Also see Alabama General Assembly, *Acts,* 7th annual sess., 1825 (Cahawba: William B. Allen, 1826), p. 48 and Alabama General Assem-

bly, *Acts,* 13th annual sess., 1831 (Tuscaloosa: Wiley, McGuire, and Henry, 1832), p. 31.

[45] The letter on women's influence appeared in the *Mobile Commercial Register,* 29 January 1828. Women's role in shaping social policy was one of the subjects of Sara M. Evans's *Born for Liberty: A History of Women in America* (New York: Free Press, 1989), p. 205.

In a memo to the author, 19 November 1998, R. Claire Snyder, assistant professor of government and politics in political theory at George Mason University, pointed out that the problem with the prevailing assumption about the socialistic origins of American social movements is that America never had full-fledged socialism comparable to that of Western Europe to inspire reforms.

John W. Quist dealt with the role of women in social reform in *Restless Visionaries: The Social Roots of Antebellum Reform in Alabama and Michigan* (Baton Rouge: Louisiana State University Press, 1998), pp. 198-199.

[46] *Impressions of America and the American Churches: From Journal of the Rev. G. Lewis* (1848; reprint, New York: Negro Universities Press, 1968), pp. 158, 180-181.

[47] The work of the women of Grove Hill who organized the female division of the Macon Academy is in T. H. Ball's *Glance into the Great South-East,* pp. 416-421. Other information can be found in Perry Outlaw's speech to the Clarke County Historical Society in 1990, "James Shelton Dickinson and the Dickinson Guards of Clarke County, Alabama," *Clarke County Historical Society Quarterly* 20 (fall 1995): 11 and in "History of the Public School System," p. 17. Also see Ball, *Glance into the Great South-East,* pp. 170, 371-373.

[48] Albert Burton Moore's observations about the education of women were in his *History of Alabama,* p. 338. James Benson Sellers noted the lack of opportunities for college education in *History of the University of Alabama,* vol. 1 (University: University of Alabama Press, 1953), pp. 161-162.

[49] Alston Fitts III wrote about Selma's debt to the Ladies Education Society for its public schools in *Selma: Queen City of the Blackbelt* (Selma, Ala.: Clairmont Press, 1989), p. 18, and in a letter to the author, 27 July 2000, as did Emily F. Ferguson in her *History of the Dallas Academy of Selma, Alabama* (Tuscaloosa: University Microfilms, 1932), p. 1. Also read Jack Nelms's "The Dallas Academy: Backbone of the Permanent School System of Selma," *Alabama Review* 29 (April 1976): 113-115.

Organizers of the Ladies Education Society of Selma included Mary Eliza Pitts (Mrs. J. F.) Conoley, Evelyn (Mrs. R. L.) Downman, Caroline Minter (Mrs. Hugh) Ferguson, Mary Ann Phillips (Mrs. Andrew) Hunter, Mrs. R. S. Maples, Mrs. Elias Parkman, Mrs. William Treadwell, Eleanor G. (Mrs. William) Waddell, and Anne Gardner (Mrs. P. J.) Weaver. Three entries in Owen's *History of Alabama,* pp. 391, 574, 1736, provided some background on the families who were involved in seeing that education was available. They seem to have been largely from the business sector of a very business-minded community. Mary Eliza Pitts Conoley, a native of Dallas County, was a recent bride at the time the educational association was getting started. Her husband, of Scottish ancestry, had arrived in Selma from North Carolina in 1833 to go into the mercantile business, so both were newcomers. Caroline Minter Ferguson was from a Georgia family and, like Mary Conoley, had a daughter who taught in the Selma schools. Hugh Ferguson, a merchant and planter, had Scottish parents who settled in Tennessee; he served the Dallas Academy as secretary-treasurer. Anne Gardner Weaver and her husband had a somewhat different background. One of the earliest settlers at Moore's Bluff, where Selma is located, Philip J. Weaver descended from a German family who settled in Pennsylvania. Beginning as an apprentice and then clerk, he found his way to Alabama, where he began a trading business that extended south to Mobile and west to Mississippi.

50 To read more about the Union community, see Doris R. James's article "Union," in *Historical Sketches of Clarke County,* p. 378. My cousin, Marion Bumpers, told me about Mima Bumpers, who was our great/grandmother.

51 The Baptist church mentioned in reference to a free school was in Gorgas, Alabama. Wayne Flynt, *Alabama*

Baptists: Southern Baptists in the Heart of Dixie (Tuscaloosa: University of Alabama Press, 1998), p. 55.

52 Prominent leaders in the Baptist church, who argued for public education, are discussed in Flynt's *Alabama Baptists,* pp. 54-55, 95. Editorials on the economic benefits of public schools appeared in issues of the *South Western Baptist* on 16 February 1854 and 23 February 1854.

Friedrich List developed an economic theory that was quite influential in the antebellum period; it was later published in *The National System of Political Economy* (1885; reprint, New York: A. M. Kelley, 1966). List believed that Adam Smith didn't appreciate the extent to which capital depended on social and intellectual conditions in a country.

53 Anne M. Boylan's *Sunday School: The Formation of an American Institution, 1790-1880* (New Haven: Yale University Press, 1988), pp. 22-25 was very helpful because it deals with the public purposes of Sunday schools. To understand the original mission of these schools, I prefer Henry Clay Trumbull's *The Sunday-School: Its Origin, Mission, Methods, and Auxiliaries,* Yale Lectures on the Sunday-School (Philadelphia: John D. Wattles, 1888), pp. 98, 105, 119.

54 Ball, *Glance into the Great South-East,* p. 197 and *Mobile Commercial Register and Patriot,* 18 May 1836.

55 "Old Gainestown Schoolhouse," *Clarke County Historical Society Quarterly* 15 (summer 1990): 7 and Frank, "Barlow Bend—Choctaw Bluff—Gainestown," pp. 6-7.

56 The affinity between pioneer educator T. H. Ball and the communities he served was evident in his book *Glance into the Great South-East.*

57 Ball, *Glance into the Great South-East,* pp. 388-389 and "Old Gainestown Schoolhouse," p. 7.

Chapter 4

A Society of Citizens and a Board of School Commissioners

ASSOCIATIONS, AD HOC groups of neighbors, and public meetings constantly brought people together for civic projects. As they joined forces, they formed public relationships. Networks grew, linking otherwise competing interests. In time, habits of working together developed and became accepted routines passed from one generation to another. Informal associations evolved into more formal ones. People organized clubs and institutions to implement their collective decisions. A compact among citizens emerged that defined the kind of community they wanted, and this compact led to standards that prescribed people's obligations to each other. All in all, a society of citizens took shape with a memory and roots. In new communities, this society, which settlers created afresh among themselves, replaced the well-established, often family-based and hierarchical social orders they had left.

A civil society doesn't have a street address or a fixed set of members like a legislature or municipal council. Yet, once developed, it becomes a political body with its own unique power. In communities where people saw to it that instruction was available year after year, they were acting as such a body. And I think of a society of citizens at work as another way of understanding the public, particularly the public as it provided for education. Individual schools came and went, but the civil society didn't; it was always there to be certain that education was available.

The Gainestown schoolhouse suggests that this community had a civil society and not just an enterprising individual, Jesse Lambard. However, the best evidence of a citizen-created society comes from large cities, which had newspapers, organization minutes, and other documents reporting what people did over a number of years. Records from Mobile, for instance, show how a society of citizens went about establishing public schools. And these records also show what public education did and didn't mean.

The Public as a Society of Citizens

Old (founded in 1702) and large (more than three thousand inhabitants in 1830), Mobile described itself as a commercial republic of free people. In 1826, its citizens demanded more control over its internal affairs. As a result, the legislature amended the city's charter, giving Mobilians the right to elect their own councilmen as well as a board of school commissioners. The act also designated county revenue to be used for education, which, in addition to federal land grants, included fines and penalties, taxes on auction sales and on damages awarded by local courts—plus 25 percent of the ordinary county tax.[1]

Expanded educational opportunities were among many improvements being made in the city. Community-building was going on at a fast clip. Cockleshells paved muddy streets, gas lighting illuminated the thoroughfares, and a theater opened. An observer reported that at one point three hundred stores and homes were under construction.[2]

Citizens also created voluntary service organizations. Fire was an ever-present danger, and Mobilians, including free blacks (mainly Creoles), formed volunteer companies following a practice of the 1820s when people put out blazes with quickly organized cooperation. After James Copeland confessed to being the arsonist responsible for the city's worst fire, citizens enrolled in the Volunteer Guard (a version of today's neighborhood watch) to assist city police. The objective was to have more eyes on the lookout for criminals. This pattern of civic/governmental collaboration continued even after Mobile's fire department had grown from two into nine companies. And the same type of cooperation characterized responses to public health threats and the plight of the poor. In many cases, civic associations developed out of the initiatives of

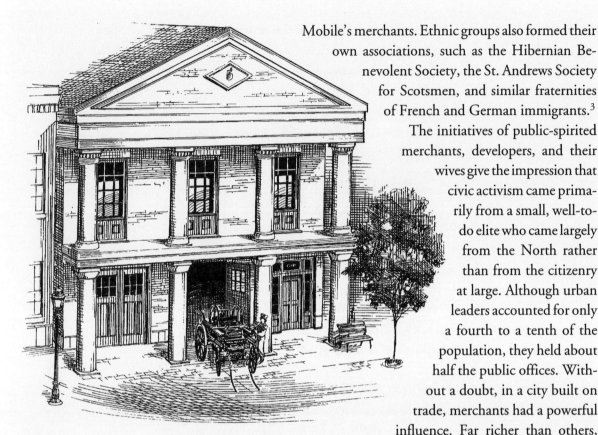

Washington Firehouse in Mobile

Mobile's merchants. Ethnic groups also formed their own associations, such as the Hibernian Benevolent Society, the St. Andrews Society for Scotsmen, and similar fraternities of French and German immigrants.[3]

The initiatives of public-spirited merchants, developers, and their wives give the impression that civic activism came primarily from a small, well-to-do elite who came largely from the North rather than from the citizenry at large. Although urban leaders accounted for only a fourth to a tenth of the population, they held about half the public offices. Without a doubt, in a city built on trade, merchants had a powerful influence. Far richer than others, they owned roughly a quarter of the property even though they made up less than 1 percent of all property holders. But working people had their own associations and made their voices heard on numerous occasions. Unfortunately, we have few records of these Mobilians and fewer still of their counterparts elsewhere in the southwestern counties. Still, there is enough evidence to sense the influence of the people who didn't get their names in the newspapers. Harriet Amos finds that "churches, fire companies, militia companies, occupational organizations, and ethnic benevolent societies offered foreign-born and native-born Mobilians, white and black, a variety of associations."[4]

The crucial question in determining the extent to which the society of citizens in a community contributes to democratic self-rule is whether that society bridges ethnic, religious, and economic divisions or reinforces them.

The evidence from Mobile is mixed. It was one of the most heterogeneous communities in the South and unlike other cities where fewer than a hundred elite families dominated society. Organizations such as fire companies and militias brought ethnic groups together, although some, like the Irish Independent Greens and the Lafayette Guards (an organization of people with French ancestry), appealed to specific parts of the population.

The mystic societies of Mardi Gras had very select memberships, yet they did connect people who competed in business. Similarly, while adversarial on one level, the Democratic and Whig Parties joined Northerners with Southerners within their respective organizations. Labor organizations (such as the Mobile Typographical Association) began as cooperative associations of employers and employees. But differences over wages eventually led to separate unions, as was the case for typographers in 1837. Working people were sufficiently well organized to strike. At the same time, labor interests fragmented as an increasing number of Irish and German immigrants competed for jobs with free blacks (Creole and non-Creole) as well as with slaves.

Black Mobilians enjoyed and suffered from the same forces of unity and separation. Creoles had strong civic associations yet tended to keep slaves at arm's length. Even so, slaves working in the city probably had some form of association among themselves and with free blacks. The opportunity was there because many slaves (about one thousand), hired out as artisans and laborers, lived apart from their masters. City officials feared what likely happened— gatherings to promote abolitionism. Evangelical Protestantism also joined black Mobilians, slave and free. The large number of black converts resulted in separate congregations in the city, whereas joint congregations with whites prevailed in rural areas (there, black church members usually sat in a balcony).

As the illustrations show, the society of citizens was subject to both centrifugal and centripetal forces. All that can be said about which was more powerful is that the forces drawing people together were strong enough at times to allow the community to act collectively on specific issues. One was education.

As I have mentioned before, the most powerful force connecting people in southwestern Alabama seems to have been the custom of calling public meetings. When problems came up, citizens met to talk about them, and there appear to have been plenty of opportunities for those conversations. In Mobile, the Alhambra coffeehouse provided space for deciding how to best assist victims of a yellow fever outbreak in 1839; the outcome was the creation of a service organization, the Can't-Get-Away Club.[5]

Not all the discussion at public gatherings was about benevolence. Nearly every major venture of any sort began with a notice: "A public meeting is being called to . . . ." Railroads were a major topic; for instance, a civic gathering in 1847 resulted in an association to promote the Mobile and Ohio Railroad. In these meetings, sponsors were undoubtedly persuasive, yet citizens made up their own minds and, on occasion, went against the organizers' wishes. In 1836, Mobilians objected to the plans for a city hall advocated by the mayor and the aldermen. The citizens weren't successful, but they weren't intimidated. Public meetings took a holiday only in the summer, when organizations found it difficult to get quorums because so many people left town in search of a cool breeze.

Since Mobile was a commercial center and cotton was its chief commodity, critics have charged that almost every conversation had to do, in one way or another, with that fiber. Even one of the local civic activists, Alexander Beaufort Meek, who served as president for the stevedores' benevolent association (the Baymen's Society) and held numerous other positions, thought the city was too preoccupied with cotton. As one visitor charged, Mobilians thought and even dreamed about little else than buying and selling the commodity that generated their livelihoods. And, in truth, the city could scarcely build warehouses fast enough to accommodate the flood of bales coming down the Tombigbee and Alabama Rivers. Along with the cotton came another flood—of families seeking their fortunes. They brought with them an agenda that resonated with Mobile's city fathers—the education of the next generation.[6]

SCHOOLING AS A COMMUNITY RESPONSIBILITY

Families had children, and children attracted teachers. The first were independent entrepreneurs or ministers turned educators. Mrs. E. Wood, Mrs. Edwards, and Mrs. D. A. Bessac founded female seminaries in Mobile. Norman Pinney, a rector of Christ Church, left his congregation to start Old

Blue College, and Bishop Michael Portier began building Spring Hill College in 1830.[7]

Though many of these institutions were praised for the quality of their instruction, the city felt compelled to see that there was enough schooling to meet a growing demand—rather than leaving the matter entirely in the hands of instructors for hire. Willoughby Barton, representing Mobile in the general assembly, won passage of the 1826 act that created a board of school commissioners (known as both a board and a commission). Elected by citizens every five years, this body was charged to "establish and regulate schools" and diffuse knowledge.[8]

Barton, a lawyer licensed to practice in 1819 who served as registrar in the federal land office, seems to have come from Augusta, Georgia. In the state legislature, he won an uphill battle to have the capital located at Cahawba on the Alabama River rather than at Tuscaloosa on the Tombigbee. Well-thought-of in the community, he was in the delegation that greeted General Lafayette on his visit to Mobile in 1825. Barton's interest in education went beyond sponsoring the board legislation; he donated land bought from Thomas Lane to the school board. Only two years after passage of the bill for which he is best known, this educational pioneer died when just thirty-eight, probably victim of one of the city's recurring epidemics. Samuel Garrow, one of the school board members, was the executor of Barton's estate, suggesting a close association among the founders of public education.[9]

Barton's bill named the first school commissioners: Samuel Acre, Henry V. Chamberlain, Silas Dinsmoor, John F. Everitt, Samuel H. Garrow, William Hale, L. W. Harris, Henry Hitchcock, Peter H. Hobart, James Johnston, Lewis Judson, William King, Addin Lewis, Abner S. Lipscomb, Elijah Montgomery, Joseph W. Moore, Solomon Mordecai, Moses Murphy, Samuel Newton, Benjamin J. Randall, Hugh H. Rolston, David Rust, Henry Stickney, and Ezekial Webb.

While Barton is properly credited with pushing through the legislation that created the school board, he was actually the agent of a group of citizens who had convened a town meeting a year earlier to lay the foundation for public education. The initial notice, headed "Mobile Academy," called people to a meeting to consider establishing an "institution" or "school." The report after the meeting refers to "Public schools" and a "uniform system," the latter suggesting that Mobilians wanted more than a single institution; they envisioned a general diffusion of education. The gathering resulted in a decision to encourage schools that would secure the long-term viability of Mobile. Having good education available would be an advantage for a city competing with New York, New Orleans, and others to become a major national port. (Mobile would eventually rank third in the country as a point of export.)[10]

The city's public schools were the direct result of that 1825 meeting. Mobile's school board drew heavily from the leadership that first brought the community together: John F. Everitt, Benjamin B. Breedin, David Rust, G. J. Mills, Samuel H. Garrow (who would serve as a board member and secretary for a quarter-century), Benjamin J. Randall, and Henry Stickney. The last five formed a committee to come up with a plan to establish "Public Schools, on principles different from those which usually govern public seminaries." What those principles were isn't clear, but the objective was to "prove that the *proper education of the young*, is an object of our increasing solicitude." Quite likely, the committee's plan became the basis for the Barton bill.

Public meetings were also used to create another important educational institution for a community—a library. In 1828, the *Mobile Commercial Register* announced a public meeting for citizens to follow up on planning begun by a library association, which had formed several years earlier. Organizers appealed to all who read, whether merchants and their clerks or mechanics and their apprentices. Like the school, a public library was seen as an institution of "common utility."[11]

The first school might have been named Everitt Academy for General John F. Everitt, who chaired the public meeting in 1825. Like other political and economic leaders in Mobile, he had migrated south from the territorial seat of government at St. Stephens. Originally from Georgia, he was a veteran of the Creek War, a merchant (with a tavern license), and a representative in Alabama's first political assemblies.[12]

Since many Mobilians had moved from commercial centers in the North to pursue their fortunes and since schools were seen as a factor in the competition with other cities, a number of the board members were merchants of New York and New England origins. Most weren't narrowly focused on their businesses and seemed to consider community-building as part of an overall strategy for economic development. In fact, some were far more interested in social issues than in their own fortunes, as was true in the case of Silas Dinsmoor, who earned his living as a land surveyor in Mobile.

Born in New England, Dinsmoor had worked on a farm in Maine before entering Dartmouth College, an institution created, in part, to educate Native

Americans. That mission evidently made an impression on the young student; he accepted President Washington's offer to head the federal agency dealing with the Cherokees and later took a similar position working with the Choctaws, which took him to St. Stephens. Committed to "civilizing" Indians, he brought that same missionary zeal to the cause of public education when he moved to Mobile. Friends described him both as a scholar and as a man of useful knowledge, wit, and humor who was given to humane impulses.[13]

Solomon Mordecai, another of the first school commissioners, was a physician from North Carolina who took great interest in the health of the community. And Henry V. Chamberlain, from Maine, also on the board, served the county as sheriff and judge.[14]

The way political, social, and economic interests flowed together was personified in the school board's president and Mobile's most active citizen—Henry Hitchcock. Part of the St. Stephens crowd, he was originally a New Englander—a native of Vermont and grandson of Ethan Allen of revolutionary fame. Well educated, he had attended Middlebury College and graduated with honors from the University of Vermont. Hitchcock had a political career as secretary of the Alabama Territory and later as Washington County's delegate to the state constitutional convention. He served as attorney general, chief justice of the Alabama supreme court, federal district judge, and as a member of the state university's first board of trustees.[15]

In 1826, when he returned from Cahawba, then site of the state capital, Hitchcock became the leading developer in Mobile and the state's first big businessman. He pursued banking and real estate ventures that earned him more than a million dollars (which he lost in a bank failure in 1837).

As a civic leader, Hitchcock not only championed public schooling (in league with his friends Silas Dinsmoor and Willoughby Barton) but also helped found the Government Street Presbyterian Church, which played a significant role

Henry Hitchcock

in the public life of the community. A devoted father, he employed Peter Hamilton, son of the Presbyterian minister and later president of the Mobile school board, as a tutor. Education benefited from Hitchcock's personal energy and enterprise, as well as from the network of people he cultivated.

The School Board as the Public's Agent?

Mobile citizens delegated much of the responsibility for carrying out the mandate from the 1825 meeting to the school commissioners. The board might have become a surrogate for the public; the theory of representative government implies that the role of the people ends when their representatives take office. That didn't happen in Mobile: citizens stayed involved to make certain that the board reflected the community's interests, as is evident in the history of the board.

The story of the school commission has three chapters. One is about meeting day-to-day challenges, primarily financial. The second is about defining what public schooling meant. And the third is about the "politics," or relationships, both within the board and between the board and the citizenry.

The Community, the Legislature, and the Money

One role the board played on behalf of the public was as conduit to Alabama's general assembly, largely on financial problems. Although Barton's bill provided funds for schools, collecting the money was another matter. With community support evident in the editorials of the *Mobile Commercial Register,* the newly designated school commissioners went back to the legislative delegation in 1829 to make county tax collectors and other officials directly accountable to them.[16]

The board was probably reacting to a series of letters in the local newspapers in 1828 and 1829 questioning why no school had been built. When commissioners reported that the board had received only $649 out of some seven thousand dollars due the school fund, citizens made it clear that they were unhappy, suggesting that the board step aside if it couldn't get the job done. Mobilians complained that there wasn't even an elementary school with significant public financing and that the children of poorer families were wholly neglected. When elections for aldermen and mayor came up in 1829, public education was a leading issue.[17]

Exactly how the school board responded isn't clear because the minutes between 1829 and 1836 haven't been found. Fortunately, a report to the public that appeared in the *Mobile Commercial Register and Patriot* of October 28, 1833, sheds some light on the situation. Evidently, a lively exchange had gone on between the commission and the citizens at a board meeting on October 18. A commission proposal to attract and fund teachers through a combination of "private with public remuneration" stirred up considerable criticism. (Teachers were to receive a fixed salary from the board as well as the income from tuition.) Commissioners responded to the complaints with a revised plan to reduce tuition in order to make instruction more widely available, a problem that must have been the source of the controversy. The board set a limit of two dollars per month on fees and supplemented teachers' salaries with an extra one dollar from public funds. In 1833, teachers could rent "the public school house" for a "modest" two hundred dollars per year, another measure designed to lower tuition.

In 1830, the board had purchased property with income from the taxes generated by the Barton bill. Commissioners allocated $2,750 for land on which to erect a new building to replace an existing frame schoolhouse apparently in use in the 1820s.[18]

According to the *Commercial Register,* the board intended to support two schools in the city, one for boys and one for girls, plus two schools for both elsewhere in the county (one in George's Settlement and perhaps another in Mount Vernon or Malone's Settlement or wherever there was a congregation of twenty students). The school year was to be ten months. Instructors in the county schools could charge a dollar in tuition and receive a salary of one hundred and fifty dollars for the school year. Communities had to furnish lodging for teachers. Also, in the county, five to ten scholars, a quarter to a half of the enrollment, could be admitted free of charge. Teachers in the city receiving public support had to accept the same number of students without charge. And the board made a similar arrangement with Mrs. Eliza Randall, who was to operate an infant school. Commissioners incorporated her formerly independent school into the public system and required her to admit five to ten children without tuition.[19]

In this same newspaper account, Henry Hitchcock, speaking for his fellow commissioners, pledged to encourage more schools to open throughout the city and county and to adopt a uniform set of textbooks so students could transfer easily. But, cautious, the board thought it inadvisable "to extend . . . the number of schools in the city, at least until those . . . mentioned [in the report] have their full complement of scholars." The success of these schools, commissioners hoped, would be a "sufficient inducement for other qualified persons to open other schools." In other words, the board's strategy was to use its limited funds as leverage to create schools and to provide "scholarships" for those who couldn't pay tuition.

Following the policies adopted in October, the board immediately employed Mr. Beattie and Mr. Lyman Gibbons along with Miss Watson, who was to assist in the female department. Gibbons further agreed to give up his plans for an independent school and teach Latin, Greek, and French to twelve students at an increased tuition of four dollars a month. This was the faculty when the school doors opened on November 15, 1833.

Encouraging schools to open was not a new policy in 1833. The year before, Mobile school commissioners had announced that they had employed H. Gates to preside over the Mobile Academy. It offered three levels of instruction from the primary to the advanced or classical; tuition ranged accordingly from three dollars to four and a half dollars per quarter. An academy by the same name had advertised in the paper since at least 1826, without any reference to support from the school board.[21]

The practice of subcontracting for and subsidizing independent teachers remained in force for almost twenty years. So did the policy of admitting a limited number of students without charge, a common remedy used throughout America. Tuition cost was a big barrier, and fees evidently affected even those with a good income. An advertisement in the *Commercial Register* urged Mobilians to send their children to New York to avoid the high cost of tuition and board at home.[20]

From the very beginning, the public schools in Mobile were both a civic responsibility and a civic frustration, the latter brought on by the discrepancy between the growing demand for free instruction and the funds available to meet that demand. By the mid-1830s, the city had twenty-seven schools and the board supported fifteen of them, which appear to have enrolled six hundred students. More expenses prompted the commissioners to petition the legislature once again, and they were given authority to audit the books of auctioneers, whose sales were taxed to support schools—though a loophole gave the circuit clerk power to withhold some of the funds.[22]

In 1835, the school board committed one hundred thousand dollars for a new school building, Barton Academy. To pay the bills, Henry Hitchcock and Silas Dinsmoor solicited donations from the community, and in December 1836 the legislature authorized a fifty thousand dollar lottery. The municipal government also loaned the board fifteen thousand dollars. Citizens continued to press the commissioners for a full account of how they spent the money they were receiving.

What does the practice of using donations and a lottery to fund the schools say about how public they were? The answer has to take into account the standard practices of the day. Most civic enterprises in Mobile were jointly funded by both voluntary contributions and appropriations from the city treasury. The local government solicited outside resources to serve the public interest, in addition to providing some services itself. People in the early 1800s didn't distinguish between what was public and what was private as sharply as we do today. For instance, municipal funds were used to grade the land and build sidewalks for the public park (Bienville Square), but donations paid for the iron fence around it. Money raised by Hitchcock and his fellow citizens didn't change the character of education any more than the fence made the public square a private park.

The 1836 act authorizing the lottery also replaced the 1826 legislation and reorganized the board, creating the position of secretary (who would serve as the fiscal officer and revenue collector). Section 11 of the new statute established a financial oversight committee consisting of three members to be appointed quarterly. (Years later, this section—and the faithfulness of the board in carrying it out—would be the subject of considerable discussion among commissioners.) The law further reauthorized a school tax equal to one-fourth of the county tax, a 1.5 percent tax on certain property sales (including the sale of slaves), and two amusement taxes. And the board was to receive two dollars on all suits in circuit and county courts.[23]

In addition, the legislation directed the board to appropriate funds for schools in the county, that is, outside the city limits. The demand for education had already spread to wards on the outskirts of the urban core. The West Ward, for instance, was a community in its own right, and its citizens were busy establishing a church and a "public school." As settlements farther out in the county grew into communities, they claimed their rights to school funding under the 1836 statute.[24]

DELIBERATIONS OVER THE NATURE OF PUBLIC EDUCATION

What kind of education did Mobilians have in mind for Barton Academy? How did the board interpret the mission it was given in 1825? Some think Mobile's public schools were simply another form of charity, that they were intended for the poor on the assumption that everyone else could and would educate their own children. I'm not sure that was the case. Mobilians appear to have been considering several options for diffusing knowledge. One was certainly to use school board revenue to favor those children whose parents couldn't pay tuition. Another was to use the money to reduce the cost of everyone's tuition. Still another option was to make schooling free to all who wanted to attend a public school. Mobilians experimented with several approaches before arriving at a decision twenty-five years later.

Henry Hitchcock seems to have supported the third option when he said that the board's objective was "to furnish public and popular instruction for the children of the great body of the population of the City." The "great body of the population" was far more than just the poor. Furthermore, if school funds were designated for the indigent, they usually paid only for a primary education. But Mobile's board had already appropriated money for everything from an infant school to classical studies.[25]

Barton Academy

Unfortunately, Hitchcock didn't see his plan

realized; he died from yellow fever in the summer of 1839. In paying tribute to him, the board adopted a statement confirming what it had said earlier about the objectives of public education. Schooling was to have a decidedly civic purpose and a community focus. Instructing the "rising generation" was critical because that generation would eventually be responsible for sustaining the city's "Religious, Literary and Political Institutions" and the values these embodied—morality, knowledge, self-government. That required "Popular Education" to "Send the Streams of Knowledge in rich profusion throughout our Community." The goal was widespread access to education, not relief for the poor.[26]

The crowning symbol of this policy was the new Barton building. A stately public academy, the architecture implied that what went on inside was of the greatest importance and the highest quality.

Thomas Fay's *Strangers' Guide to Mobile* for 1839 described what was going on in Barton Academy "to meet the increasing wants of the public" (this was the second year in the new building). A. S. Vigus, who had been teaching in Montgomery, organized a classical and scientific department for boys, and Misses Ogden and Camp supervised a primary school for both boys and girls. School commissioners announced that they intended to open an advanced female department in October and to hire "an experienced teacher on the Monitorial System." This system promised to increase the number of students who could be instructed and, as a result, lower the per student cost, which would make lower tuition possible.[27]

The board also had to consider its responsibilities to communities outside the city. The same year Barton opened (1836), it appropriated six hundred dollars to T. Malone for a school on Saw Mill Creek, where there were twenty students, and a similar amount to another school between Chicasabogue and Bayou Sarah. Given this large scope, the board created a committee to oversee and employ teachers for a countywide array of public schools.[28]

Unfortunately, a familiar major obstacle threatened the board's ambitious plan—twelve thousand dollars in debts. Reluctantly, the commissioners had to charge tuition "for the present," but thought they could hold the fee to less than that of independent schools by not charging teachers for the use of the classrooms. As before, commissioners anticipated using their funds to pay for the education of children who couldn't afford the tuition.[29]

BOARD POLITICS

The extent to which school boards are faithful representatives of the public is determined by the relationships they form with the citizenry of their communities. Even if periodic elections provide all the legitimacy that legislative bodies need (which I seriously doubt), election campaigns alone don't allow school boards to build the kind of relationships that enable them to understand the larger and enduring interests of a community.

These boards can become estranged from their communities in several ways. They may be consumed by their own internal politics. The public may become an abstraction when the citizenry the board consults narrows to a small group of personal friends. Relationships among members may become unwholesomely congenial or unnecessarily adversarial. A board loses legitimacy if it becomes a private club or if it divides into factions, which happens when members begin to represent particular parts of a community or special interests within it.

When, for whatever reasons, boards become dysfunctional, the signs are obvious. A single individual or small clique dominates the whole group. The board becomes preoccupied with its power rather than its responsibility. At the extreme, it is unable to muster a quorum for meetings. The Mobile school commission began to exhibit some of these symptoms in the post-Hitchcock era.

Initially, commission members were people who crusaded for public schools and, until 1839, the board appears to have had a keen sense of its role as the public's agent—as well as its ability to function effectively. Later, it appears to have lost touch with the citizenry and may have become absorbed in infighting. Eventually, the situation deteriorated until the legislature had to step in and reorganize the board. For a period, the public was left without an effective agent to represent its interests.

The trouble started when the paint was still fresh on the Barton building. In 1837, land and other property values fell as cotton exporting became erratic. In addition, Alabama began to feel the economic tremors from a faraway dispute between President Andrew Jackson and champions of a national bank. It wasn't a good time for the school board to pay off its debts. Making matters worse, Jim Copeland's arson turned a good part of Mobile into ashes in 1839, and the city's liability rose to more than half a million dollars, forcing the municipal government to default on its loans, an unheard-of failure at the time.[30]

Financial pressures on the school board grew as Mobile's economy continued to decline. Despite earlier pronouncements, commissioners agreed to a policy that allowed free schooling to become synonymous with charity. On October 31, 1838, the board authorized a special school "for the Instruction of the Children of the *Poor Exclusively*" in the three primary subjects (basically, the three Rs). Parents still had to pay a dollar in monthly tuition for each child, though the fee was dropped by January 1839 when cash became so scarce that people couldn't even pay for groceries. Initially, the free school consisted of a department for boys, but the board planned to open a similar one for girls in February 1839. Although a seemingly practical response to compelling economic circumstances, this type of free school, intentionally or not, reinforced economic segregation in Mobile's educational system.[31]

The argument for the change in policy was practical: something had to be done to deal with rising costs. And the response to the new school clearly demonstrated the need; enrollment soared despite any stigma attached to an institution for the poor. By the end of its second year, 1839, the free school had registered 150 children, a significant number compared to a total Barton enrollment of 350. At the same time, commissioners took steps to reduce or eliminate tuition in the other schools they were subsidizing. For example, in 1843, Professor Schuyler Clarke was allowed to use a room in Barton without paying any rent if he accepted whatever payment parents could afford (even if it was nothing).[32]

The demand for education in the county put even more pressure on the board. Smaller communities, including the Creole communities of free black Alabamians, wanted funds either for schools they had already built or for new ones. In 1839, commissioners were trying to provide instruction in Spring Hill, the McGill's and Goff's settlements, the Mason and Scott communities, Bayou La Batre, and Mount Vernon. A year later, the legislative delegation recognized these communities by authorizing the election of school board members by wards in the city and by beats elsewhere in the county.[33]

In 1840, the school commission faced its most serious crisis. How it came about is summarized by Harriet Amos, and I have drawn on both primary sources and the information she gathered for *Cotton City* to tell one of the most interesting stories in the annals of public education. Expenses, doubtless compounded by the debt on Barton Academy, led to a sheriff's sale of the building that year for fifteen thousand dollars. Fortunately, a group of citizens headed by Samuel P. Bullard and Daniel Chandler saved the day—with the aid of generous extensions of time for repayment by the man who had bought the building, Thomas McGran. Bullard, who had helped the city out of bankruptcy, raised collateral for a bank loan to repurchase Barton by persuading citizens to sign personal notes and pledge their property. (He later acknowledged the board's debt to Samuel W. Allen, John A. Campbell, Daniel Chandler, James Innerarity, Solomon Mordecai, and James Sanford as well as to the firm of Ledyard, Hatter, and Company.) Despite these sacrifices, school commissioners would have to work a decade to retire a debt that reached nearly thirty thousand dollars.[34]

Not unaware of their precarious financial situation before the sheriff's sale, school commissions had already begun to apply for more loans, to collect what money could be had from the sixteenth-section lands, and to raise revenue by renting Barton to independent schools and civic organizations (such as the Franklin Society). Commissioners had also reversed the policy of letting teachers use the academy without charge and had suspended the free school. Given these measures, board members like Bullard had been confident that the citizenry of Mobile would see them through any crisis—that "every liberal minded and intelligent Citizen" would help the schools.

Daniel Chandler and Sarah Campbell Chandler
Daniel Chandler was especially interested in the education of women. In an 1835 address at the University of Georgia, he proposed that they be provided the same opportunities for higher education as men. His remarks encouraged the Georgia legislature to establish its first women's college, Wesleyan Female College. Sarah Campbell Chandler, from Georgia like her husband, was a sister of John A. Campbell, who was her husband's law partner and, later, served as a justice of the United States Supreme Court.[35]

(The commission may also have been encouraged by the prospect of the first state appropriations for schools in 1839 and 1840.) The terms of this board ended, however, and a new board chaired by Robert L. Walker took office in the fall of 1840. By then it was clear that the crisis was more serious than anticipated.[36]

Perhaps because of differences over how to respond to financial problems, the Walker board began to fall apart. Commissioners cut even more deeply into the budget and discontinued the already suspended free school. The community may have disliked these austere measures, and some board members could have challenged the recently elected president. On April 1, 1841, Walker resigned, along with commissioners George E. Holt and Jacob G. Collins. Who replaced them? Bullard and Chandler. Whatever influence these two old hands might have had, however, it didn't solve the problems within the commission. After a called meeting on April 1, board members failed to show up for eight meetings in a row. They met to approve loans on December 9, 1841, but subsequently failed to assemble a quorum during most of 1842.[37]

Before leaving office in 1840, Samuel Bullard had reported at length on the financial condition of the schools and the number of pupils in attendance. He and the executive committee believed that their actions had benefited the community. Bullard's report emphasized the good record of the tuitionless schools and their importance to the public, and he ended with the hope that free schools would soon be established throughout the city and county. He made a similar financial report when he returned as board president, replacing Robert Walker in 1841.[38]

Still something wasn't right in the board. Maybe members had personal differences among the members. Maybe they disagreed over means (since commission minutes suggest that most everyone agreed that free schooling was the objective). Schools exclusively for the poor could have been the dividing issue. The minutes, while silent about the reasons, show that the board collapsed, unable to muster a quorum. In February 1843, the state legislature stepped in and named a new commission to be chaired by John A. Cuthbert. Both Bullard and Chandler retained their seats, which gives some idea of the internal politics. The new board also included Josiah C. Nott, a local physician known for his theories on race, and Walter Smith, a general in the militia, Mobile city recorder, and coeditor of the *Mobile Daily Advertiser*. A former board member, the general was destined to play a major role in the 1850s.[39]

The legislature explicitly required the commissioners to resume meeting by the first of March. And it made the new board self-perpetuating, ending the practice of public elections; members could now appoint their own successors. Mobilians no longer controlled their schools through a board of their choosing, a change that would prove unacceptable in time.

The legislature also put severe financial restrictions on the board. Commissioners had to liquidate the balance of the debt before funding instruction. And they weren't allowed to raise revenue by selling or encumbering school property. Not only were the Mobile schools in trouble, but to make matters worse, the state bank collapsed, which caused the government to default on its payments in 1843. (Recall that the federal funds for education had been used as bank capital.) The financial crisis in education spread statewide.

Despite the legislative directive to resume meeting and despite a promising start, the Cuthbert board soon began to show signs of failing like its predecessor. Members met in February and March of 1843 but couldn't marshal another quorum until July 20. After that session, no meetings occurred until December 20.[40]

When the commissioners did meet in 1843, they talked about consulting with "the business portion of the Community" and indicated that this influential group was unhappy with the board's management of school funds. In response, the commission appointed a review committee as called for in the 1836 legislation. It consisted of Bullard, Chandler, and Joseph Lesesne. Their report was highly critical of past practices, presumably by the Walker board since the Bullard-Chandler duo was leading the charge. Prudent management, the three said, could have "put a sound English education within the reach of the poorest child." But their inability to determine the true financial situation under the previous board forced the new commissioners to defer any expenditures for six to seven months, the time they estimated it would take to retire the debt. The review committee was equally critical of the earlier policy of not charging instructors rent for space. Savings to parents from lower tuition, board members said, had been insignificant.[41]

Bullard, Chandler, and Lesesne wanted to rouse the new board to action through committees, with responsibilities spelled out for members. (Citizen boards organized themselves in this fashion since they had few, if any, staff members.) Past school commissions had had numerous committees, so the proposed scheme wasn't entirely new. The issue seems to have been getting commissioners to be more accountable. Charges of fraud and self-dealing (conflict of interest) were in the air, and the committee report emphasized the importance of examining revenue collections quarterly, as prescribed in the law.

Constrained by debt, the commission continued to lease space in Barton to independent teachers and used the rent, along with revenue from city taxes, to make education more accessible. In 1844, the board provided scholarships, allowing additional students to take classes from Schuyler Clarke. This wasn't a consistent practice, however. Professor William Merrill, a subsequent lessee, offered to operate a free school but was charged an annual rent of seven hundred dollars, which likely precluded free instruction.[42]

COLLABORATION WITH FAITH-BASED ORGANIZATIONS: PUBLIC SCHOOLS IN CHURCHES

John Cuthbert's reign as board president ended abruptly in 1844 when he refused to pay for a bond that would protect the board against any misuse of funds on his part. Cuthbert objected to spending his own money for a bond when he wasn't being paid a salary. Samuel Griffith Fisher, the vice president, replaced him in 1845 and presided over a board that seems—despite a few failures to assemble a quorum—to have gotten its act together. With reducing tuition as its major objective, the commission found particularly strong allies in churches that were prepared to offer a totally free education to all comers. In addition, the churches would continue their parochial schools (which charged tuition) and their schools for orphans.[43]

On May 25, 1846, without any record of extensive discussion or debate, the board began to fund public schooling in religious institutions. The minutes read, "The Rev. McGlashan asked for an appropriation of $25 per month for three months to aid the Bethel Free School," an institution founded by the Presbyterian Church in 1845. The secretary of the board was immediately authorized to appropriate the amount requested because of the school's "peculiar claims on the community." This and similar appropriations to other churches were made with the restriction that classes had to be open "without distinction of faith."[44]

Strange as this practice appears from today's perspective, it may not have struck Mobilians as exceptional. The city had a long tradition of civic/governmental collaboration, which may be the reason there is no record of any board discussion of what we might call a "faith-based" initiative.

Besides money from the school board, revenue for the Bethel Free School came from the city government (an additional thirty-five dollars per month) and from donations. Several civic associations and churches rallied community support. One was the Mobile Port Society, which was organized in 1835 by the men of the Government Street Presbyterian Church and met in Henry Stickney's home. Another was an association of Presbyterian women. With this assistance, enrollment at the Bethel school grew rapidly to 223 students during the first six months. Later McGlashan opened a similar school for Creole children at the urging of Creole citizens. (It's discussed in the next chapter.)[46]

Mobilians had recruited Alexander McGlashan from the American Seaman's Friend Society to be chaplain at the Bethel Church (sometimes called Seaman's Bethel because of its ministry to visiting sailors and local watermen). The initial purpose of Bethel was to provide laboring men on the waterfront with "a means of moral and social improvement," but McGlashan soon expanded the church's ministry to the whole city.[45]

The state legislature sanctioned this arrangement for financing public education in 1846. A new law allowed citizens to designate their tax payments either for schools operated by churches or for the general school fund. The legislature specifically directed the school board to pay up to eight hundred dollars a year to the Methodist Free School, with the stipulation that the instruction had to be available to children of all denominations. This school may have grown out of a cooperative venture with the Unitarians. In 1842, Charles Dall, a Unitarian minister who was teaching reading in a Sunday school, began to offer weekday classes to twenty children at the Jackson Street Methodist Church. Later, Methodists continued the program as a free school at the Franklin Street Church.[47]

Even though the board approved the Bethel subsidy without opposition, commissioners objected to the legislative directive to pay the Methodists and tried to have it repealed—perhaps because of concern (surely among Presbyterians) about favoritism and inequitable distribution of resources.

In 1851, commissioners began supporting other denominational efforts: the Trinity Parish Free School (presumably an institution of the Trinity Episcopal Church) and the Catholic Public Free School. Later that same year, they financed three more schools, each institution receiving from five hundred to thirteen hundred dollars. These weren't the only institutions the board supported, however; minutes list eleven annual appropriations in addition to those for schools operated by four churches. County schools, including one organized by the Malones and Chastangs, collected between one hundred fifty and two hundred dollars a year. The Creole Free School (possibly at the Bethel Church), said to have had sixty to seventy students, got two hundred dollars in 1851.[48]

The total board appropriation for church-sponsored schools wasn't large—$4,200 in 1851. The municipal government added $77.50 per month for each of the schools on the grounds that they served the city. This money made a huge difference to hundreds of students. Of all the denominations, the Catholic Church provided most of this free instruction in what it deliberately called "Public Free Schools." Recall that these were in addition to parochial schools and distinct, in the church's view, from "Orphan Schools" for the poor and parentless—distinctions spelled out in a communiqué sent to the Mobile school board. Catholics alone reached as many as six hundred youngsters a year.[49]

Catholics began providing education for the community in 1832 when a priest, Gabriel Chalon, taught classes without charge. In time, the Sisters of Charity and the Brothers of the Sacred Heart operated four free schools: one for boys, one for girls, one for boys and girls, and one for Creoles. In addition, the church founded its own academies: the Visitation Academy (for girls) in 1833 and, in the 1840s, the McGill Institute (for boys) and the Cathedral School for Girls. These charged tuition, which was used to fund the free schools. Catholics also founded orphanages: the Industrial School for Boys and a similar school for girls.[50]

Were the free schools sponsored by churches public, or were they merely nineteenth-century versions of colonial charity schools? In an era of self-rule, did Mobilians intend to turn the clock back to a way of providing education that was characteristic of a less-democratic past, or were they only responding to a financial crisis by enlisting the help of churches? What did the Catholic Church have in mind by calling its school "public" and "free," not just "free"? There doesn't seem to be any

In addition to church schools, the city was filled with entrepreneurial institutions whose advertisements crowded the pages of the local papers; among them the Dauphin Academy, the Mobile High School, the Episcopal Female Seminary, and the French and English Day School. In the November 28, 1850, issue of the *Mobile Daily Advertiser,* Mrs. Watkinson respectfully announced that her School for Young Ladies would be opened on the first Monday in November. Madame Esperance Palagi, "Professor of Vocal and Pianoforte Music," made the same offer, and Professor S. Bernard, also respectfully, informed the "young Gentlemen of Mobile that his EVENING CLASSES will be re-opened." Bernard offered French, Spanish, bookkeeping, surveying, penmanship, and commercial arithmetic, charging five dollars per month. Education was available—at a price.

question that the church schools weren't parochial with sectarian agendas; they couldn't have received public money if they had been. Were they exclusively for the poor, as was the board's free school in 1839? That depends partly on how "poor" is defined. It can mean "destitute," the usual definition. And, surely there were such families in the city, especially during periods of economic recession. But the free schools may have been populated largely by the sons and daughters of working people who found the tuition charged by other institutions too high, especially if they had more than one child, which was common then.

Regardless of how many of their students were truly impoverished and how many were simply priced out of the other schools, I think the church-sponsored institutions have a place in the evolutionary chain of public education. They were funded for public purposes. As the school board acknowledged, these schools had claims on the community because of what they did for it. And providing education through faith-based institutions was consistent with the way other city services were provided in the nineteenth century—through collaboration between governmental and nongovernmental organizations. The church-sponsored schools strike me as less sectarian or charitable than civic. Many denominations have entered public life with nondoctrinal agendas.

THE EVOLVING CONCEPT OF PUBLIC EDUCATION

Between 1826 and 1850, deliberations over the public's obligations for diffusing knowledge had progressed to the point that Mobilians were clear about the need to provide schooling for all citizens by making it as inexpensive as economic circumstances allowed. They were less certain about whether that should be done by creating special schools for the poor. It is difficult to say whether the 1839 free school was established because of financial expediency or educational philosophy. Significantly, the Alabama legislature didn't earmark school funds exclusively for the poor as Georgia had done, which is some indication of attitudes in the state. Yet, as noted, while Mobilians rejected sectarian distinctions, they accepted economic segregation by establishing one school "for the poor *exclusively.*"

Citizens of Mobile were also undecided about what public direction of education involved. Were contracts with independent teachers sufficient, or did the board have to establish schools and provide instruction itself? The scope of the public's obligation was another issue. The practice seems to have been to offer the full range of subjects from the elementary to the classical level at the city's expense; though that would be contested later when some board members argued that the public should pay only for primary schooling.

The citizenry was relatively certain about why education should have public support, even if people were divided on the means of providing it. Educating children was only one of many reasons; the well-being of the community was equally important. Those two motives reinforced one another. Families with school-age youngsters made common cause with developers and merchants, who wanted schools that would provide the mental capital needed to spur the economy and make towns more competitive. The working people of the city and yeoman farmers in the county had other, though no less compelling, reasons. Among them, the obvious: instruction at a price they could afford.

To put education in Mobile in the context of what was happening in other Southern cities, Natchez, Mississippi, is a useful point of reference. It was also a French settlement with a large Catholic population. Several schools conducted by independent teachers were in operation by 1801. Tuition was high, even though incomes ($124 per capita for free citizens in 1860) may have been lower than in Mobile. The equivalent of Barton Academy, a public school funded by a city, the Natchez Institute, didn't open until 1845. It accepted the city's white children free of charge provided they were at least six years old and had been vaccinated. Catholic children went to the institute, but the church, concerned about conversion to Protestantism, opened its own denominational free schools in 1847. There are said to have been a few schools for free black Mississippians, though apparently none with public funding.[51]

According to a study by Julia Nguyen, "pupils from varying family backgrounds and different economic situations studied together" in Natchez, though some citizens were quite class-conscious. Among the wealthy, the social position of an institution and its students were important considerations in choosing a school. They felt that the "right school" could secure or improve a child's standing in society. That same attitude may have been present in Mobile.

Historians such as Rush Welter have argued that working people, in particular, saw universal education as a means of securing the political rights of citizens or, as Welter puts it, as "an intellectual resource against authority." Universal, common education was also a way to promote equity by countering class distinctions and privilege. Citizens with these concerns were most likely to have insisted that boards do more than stimulate the growth of schools and provide for the children who couldn't pay fees. They held to the notion that education should be available to everybody on the same basis.[52]

Some might argue that Mobile's and Natchez's concern with education was only characteristic of large cities, that it was primarily an urban phenomenon. Rural counties, however, were also founding schools at a similar rate. Historians of Clarke County reported that no community of any size was without some kind of educational institution.

Lack of instruction obviously plagued areas where families were too scattered to sustain a school. Parents probably continued to rely on neighbors, such as the Moncriefs and Greens, who were willing to tutor other children. We don't have any way to know how much of that was going on, but later in the book there is a description of how one rural family, the Masseys of Choctaw County, filled the void. I suspect there were many others like them.

NOTES TO CHAPTER 4

1 Information on Mobile was from City of Mobile Census Records 1830, Alabama Department of Archives and History, Montgomery, Ala.; Charles Grayson Summersell, *Mobile: History of a Seaport Town* (University: University of Alabama Press, 1949), p. 12; and Alabama General Assembly, *Acts,* 7th annual sess., 1825 (Cahawba: William B. Allen, 1826), p. 35.

2 Weymouth T. Jordan, *Ante-Bellum Alabama: Town and Country* (1957; reprint, University: University of Alabama Press, 1987), pp. 10-11.

3 One of the best sources on Mobile's society was the chronology of names and dates of significant events in Caldwell Delaney, ed., *Craighead's Mobile: Being the Fugitive Writings of Erwin S. Craighead and Frank Craighead* (Mobile: Haunted Bookshop, 1968), pp. 102-107. Harriet Amos also had a lengthy discussion of social services in Chapters 6 and 7 of *Cotton City: Urban Development in Antebellum Mobile* (University: University of Alabama Press, 1985), pp. 151-152, 177-178.

4 My descriptions of Mobile's ethnic groups, social clubs, churches, and labor organizations in this section are based on Amos, *Cotton City,* pp. 58-59, 63-65, 76-77, 84, 88-90, 110-112, 145.

5 Delaney, *Craighead's Mobile,* pp. 104, 109; Richard B. Redwood, Jr., *The Redwood Family of Mobile* (Mobile: Willowbrook Press, 1993), p. 25; and Amos, *Cotton City,* pp. 116, 121, 173, 196.

6 Amos, *Cotton City,* pp. xiii, 78, 177 and Jordan, *Ante-Bellum Alabama,* p. 12.

7 Bama Wathan Watson, *The History of Barton Academy* (Mobile: Haunted Book Shop, 1971), pp. 10-12. Watson, consistent with the practice at the time, lists women by their married names.

8 Alabama, *Acts,* 7th annual sess., 1825, pp. 35-36.

9 Sources that helped identify Willoughby Barton included a note dated October 6, 1982, in the Oakleigh collection at the Historic Mobile Preservation Society; an article by Cammie East, "Who Was Willoughby Barton?" *Port City,* 7 November 1982; a reference by William H. Brantley in *Three Capitals: A Book about the First Three Capitals of Alabama* (University: University of Alabama Press, 1976), p.

190; and a brief discussion by Peter J. Hamilton in *Mobile of the Five Flags: The Story of the River Basin and Coast about Mobile from the Earliest Times to the Present* (Mobile: Gill Printing Company, 1913), pp. 253-254. Barton's death is recorded in Johnnie Andrews, Jr., comp., *Mobile Records, 1812 to 1834: A Compendium of Historical and Genealogical Records of Early/American Mobile* (Prichard, Ala.: Bienville Historical Society, 1984). These records showed that he was from Augusta, Georgia.

10 Mobilians may have been motivated to provide free education, in part, by the community's experience with an 1819 epidemic that left a number of children destitute. The city provided schooling for the orphans. Paul Wayne Taylor, "Mobile: 1818-1859 as Her Newspapers Pictured Her" (master's thesis, University of Alabama, 1951), p. 60. Also see *Mobile Commercial Register,* 10 May 1825 and 24 May 1825 and Poore, *Alabama's Enterprising Newspaper,* p. 61.

11 *Mobile Commercial Register,* 3 May 1828.

12 John Everitt's career can be traced by looking at Brantley, *Three Capitals,* p. 24; Jacqueline Anderson Matte, Doris Brown, and Barbara Waddell, comp., *Old St. Stephens: Historical Records Survey* (St. Stephens: St. Stephens Historic Commission, 1999), pp. 56, 60, 69; and Thomas McAdory Owen, *History of Alabama and Dictionary of Alabama Biography,* vol. 3 (Chicago: S. J. Clarke Publishing Company, 1921), p. 555.

13 Peter J. Hamilton wrote about Silas Dinsmoor in *Colonial Mobile,* ed. Charles G. Summersell (1910; reprint, University: University of Alabama Press, 1976), pp. 552-553. There was more in *The Reminiscences of George Strother Gaines: Pioneer and Statesman of Early Alabama and Mississippi, 1805-1843,* ed. James P. Pate (Tuscaloosa: University of Alabama Press), p. 41.

14 Robert J. Zietz mentioned board members Mordecai and Chamberlain in *The Gates of Heaven: Congregation Sha'arai Shomayim, The First 150 Years, Mobile, Alabama, 1844-1994* (Mobile: Congregation Sha'arai Shomayim, 1994) p. 2, as did Willis Brewer in *Alabama: Her History, Resources, War Record, and Public Men, from 1540 to 1872* (1872; reprint, Spartanburg, S.C.: Reprint Company, 1975), p. 396.

15 Thomas McAdory Owen chronicled the career of Henry Hitchcock in *History of Alabama,* pp. 816-819. Hitchcock is also referred to in Brewer's *Alabama: Her History,* p. 394 and

Jacqueline Anderson Matte's *The History of Washington County: First County in Alabama* (Chatom, Ala.: Washington County Historical Society, 1982), p. 57. The most extensive biography I found was William H. Brantley, Jr.'s "Henry Hitchcock of Mobile, 1816-1839," *Alabama Review* 5 (January 1952): 3-39.

16 *Mobile Commercial Register,* 20 February 1829.

17 Letters criticizing the Mobile school board appeared in the *Mobile Commercial Register,* 11 October 1828, 15 October 1828, 22 October 1828, 25 October 1828, and 27 February 1829.

18 Bessie Mae Holloway reported on events in Mobile's educational history in the 1830s and 1840s in "A History of Public School Education in Mobile, Alabama, for the Child under Six Years of Age, 1833-1928" (Ph.D. diss., Auburn University, 1983), pp. 9-19. Other sources included Watson's *History of Barton Academy,* pp. 12-13; Hamilton's *Mobile of Five Flags,* p. 254; and Harriet Bomar Ellis' "Mobile Public School Beginnings and Their Background" (master's thesis, Alabama Polytechnic Institute, 1930), p. 19.

19 *Mobile Commercial Register and Patriot,* 28 October 1833.

20 *Mobile Commercial Register and Patriot,* 8 October 1832.

21 *Mobile Commercial Register,* 17 January 1826 and 2 November 1832.

22 Primary sources for education in Mobile in the mid-1830s were Alabama General Assembly, *Acts,* annual sess., 1836 (Tuscaloosa: David Ferguson, 1837), pp. 49-50. Secondary accounts included Delaney, *Craighead's Mobile,* p. 49; Nita Katharine Pyburn, "Mobile Public Schools before 1860," *Alabama Review* 11 (July 1958): 177; and Amos, *Cotton City,* pp. 180-181.

23 Alabama, *Acts,* annual sess., 1836, pp. 48-51.

24 Alan Smith Thompson, "Mobile, Alabama, 1850-1861: Economic, Political, Physical and Population Characteristics" (Ph.D. diss., The University of Alabama, 1979), p. 228.

25 Bama Watson reproduced the Mobile School Board Minutes of 23 August 1836 in her *History of Barton Academy,* pp. 15-18. These pages had the Hitchcock committee report.

26 Mobile School Board Minutes, 1836-1845, 17 August 1839, p. 50.

27 Thomas C. Fay, *Strangers' Guide for 1839: Embracing Names of Firms, the Individuals Composing Them, and Citizens Generally; Together with Their Professions, Residence & Number, Alphabetically Arranged, with a Cross Index* (Mobile: R. R. Dade, n.d.), pp. 2-4.

28 Mobile's school board recorded its appropriations for education outside the city in its minutes of 7 December 1836, p. 13; 1 March 1837, p. 20; and 1 September 1837, p. 31. Harriet Bomar Ellis used these pages in her account of these appropriations: "Mobile Public School Beginnings and Their Background" (master's thesis, Alabama Polytechnic Institute, 1930), p. 20. Also see Pyburn, "Mobile Public Schools," p. 180.

29 Watson, *History of Barton Academy,* pp. 15-18 quoting Mobile School Board Minutes, 23 August 1836.

30 Thompson, "Mobile, Alabama 1850-1861," pp. 73-76.

31 Mobile School Board Minutes, 1836-1845, 31 October 1838, p. 41 and Ellis, "Mobile Public School Beginnings," p. 23 citing Mobile School Board Minutes, 1836-1845, 2 January 1845, p. 44.

32 Mobile School Board Minutes, 1836-1845, 12 December 1839 as cited in Pyburn, "Mobile Public Schools," p. 181; Mobile School Board Minutes, 1836-1845, 31 July 1840, p. 66; and Mobile School Board Minutes, 1836-1845, 2 August 1843, p. 102 as cited in Ellis, "Mobile Public School Beginnings and Their Background," p. 24.

33 Alabama General Assembly, *Acts,* annual sess., 1839 (Tuscaloosa: Hale and Eaton, 1840), p. 113 and Pyburn, "Mobile Public Schools," pp. 180-181 citing Mobile School Board Minutes, 1836-1845, 12 December 1839.

34 Mobile School Board Minutes, 1836-1845, recorded commission discussions and debts (including a $15,000 city loan) between July 31, 1840, and December 9, 1841, pp. 63, 65, 74-75. Amos covered this period in *Cotton City,* pp. 181-189, as did Ellis in "Mobile Public School Beginnings," pp. 24-25.

35 Owen, *History of Alabama,* pp. 293, 315.

36 Mobile School Board Minutes, 1836-1845, 8 August 1840, p. 67 and Amos, *Cotton City,* p. 182 citing Mobile School Board Minutes, 1836-1845, 31 October 1838, 8 June 1839, 8 July 1839, 21 August 1839; 14 February 1840; and 4 November 1840, pp. 50-67.

37 Mobile School Board Minutes, 1836-1845, 1 April 1841, p. 72.

[38] Mobile School Board Minutes, 1836-1845, 31 July 1840 and 9 December 1841, pp. 63-67, 74-75.

[39] The legislative intervention in 1843 and the reorganized Mobile school board are discussed in Alabama General Assembly, *Acts,* annual sess., 1842 (Tuscaloosa: Phelan and Harris, 1843), pp. 58-59; Mobile School Board Minutes, 1836-1845, 31 July 1840, 24 February 1843, and 3 March 1843, pp. 63, 66, 80; R. P. Vail, *Mobile Directory, or Strangers' Guide, for 1842* (Mobile: Dade and Thompson, 1842), p. 53; Ralph E. Poore, Jr., *Alabama's Enterprising Newspaper:* The Mobile Press Register *and Its Forebears, 1813-1991* (Mobile Municipal Archives, Mobile, Alabama, photocopy), p. 38; and Stephen B. Weeks, *History of Public School Education in Alabama,* U.S. Bureau of Education Bulletin, 1915, no. 12 (Washington, D.C.: Government Printing Office, 1915), p. 28.

The Mobile delegation to the general assembly, which probably had a hand in reordering the board, consisted of John A. Campbell, W. D. Dunn, John Ervin, T. W. McCoy, and T. L. Toulmin. Brewer, *Alabama: Her History,* pp. 432-433.

[40] The failure of the school board to assemble a quorum was dutifully noted in the Mobile School Board Minutes, 1836-1845, pp. 98-105.

[41] Mobile School Board Minutes, 1836-1845, 3 March 1843 and 10 March 1843, pp. 82, 84-85.

[42] Leases for Barton in the mid-1840s appeared in the Mobile School Board Minutes, 1845-1852, 2 October 1845 and 15 July 1848, pp. 6, 24, and were discussed by Harriet Amos in *Cotton City,* p. 183.

[43] Mobile School Board Minutes, 1836-1845, p. 116, recorded John Cuthbert's resignation.

[44] The first appropriations to church-sponsored schools were found in Mobile School Board Minutes, 1845-1852, 25 May 1846 and 12 January 1847, pp. 11-12, 15. Paul Wayne Taylor also mentioned this practice in "Mobile: 1818-1859 as Her Newspapers Pictured Her" (master's thesis, The University of Alabama, 1951), p. 63.

Appropriations to church-sponsored schools may have prompted little discussion in the Mobile school commission because it was a common practice in the country to rely on "faith-based" institutions to carry out civic objectives. Maryland, for example, has a tradition of county free schools staffed by clergy, which dates back to 1696. The schools were financed with public money. The schoolmasters, however, were of the Church of England. Maryland churches also established schools, some of which received state free school funds. Most, however, were parochial and supported by donations. Collaboration between church and state was evident in 1828 when Baltimore created its first public school—in the basement of a Presbyterian Church. In 1853, the state was allocating about $63,000 to "all types of public schools." Leo Joseph McCormick, *Church-State Relationships in Education in Maryland* (Washington, D.C.: Catholic University of America Press, 1942), pp. 18-41, 154-167.

[45] Augusta Norden, "Research on the Seamen's Bethel" (Spring Hill College, Spring Hill, Alabama, 1971, photocopy), pp. 1-2 and Charles D. Bates, ed. *The Archives Tell A Story of the Government Street Presbyterian Church, Mobile, Alabama* (Mobile: Gill Printing Company, 1959), pp. 108, 123.

[46] Bates, *Archives Tell a Story,* p. 122 and Taylor, "Mobile: 1818-1859," p. 63.

The Presbyterian Church's efforts on behalf of black Creoles is the subject of Alexander McGlashan's "Report on the Creole Free School, from March 13, 1849, to January 1, 1850," *Mobile Daily Register,* 17 January 1850. According to the article, "A committee was appointed . . . to enroll the names of those entitled to an education at the Mayor's Office, to visit the School, and see to it that none attend the School except those thus entitled." The *Mobile Daily Register* for February 9 and 19, 1850, has additional details about the Free Creole Colored School, which was operated by the Presbyterians and partially financed by the school board.

[47] Alabama General Assembly, *Acts,* annual sess., 1845 (Tuscaloosa: John McCormick, 1846), pp. 192-193; Amos, *Cotton City,* p. 184; and Mobile School Board Minutes, 1845-1852, 12 January 1847 and 12 October 1848, pp. 15, 26-29.

[48] The Mobile school board recorded its contributions to church-based free schools in the 1850s in its 1845-1852 book of minutes, 6 January 1851, 4 June 1851, and 5 November 1851, pp. 54, 68, 73-75.

Oscar Hugh Lipscomb describes the efforts of the Catholic Church to educate the free black Creole children of Mobile in "The Administration of Michael Portier, Vicar Apostolic of Alabama and the Floridas, 1825-1829, and First Bishop of Mobile, 1829-1859" (Ph.D. diss., Catholic University of America, 1963), pp. 231-232.

[49] A typed copy of the Catholics' petition to restore public funding to their schools is included between pages 126 and 127 of the 1845-1852 board minutes.

[50] For a more complete account of Catholic education in Alabama, see Sister Mary Stanislas Donoghue's "History of Catholic Education in Alabama" (master's thesis, The University of Alabama, 1935), specifically pages 25, 31-35, 43-44, 58-59. In addition, refer to Amos, *Cotton City,* p. 184.

[51] Julia Huston Nguyen, "The Value of Learning: Education and Class in Antebellum Natchez," *Journal of Mississippi History* 61 (1999): 237-263.

[52] Rush Welter, *Popular Education and Democratic Thought in America* (New York: Columbia University Press, 1962), pp. 48-49.

Chapter 5

WHAT THE PUBLIC DID
AND DIDN'T ACCOMPLISH

DESPITE EVIDENCE of public schooling throughout the six counties of the old southwest (and elsewhere in Alabama) and despite Mobile's progress, there is a widespread perception that there was no public education in the state or in the South until after the Civil War.

This perception is rooted in cultural stereotypes. Northerners caricatured Southerners the same way that the English caricatured the Celtic people of Scotland, Wales, and Ireland. Since many Southerners emigrated from those countries, the comparisons came easily. Ironically, white Southerners then used nearly identical stereotypes in describing black Southerners. The in-group always seems to find the out-group lazy, immoral, unruly, and either stupid, uneducated, or both.

Northern and foreign visitors left reams of anecdotes illustrating what they assumed was the prevailing attitude toward education below the Mason-Dixon line. They quoted Southerners saying things like, "I have always been cheated most by men who could write," or "Do you suppose I am fool enough . . . to believe there is any benefit in learning to write?" One Southerner, asked whether he liked to read, said bluntly, "No, it's damned tiresome."[1]

Federal statistics reinforce the charge that Alabamians cared little about formal instruction. Only 35.5 percent of their children were registered in schools in 1850, as compared to the national average of 56.5 percent. By 1860, the census credits Alabama with no more than 46 percent of school-age children enrolled, far below the national average of just under 60 percent. These figures are especially significant because they are not simply about education; they cast doubt on the effectiveness of citizens "exercising their collective capacities" in teaching their children.[2]

THE NETHER REGION

Given both the perceptions and the statistics, the history of Southerners in education became a history of a people who wouldn't school their young. Known for its economic system, its peculiar social structure, and its distinctive intellectual tradition, the South was labeled the deviant in a nation dedicated to universal public education. Southern educators, perhaps trying to secure more funding for their schools, often joined in these gloomy assessments of the region's commitment in the hope that it would benefit their cause.[3]

The Reverend Amory D. Mayo bashed the South for its educational backwardness in his pioneering chronicle of the public school movement. In the Confederate states, Mayo writes, "schooling was modelled on the old English idea,—colleges and academies, . . . largely administered by the Protestant clergy, for the superior class; supplemented often by the best schools in the North and European study." He found no evidence of an "established system of education like the Northern common school" for the millions of nonslaveholding whites.[4]

Ellwood P. Cubberley liked Mayo's conclusions and incorporated them into his study of American public education: Southerners had taken the position that education is a private matter in which the state has no right or need to interfere, he said. Their schools had been established by those who could afford them or by charitable organizations, like churches, which felt an obligation to the orphaned and poverty-stricken. Southern laws were benevolent in purpose but restricted in scope, authorizing aid only for the poor.[5]

This interpretation is still in vogue, even in Alabama. Recent publications report that the antebellum citizenry had little appreciation of the importance of public education because people considered the instruction of children a purely private responsibility and not an obligation of the state. Wealthy planters used private tutors or organized schools that served only their class, and they regarded publicly funded institutions as schools for the poor.[6]

Most of the indictments assumed that the antebellum South was a two-tiered society, in which an aristocracy of planters dominated yeoman farmers, "poor white trash," and, of course, slaves—assumptions about planters and farmers that historians like Frank Owsley later demonstrated weren't entirely valid. Critics also jumped to the conclusion that the Southern social order precluded universal public education, since a caste system is the antithesis of the kind of democratic society thought to have produced public schools.[7]

Many believed common schools couldn't have existed in the South before the Civil War because they were convinced that the values of people like those in the southwestern counties were different from the values of other Americans—that the things Southerners prized were incompatible with the ideals of public education. John C. Calhoun of South Carolina was the perfect example for these critics. Calhoun did, in fact, reject democratic ideals in such works as his *Disquisition on Government,* where he insisted that inequality is indispensable to social order and progress, pointedly objecting to educating lower-class whites on the grounds "that it would 'do nothing for them.'"[8]

Adding more evidence, articles denouncing the rationale for public education appeared in popular journals like the *Southern Quarterly Review* (edited by William Gilmore Simms, a widely read novelist and poet). In October 1852, the magazine published a speech by James Simmons, "Instruction in Schools and Colleges," which was prompted by the opening of free schools in Charleston, South Carolina. Simmons didn't share the enthusiasm of Americans "fond of boasting" about the benefits of public education. Even though political and religious leaders alike called for public schooling on the grounds that it was the palladium of liberty and the guide to eternal salvation, he rejected both claims, arguing that education can't change man's nature because it is merely an instrument that will serve either good or evil purposes. Education is not the engine of freedom, Simmons insisted, and nothing could be more absurd than encouraging "people to read and judge for themselves."[9]

Simmons was equally disturbed by the assumption that everyone should be educated. Not so, he said: society should determine a child's "probable destiny," based on social position and financial resources, and then train that youngster "in accordance with the condition in which he is expected to commence his career." Furthermore, the South Carolinian warned, children with different destinies should *not* be educated together because the "better" social classes would have serious reservations about their children attending schools with the offspring of the great unwashed.[10]

No Scrooge, Simmons wouldn't deny common folk some education; he merely wanted to limit their schooling—and society's obligations to them. Every child should be taught to read, write, and cipher, he felt, because it was a necessary minimum required by the time. Beyond that, education should be based on the ability to pay for it.

Though obliged to "foster" learning, the government shouldn't actually operate schools, from Simmons's point of view. The state only needed to see that children had opportunities to master the three Rs; it should never become directly involved in schooling—certainly not to the extent of imposing taxes. The government had no more right to levy a tax for a school than it had for a church. And, if public education meant that people would be required to send their children only to state schools, it would be "absolute tyranny." Exactly as the critics charged, here was a Southerner who believed that education was a private matter and that instruction in anything beyond the basics was a privilege, not a right.

Simmons and Calhoun were perfect witnesses for the indictments leveled by Mayo and Cubberley. But neither historian noticed that Simmons had openly admitted that his views on education were *not* representative of most Southerners. In fact, Simmons said that most of his contemporaries wanted to elevate the character of their schools, provide more instruction, and make all more learned. The majority of the articles in the *Review* and other journals of the period bore him out: they endorsed free schools. Simmons's only justification for his contrariness was an unshakable conviction that public education was born of an idealism as impractical as it was undesirable.

THE SCOREBOARD

Mayo's and Cubberley's criticisms weren't entirely without merit. Even the most favorable analysis of public education in Alabama wouldn't show that a uniformly resolute citizenry provided schooling on a par with that of the older states in New England. There was opposition and, worse, indifference to the cause of universal instruction. Yet despite what the critics charged, and even taking into account federal statistics, the fact is that the number of public schools in Alabama, in general, and in the southwestern counties, in particular, increased rapidly during the first half of the nineteenth century. Progress wasn't confined to Mobile. Clarke County's seventeen schools in 1840 had increased to thirty by 1850 and then to forty-four by 1860. The growth was primarily in public institutions. Counties funded this expansion more from community sources than from taxes (Mobile was the exception). In Clarke, almost all financial support ($5,349) came from local sources; the 1850 census doesn't show any revenue from federal grants or taxes, although the county had $7,632.42 in land-grant endowments. Critics have made a great deal out of this difference on the grounds that taxes show a greater commitment to education than donations. Certainly voluntary contributions allowed the very wealthy to avoid their civic duty if they were so inclined (as some presumably were).[11]

Not only did the number of schools increase, so did enrollments. Of the six southwestern counties, Mobile led in students registered; Washington was at the bottom. Clarke County was in the middle with 682 youngsters enrolled by the end of the 1840s, a number equally divided between boys and girls.

Statewide, Alabama experienced an impressive 117 percent growth in public school attendance between 1850 and 1860. Champions of state aid claimed that a legislative appropriation of $100,000 in 1854 produced this increase; but while this revenue surely helped, that claim seems exaggerated. The rate of increase in student enrollment before the state intervened appears to have been about the same as after. Keep in mind, too, that state revenue accounted for less than 15 percent of all public school funding. That amount of money couldn't have been too influential.[12]

Even though the South had more private schools than other regions, the charge that these institutions provided most of the education doesn't stand up. In 1860, Alabama had about ten thousand students in private institutions out of a school-age population of more than two hundred thousand children, a proportion only fractionally greater than the national average of 4.9 percent. To be sure, private schools, though not in the majority, were more common in planter counties like Dallas, Greene, and Lowndes. In the southwestern counties, there were comparatively higher percentages of these schools in

Choctaw, Monroe, Washington, and Wilcox. (A more extensive analysis of educational statistics is provided in Notes to this chapter.)

As for the difference between the number of children enrolled in all Alabama schools and the national average, which was reported in the 1850 federal statistics, information collected by county officials in 1856, 1857, and 1858 paints another picture. Although these reports don't show that Alabama met national averages, they do indicate that the state was only somewhat off the mark and not hopelessly behind. According to state figures, the proportion of the school-age population enrolled in all institutions during these years ranged from 53 to over 57 percent, compared to a national average somewhere between 57.6 and 59.6 percent. In support of these local statistics, Alabama's school superintendents testified that more than half of the school-age population was in school. Still, conscientious Alabamians took little comfort from their own data; as in Mobile, they worried about the sizeable number of children who were not in class.[13]

Literacy rates may help explain why people weren't satisfied. Alabama had far more white illiterates than Michigan, a state of comparable size and age. In 1850, there were 33,757 whites in Alabama who couldn't read or write compared to only 7,912 in Michigan. And, even though illiteracy grew by 120 percent in Michigan during the next decade and by just 17 percent in Alabama, Michigan still had only 17,441 illiterates in 1860 while Alabama had 37,605.

It isn't difficult to understand why Michigan was able to keep its number of illiterates low. The state had nearly twice as many pupils enrolled as Alabama, even though the school-age populations in the two states were about the same. The best that can be said for Alabama is that by 1860 it was spending only ten thousand dollars less on schools than Michigan—without having significant revenue from taxes. Also, the number of public schools was increasing at a faster rate in Alabama.

Considering all the evidence, Alabama, in general, followed the national trends in education. Throughout the country, communities had built the first schools in response to popular demand before legislatures came to their aid. These schools were organized by families, churches, town councils, ad hoc groups of citizens, and enterprising teachers, just as they were in Alabama.

Some were selective in their enrollment and expensive; others were charitable ventures for the poor. Most were called "common," meaning elementary or "common pay" schools. (Nearly all charged tuition.) As true in Alabama, these institutions were usually intended to serve all citizens in a given area or community and were financed by everything from fees collected by town treasuries to donations made in fund-raising campaigns. The number and size of these schools increased rapidly during the first half of the nineteenth century. And their success was reflected in the dramatic growth of literacy. That is pretty much what happened in antebellum Alabama, although the illiteracy rate there remained much higher than in the nation as a whole.[14]

By the late twentieth century, public education in the state had fallen so far below national averages that people "thanked Mississippi" for keeping Alabama from being dead last. But in 1860, the state wasn't that far off the pace. And it was actually doing better than its more established neighbor, Georgia. Modern deficiencies aren't genetically predestined.

WERE THE PUBLIC'S SCHOOLS GOOD SCHOOLS?

Numbers only describe the amount of instruction going on, not the quality. How good were the first schools? Opinions varied. Some reform-minded educators were very critical, describing them as pine-pole pens furnished with rude benches and broken slates. Tattered spelling books, scattered on the floor, could be seen through cracks in the schoolhouse walls. The character of the buildings, critics said, matched the competence of the instructors—people of "a very low grade" who had "resorted to teaching because they had proved unfit for anything else." Perhaps these were accurate reports, but educators in other states said much the same thing, suggesting that the comments may have reflected a certain bias on the part of the critics. For example, Iowa's chief state school officer used nearly identical language in condemning his state's school buildings.[15]

Others familiar with education in Alabama had a more positive view of the public's schools. Yet they weren't uncritical, commenting often, for instance, on the brutal

It is only a footnote to history, but Thomas Hart Benton, Jr., Iowa's superintendent of public instruction—who thought its schoolhouses were inferior—had an opportunity to see the quality of Alabama's schoolhouses firsthand. As a Union colonel in the 29th Iowa, he participated in the capture of Spanish Fort in Baldwin County and may have marched past some Alabama schools.[16]

discipline teachers used. Not much older than their students, some would establish order by taking good-sized boys across their laps and, before the entire school, wearing out "a half dozen keen hickories on them." John Massey, whom you will remember from his descriptions of frontier life in Choctaw County, left one of the richest accounts of what schooling was like between 1846 and 1859. Massey's father, a soldier in Andrew Jackson's army, established the family farm "four miles south of Okatuppa Creek"; it was "hilly, with scarcely a level spot" and definitely not plantation country.[17]

The Masseys lived several miles from their nearest neighbors. Yet, even in this rural area, some education was available. John Massey's instruction began in a neighbor's school when he was eleven or twelve. In the summer of 1846, after Michael Hennessee left, "professor" John James took over the teaching. (Evidently the school was only in session when a teacher could be found.) James began to teach for the benefit of his sons and other boys in a neighborhood that embraced five or six miles. The school building was an old log house. As to the quality of instruction, Massey recalls that "the one thing above all else required in this school was *good lessons*" in spelling, reading, and writing. He responded well to these demands because his father had been teaching him at home from the time he was six.[18]

Massey studied grammar and arithmetic while reading McGuffey's new series of books, a curriculum he found both interesting and satisfying. Unfortunately, his schooling was interrupted in 1848, when his father died and he had to take over management of the family farm at age fourteen. Without any inheritance, he couldn't pay school tuition, but James agreed to tutor him at home in the evening. The next year, the community employed a new teacher, Dr. A. J. Graham, who introduced Latin. As duties allowed, Massey attended Graham's classes for two to three months a year. Teachers turned over frequently but, in Massey's judgment, the quality of instruction didn't suffer. Graham was followed by James A. Kimbrough, remembered as having had a "good English education," and later by A. J. Allen, a graduate of the Naval Academy at Annapolis, who though never intoxicated at school, was suspected of being fond of strong drink. "A well-educated man," Allen introduced students to Thomas Jefferson and Sir Walter Scott. By 1851, Allen's school was enrolling both boys and girls ranging in age from ten "to grown young men and women." The curriculum included arithmetic (some algebra), grammar, geography, and spelling.

The following fall, Massey started teaching others what he had learned. And, in January of 1854, when about twenty, he began taking more advanced courses at an academy in Pierce's Springs, Mississippi. From there he went to the University of Alabama in 1859, teaching between sessions on a certificate awarded in Choctaw County. He lectured at the university before volunteering for the Confederate Army. This wealth of firsthand experience didn't lead Massey to conclude that instruction in the public's schools was terrible, and he certainly didn't consider his teachers people of "low grade."

THE EDUCATION OF BLACK ALABAMIANS

Conclusions about education before 1865 apply, of course, largely to schooling for only one group of Alabamians. Whatever education white children received, black youngsters received far less. Even though some plantations provided rudimentary instruction in reading and writing, literacy among slaves was limited; it is generally believed that 90 percent were unable to read. Still, the experiences of nineteenth-century African-Americans have something to tell us about the public for public schools.

Choctaw County was, as its name implies, originally home to the Indian tribe of the same name. Schools there were a part of community-building, like others in the southwest. Among them were the Choctaw Male and Female Seminary at Mount Sterling, the DeSotoville Male and Female Academy, the Male and Female High School at Pushmataha, and the Providence Union Academy two miles west of Butler. Some, like the DeSotoville school, were well housed and offered four levels of instruction up to high school. In 1850, the county had a total of twenty-eight schools, twenty-eight teachers, and 420 students. In 1858, state records reported considerable growth—forty-four public schools with 1,141 enrolled. Of the total, seven academies had 239 students. No private schools were listed, but eight had been reported in 1856.[19]

A powerful reason for assuming that few black Southerners were educated is that teaching them was expressly forbidden by law. This prohibition was a response to the 1831 rebellion led by Nat Turner, a slave who was a preacher in Southampton County, Virginia. About one hundred blacks and fifty-seven whites died in the uprising. In 1832, the Alabama legislature, like others in the South, made it illegal for "any free person of color to settle within the limits of this state," illegal for free blacks to associate with slaves except with permission of their owners, and illegal for anyone to "attempt to teach any free person of color, or slave, to spell, read, or write." The penalty was a fine of "not less than two hundred and fifty dollars, not more than five hundred dollars."[20]

Given these restrictions, it is often assumed that Alabamians of African descent had no public life, no role in community-building, and no schooling. Conventional wisdom holds that nothing changed until after the Civil War—and then only as a result of outside assistance. There were important exceptions, however, and they tell a powerful story about how some black Alabamians created a semblance of a public world and educated themselves under unimaginably difficult circumstances. They played a great game with a poor hand.[21]

In 1860, 114 black Alabamians were attending public schools, most of them in Baldwin and Mobile Counties. Phillip Joseph, who edited the *Mobile Nationalist* after the Civil War, was one of them. Horace Mann Bond uses him as an example of free blacks who were educated entirely in public schools at public expense. Joseph apparently attended a segregated institution, although there is some evidence that a few mulatto children attended schools for whites.[22]

The Skipwith School

In addition, certain plantation owners continued to educate some of their slaves in defiance of the law. At least one plantation in Alabama had schools organized *by* slaves *for* slaves. This extraordinary case is described in the letters of the Skipwith family of Greene County. The Skipwiths were the property of Virginia planter John Hartwell Cocke, an innovator in farming and a social reformer. His Hopewell plantation, near Greensboro, housed infant, night, and Sunday schools for slaves. Lucy Skipwith, the principal household servant, taught in all of them, with help from a nearby white minister, C. B. Eastman, who provided a blackboard and slates. Skipwith's letters to Cocke describe this remarkable educational program in detail.[23]

Skipwith, and what were surely her allies in the families on the Hopewell plantation, maintained something like a community school. Though enslaved, these and probably other black Alabamians joined forces to provide education for a collective future that they were denied in the present. Their schools also belong in the genealogy of public education.[24]

Sunday schools evidently provided a good deal of the education that slaves received. Several denominations were especially active in this work, including the Episcopalians and Presbyterians. Many black Alabamians learned to read in these schools and, in some instances, may have been doing the teaching themselves. They were most likely to have been instructing others in their own churches (though the law required them to secure white ministers). Travelers to the state in the 1840s were impressed by the work of the African Methodist Episcopal church in Mobile with its congregation of about a thousand people. And the black community was building a second church.[25]

State Street African Methodist Episcopal (AME) Church

Black Baptists in Mobile may have been doing even more teaching than their Methodist counterparts. The Stone Street Baptist Church was organized under a brush arbor around 1806, if local lore is accurate. It then merged with a semiautonomous branch of the Saint Anthony Street Baptist Church, making it a legal affiliate of a white church. The congregation later refused to submit to the rules of the Saint Anthony Church and in 1845 affiliated with the St. Francis Street Baptist Church. These and similar congregations around the state could have created the foundations for public life.[26]

THE CREOLE EXCEPTION

Even before the ink was dry on the 1832 law prohibiting the education of black Alabamians, the 1833 general assembly made a significant exception for free Creoles in Mobile and Baldwin Counties. That is why Phillip Joseph got to attend a public school. The rationale was the "treaty made between the French republic and the United States of America, in . . . 1803," which legislators interpreted as giving inhabitants of French Louisiana the full rights of American citizenship. Since the meaning of that treaty was a matter of considerable dispute, I suspect there may have been other reasons, even though the Adams-Onis Treaty of 1819 did much the same thing for Creoles who had been citizens of Spain when that country held a large portion of south Alabama. Legislators aren't in the habit of looking up old treaties for no reason.[27]

My suspicion is based on the text of the house journal for the 1833 assembly. William R. Hallett represented Mobile County, with the support of Henry Chamberlain and John J. Ormond (Lawrence County). Hallett presented a petition of Faustin Collins and others "to authorize the instruction of certain free persons of color." Evidently the Creole community had some political clout. Despite several efforts to delay the bill, it passed on a thirty-five to twenty-two vote. Opposition came largely from Black Belt counties where there was a heavy concentration of slaves, though there were exceptions like the delegations from Dallas County. North Alabama counties, even some with numerous plantations, also supported the amendment. The southwestern counties split their votes: Clarke joined Mobile and Baldwin in favoring the bill; Choctaw, Washington, and Monroe did not.

Studies of Creole communities show they had a tradition of pressing for autonomy, a public life rich in civic associations (like the Creole Fire Department and Social Club in Mobile), and a passion for learning. Descendants of the earliest French and Spanish settlers, Creoles "socialized with one another, attended church together, provided an education for one another's children, and arranged for the marriage of their children within the clan." Because schooling was a priority, these free blacks employed tutors, sent their children out of the region, or created their own schools. In the lower South,

87 percent could read and write, which was probably about the level of literacy of Creoles on Alabama's Gulf Coast.[28]

The census of 1850 shows that only twelve of the 734 free adults in Mobile were illiterate. These people were very industrious, pursuing over twenty different occupations, several requiring more than rudimentary knowledge.[29]

Apparently, some time elapsed before free black Mobilians saw the full effects of the 1833 exemption. A Unitarian minister, Henry B. Brewster, offered and then withdrew his offer to open a Creole school in 1845. A year later, the city council authorized A. Sellier to teach Creole children for a year, and he gave municipal officials a list of those he intended to enroll (those who met the legal requirements of being direct descendants of the colonists). But no one is sure of what happened after that.[30]

Evidence of a school appears in an April 1849 edition of the *Mobile Register and Journal:* "We are pleased to learn that a free school has been opened for the Creole population of this city." The paper went on to say that the school was not only a necessity but also a right and privilege of these "American citizens." The *Alabama Tribune* joined in saluting the new school, and a white business-man, Alexander Stoddart, donated fifty dollars to its support. Alarmed by these developments, the New Orleans press charged that the Alabama school was part of an abolitionist plot. The *Mobile Daily Advertiser* responded that the city was acting within the law and that the same practice was going on in Louisiana, where there was also a large black Creole population.

The newspapers were apparently referring to the Creole school that Alexander McGlashan opened in March of 1849. McGlashan said the initia-tive had come from a committee of free Creoles. Faustin Collins, who had evidently led the group petitioning the legislation to recognize the right of Creoles to an education, was on the committee, along with Lawrence Brour (Brue), Joseph B. Laurant, and John A. Collins. (As some indication of who these people were, John Collins is listed in the city directory of 1837 as a skilled artisan, a carpenter.) This group acted as a board of trustees, visiting classrooms and raising money like other local trustees. The need for the school was obvious; in the first year, only five or six out of eighty students could read. Attendance grew to 103 pupils, almost equally divided between boys and girls. McGlashan was pleased with their progress, noting that "discipline has been

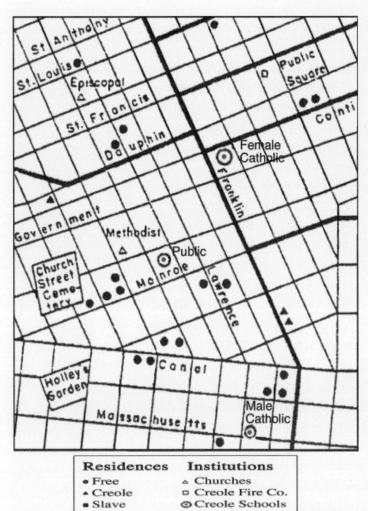

Residences	Institutions
• Free	▵ Churches
▴ Creole	▫ Creole Fire Co.
▪ Slave	◎ Creole Schools

Map of the homes and institutions of black Mobilians between 1856 and 1859. Note the location of two Catholic schools and one public school.

good, and as to the thoroughness, we have seldom attended an examination where the schools were more thoroughly drilled in the studies which they were pursuing than were the scholars of the Creole school."[31]

As true of all educational ventures in Mobile, financing was a constant problem, and McGlashan kept reappearing at school board meetings asking for funds to pay off debts. The Creole community was doing its part; a fair provided the largest source of income, and the Creole Fire Company No. 1 allowed the school to have the proceeds from a ball held in its building. The Presbyterian minister also reminded the school commission that Creoles paid taxes and deserved a return in public money. Eventually, the city school commission responded. In 1854, the board acquired the title to the building and lot and assumed direct responsibility for managing what was now a fully public school. Despite several attempts to close this school, the board continued to come back to the same conclusion: "It is expedient to continue the Creole school."[32]

In 1856, the board received a request for another Creole school where some descendants of Dr. John L. Chastang lived. The prime mover seems to have been Zeno Chastang, a grandson who became a trustee of this school that was established in northern Mobile County.

During this same period, the 1850s, the Catholic Church maintained two schools for Creole children: one operated by the Brothers of the Sacred Heart (for twenty boys) and one by the Sisters of Charity (for fifty girls).[33]

AFTER THE CIVIL WAR

The way black Alabamians went about creating schools after 1865 suggests that something resembling public practices may already have been in place. Immediately following the Civil War, they did exactly what whites had done earlier—parents, ministers, and other members of the community joined forces. This pattern was repeated over and over. In Clarke County, at Mount Zion, three black men "who were very interested in this project and were later made the school's first trustees, were asked to find a site and get the land.... These men had a friend [white] in the community who was and still is interested in making a better community . . . so willing he gave two acres of land . . . later deeded to the State." In other communities, one of Alexis de Tocqueville's voluntary associations—the Bladon Springs Association, or the Women's Home Mission Society of the Baptist Church in Manilla, or the Free Mission Association at Barlow's Bend—organized schools.[34]

Black Alabamians in rural areas had less access to education than those in towns and cities. Most of their schools were founded in the latter part of the century. The first one in Clarke County opened in 1866 or 1867 at Mackey Branch, where local founders (unnamed) arranged for classes in a church. Others included the West Bend School, opened in 1884; the Eberneezer School, started by Reverend Lin Hayes and his neighbors in 1885; and Harper High in Jackson, organized in 1890 by Tom Williams, Gail Daffin, and Robert Thomas. A year later, ministers and citizens in Thomasville resolved to establish a school, and in 1898, C. C. Scott convinced six friends in Walker Springs to help him do the same. They finally succeeded in 1903 with the opening of the Alberta School. This was about the time the Johnson family founded the Good Hope School.

Certainly, national philanthropies like the Rosenwald Fund helped bring education to Coffeeville, Mount Zion, and the Wilson Hall Chapel area. But they were supporting actors for C. C. Scott, the Johnsons, and others we know little about. I believe that the complete record of the educational efforts of these Alabamians has yet to be uncovered.[35]

WHY DID THE FOUNDERS DISAPPEAR?

The definition of the public introduced in the first chapter includes the Chastang family and their neighbors as well as John Pierce and the people who helped maintain his school. The public was exercising its collective abilities in towns rallied by civic associations like the Grove Hill Sewing Circle and ad hoc groups like the one that called the 1825 meeting in Mobile.

So why have these people and what they started been largely forgotten? Why have lessons about the importance of communities often been ignored? In part, it appears to have been the accidental fallout from a good cause—the effort to get the state government to meet its responsibility for education by appropriating tax revenue.

In 1923, John Simpson Graham, editor of the *South Alabamian* and a legislative representative, equated "public" exclusively with "tax-supported." In his *History of Clarke County,* he said what everyone else was saying. Labeling all earlier institutions "subscription schools," Graham maintained that there were no public schools in Alabama until the legislature created a state system in 1854. He didn't acknowledge the public that organized the first schools, despite evidence of widespread citizen involvement. He did mention Caleb Moncrief but described him only as an early settler. He listed schools like the Macon Male and Female Academy in Grove Hill and commented on those who taught in them but said nothing about the Grove Hill Sewing Circle.[36]

Contending that the public's first schools weren't really public because they had more voluntary support from the community than state tax revenue doesn't seem justified. After all, we refer to many institutions today that have substantial income from sources other than tax dollars as "public." We don't call public radio "subscription radio" because it raises funds from donations. And we continue to call state universities "public" even though most of their income no longer comes from their legislatures.

The reason for equating public schools with tax support was to help make the case that all children were entitled to completely free instruction. What that meant—and how much it meant—is captured in a story my grandfather, David Chapman Mathews, told me. He was superintendent in Clarke County at about the time Graham was writing, and the schools still weren't fully funded. Lack of tax revenue and the resulting disparities in educational opportunities were dividing the county. Some communities had enough money to offer nine months of instruction (though parents had to pay five to ten dollars to supplement county funds). In areas where people were poorer, schools were open for only five months. The difference promoted class distinctions, even though children attending schools with terms of different lengths were often related to each other. My grandfather explained that "one brother might live in Grove Hill and own a store. His children would get to go to school for nine months. His brother might live across the creek on a farm, and his children would get only five months of schooling." This offended my grandfather's sense of fairness: "Coming from the country or rural area, naturally, my sympathies were with the country child. I despised the disparity; it was un-American, undemocratic, and not Christian to have such a distinction."[37]

On becoming superintendent, he recalls, "I swore a mighty oath that I was going to change the system. I was going to give that country child the same length of school that the law promised." With an outpouring of public support, he succeeded. In 1922, the citizens of the county taxed themselves and by an overwhelming margin of 1,137 to 183, approved a one-mill tax on each dollar of property value. They also voted for a three-mill property tax by an equally impressive 1,117 to 238 majority. Each levy was in effect for ten years.[38]

By the 1920s, both local and state tax revenue had become the principal sources of school funding. No one concerned about public education wanted anyone to forget that. So educators and political leaders had little incentive to tell the story of Caleb Moncrief or the Grove Hill Sewing Circle.

NOTES TO CHAPTER 5

[1] Grady McWhiney described the Celtic connection to the South in *Cracker Culture: Celtic Ways in the Old South* (Tuscaloosa: University of Alabama Press, 1988). The quotations came from Chapter 8.

[2] The federal census data was in James Dunwoody Brownson DeBow, *The Seventh Census of the United States: 1850* (Washington, D.C.: Robert Armstrong, 1853), pp. lix, 414; J. D. B. DeBow, *Statistical View of the United States . . . Being a Compendium of the Seventh Census,* vol. 4 (Washington, D.C.: A. O. P. Nicholson, 1854), p. 144; Joseph C. G. Kennedy, *Population of the United States in 1860; Compiled from the Original Returns of the Eighth Census, under the Direction of the Secretary of the Interior* (Washington, D.C.: Government Printing Office, 1864), p. 592; and *Statistics of the United States in 1860; Compiled from the Original Returns and Being the Final Exhibit of the Eighth Census, under the Direction of the Secretary of the Interior* (Washington, D.C.: Government Printing Office, 1866), p. 507.

[3] In "Education in the Forming of the American South," *History of Education Quarterly* 36 (summer 1996): 44, John Hardin Best also concludes that educational history "largely ignores the South, which is dismissed as 'backward' or treated somewhat condescendingly as peripheral to the progress of the nation."

[4] Amory D. Mayo gave his version of the educational history of the antebellum South in *The Educational Situation in the South* (n.p., n.d.), p. 4.

[5] Ellwood P. Cubberley, *Public Education in the United States: A Study and Interpretation of American Educational History* (Boston: Houghton Mifflin, 1947), pp. 408-409.

Cubberley's judgment about the deficiencies of education in the old South was shared to a large extent by his Southern counterparts, notably Charles W. Dabney, who wrote *Universal Education in the South,* and Edgar W. Knight, whose *Public Education in the South* became the standard reference on Southern school history. Like Cubberley, Knight concludes that "the response to the antebellum educational revival was not so prompt and effective there [in the South] as in some other parts of the country." Most Southern states, he explains, "passed rather slowly through the process of democratizing education, and the principle of public education, as it is understood today,

was not early and fully accepted by any of them." Charles W. Dabney, *Universal Education in the South,* 2 vols. (Chapel Hill: University of North Carolina Press, 1936) and Edgar W. Knight, *Public Education in the South* (New York: Ginn and Company, 1922). (See Knight pp. 263, 266 for specific information.)

[6] Alabama State Department of Education, *History of Education in Alabama* 7 (1975), p. 6.

[7] The view that planters dominated the Old South persisted until Frank L. Owsley challenged it in 1949. Owsley believed that the planter class received disproportionate attention and argued that the conventional account of Southern castes is seriously flawed. He demonstrated that "plain folk" owned productive farms situated beside the larger plantations, had substantial political power, and moved readily across social lines to become planters and professionals themselves. This farming, or yeoman, citizenry flocked to the public schools in the 1850s. Frank Lawrence Owsley, *Plain Folk of the Old South* (1949; reprint, with an introduction by Grady McWhiney, Baton Rouge: Louisiana State University Press, 1982).

[8] John C. Calhoun's ideology is seen as an attempt to provide an intellectual defense for the economic necessities of the new cotton kingdom. Cotton planting was no gold mine for the seaboard states because of technical limitations in getting the cotton fiber off the seed and spun into a fine thread. That is one of the explanations for why planters there were willing to admit that slavery was a necessary evil and thought it would soon die a natural death. The improvement of textile machinery, the perfection of the cotton gin, and the opening of fertile cotton lands in the southern frontier, however, made slavery economically valuable in the new southern states. This economic change is said to have prompted a change in the South's social philosophy. *The Works of John C. Calhoun,* ed. Richard K. Crallé, vol. 1 (New York: Appleton, 1851); Virginius Dabney, *Liberalism in the South* (Chapel Hill: University of North Carolina Press, 1932), p. 146; and Vernon Louis Parrington, *The Romantic Revolution in America, 1800-1860,* vol. 2 of *Main Currents in American Thought* (New York: Harcourt, Brace and World, 1954), pp. 57, 59.

[9] James Simmons, "Instruction in Schools and Colleges," *Southern Quarterly Review* 6 (October 1852): 460, 467-469. The *Review* itself was a topic in *The Conservative Press in Eighteenth- and Nineteenth-Century America,* ed. Ronald

Lora and William Henry Longton (Westport, Conn.: Greenwood Press, 1999), pp. 183-188.

[10] All of the Simmons quotations were from "Instruction in Schools and Colleges," pp. 461-462, 467.

[11] Stephen B. Weeks, *History of Public School Education in Alabama,* U.S. Bureau of Education Bulletin, 1915, no. 12 (Washington, D.C.: Government Printing Office, 1915), p. 41 and Historical United States Data Browser, available at http://fisher.lib.virginia.edu/census/.

[12] To determine the annual rate of enrollment growth after the 1854 appropriation, I relied on the state superintendents' reports, which showed public school enrollment increasing from 89,160 to 98,274 between 1856 and 1858. That is about 5 percent annually. Calculating the rate beforehand was more difficult. Federal census data showed total enrollment growth from 1850 to 1860 but not public school enrollment. The only public school data was for daily attendance, which is naturally lower than enrollments. In order to get some idea of enrollment in public schools, we used the attendance data to make an estimate. Then we compared the estimated public school enrollment in 1850 to that in 1860 and arrived at an annual growth rate. Assuming the increase was constant, the yearly increase over the decade was also about 5 percent, just as it was between 1856 and 1858. This suggests that state funding alone doesn't account for the progress made in the 1850s. Even if, as was probably the case, the rate accelerated with each year, the conclusion is still valid. Furthermore, state tax revenue in 1860 produced only $63,845 out of the $489,747 spent on public schools in Alabama.

Calculations of the ratio of public to private schools in various counties were taken from a survey done by county superintendents in 1856 and reported in *Annual Report of William F. Perry, Superintendent of Education, of the State of Alabama, Made to the Governor, for the Year 1856* (Montgomery: Smith and Hughes, 1857), p. 49; *Statistics of the United States in 1860,* p. 506; and Kennedy, *Population of the United States in 1860,* p. 592.

[13] The claim that there was little public schooling in antebellum Alabama seems open to question, but determining what was really happening in education requires a closer and also broader look at performance.

In order to put Alabama's record in context, my colleagues and I collected census data from the states of Michigan and Georgia. We then did a series of analyses. In the first, we compared public education in the nation as a whole with schooling in Alabama, Michigan, and Georgia in 1850 and 1860, using federal data. We looked at students registered or enrolled, based on what families said, and at average daily attendance, based on what educators said. Then we took into consideration different figures for registration and attendance based on surveys done by the state superintendents of Alabama in 1856, 1857, and 1858.

In doing this analysis, I realized that a reinterpretation of the data could appear to be a defensive reaction to the charge that there was little public education in Alabama. I certainly didn't want to give that impression, especially since many Alabamians living in the antebellum period were themselves critical of the number of children not being educated. Nonetheless, I couldn't escape the conclusion that the federal enrollment percentages, by themselves, were misleading. Inconsistencies and complexities became obvious once these figures were put alongside other information.

The data up to 1850 showed clearly that Alabama was behind the nation, neighboring Georgia, and Michigan in nearly every category. One exception was in funding education. According to federal reports, the state was outspending Michigan almost two to one and Georgia by a wide but less dramatic margin. The way the money was raised was different, however. About half of Michigan's revenue came from taxes, while Alabama relied more on other public funds such as income generated from subscriptions (donations). What do these statistics say about the public? The answer would seem to depend on whether the public is considered primarily as taxpaying citizens. If the public is more than that, then Alabama's schools can be considered to have had considerable public support.

Next, we looked at what happened in Alabama after 1850. The effort citizens were putting into strengthening education—and the progress they were making—was impressive. The state was improving much faster than the country as a whole, often faster than even Michigan. For instance, while the nation experienced less than a 6 percent increase in the percentage of school-age children enrolled during this decade and Michigan less than 4, Alabama's enrollment grew by nearly 30 percent.

Alabama's progress in education also compares favorably with its more developed neighbor, Georgia. In 1850, Georgia, with a larger school-age population, was slightly ahead of Alabama in total enrollment, in attendance, and in the number of public schools—though not in revenue spent on education. Ten years later, Alabama had taken the lead in all of these categories.

In addition, my colleagues and I analyzed the information we had collected to see what it said about the contention that Alabamians preferred private to public institutions. First of all, I don't believe the distinction made between "public" and other schools meant the same then as it does today. Academies not listed as "public" weren't necessarily "private." And even if all of them are classed as private, they served just a fraction of the young people. Alabama had more academies than many other states. But there were just slightly over 200 of these institutions in 1860 compared to nearly 2,000 "public schools." Furthermore, public school attendance between 1850 and 1860 increased over 100 percent, while attendance in academies and other institutions grew 30 percent.

All in all, the picture these statistical comparisons give of what really happened remains rather muddled; they don't support strong generalizations. Debates over the data could go on forever. We used state statistics to counter federal numbers. Critics of our conclusions might demand, not unreasonably, state-to-state comparisons. That would be very difficult to do, however, because states varied in what they counted and in the way they reported. Michigan and other states, for instance, showed more students attending school on a daily basis than parents said were enrolled. The census report couldn't explain the discrepancy except to say that either the schools or the families (or both) were in error. Rather than go into more statistical analyses, I decided to write about the Alabamians who were distressed by the undeniable fact that nearly half of the school-age population wasn't in a classroom. That was unacceptable even if it was the national average.

The federal sources were DeBow, *Statistical View of the United States*, pp. 142-145 and *Statistics of the United States in 1860*, pp. 506-509. For state statistics, we used *Annual Report of William F. Perry, 1856*, pp. 4-6, 49; *Report of William F. Perry, Superintendent of Education, of the State of Alabama, Made to the Governor, for the Year 1857* (Montgomery: N. B. Cloud, 1858); pp. 3-5, 74-75; and *Report of Gabriel B. DuVal, Superintendent of Education, of the State of Alabama, Made to the Governor, for the Year 1858* (Montgomery: Shorter and Reid, 1859), pp. 3, 7, 52-53. (We noted that the school-age population for 1856 and 1857 includes children 6 to 21 years old. In 1858, no school-age specifications were given. Also, some counties didn't give the

state superintendent the information he requested, so the tally is incomplete.) These reports were also the source of information on illiteracy. All of this information was put onto charts, which are available at the Kettering Foundation in Dayton, Ohio.

[14]   In preparing a general overview of national trends in schooling, I drew on the history of public education written by Carl F. Kaestle, *Pillars of the Republic: Common Schools and American Society, 1780-1860* (New York: Hill and Wang, 1983), p. xi.

[15]   William F. Perry was very critical of the quality of the early schools and their teachers in "The Genesis of Public Education in Alabama," an article published in *Transactions of the Alabama Historical Society: 1897-1898*, ed. Thomas McAdory Owen, vol. 2 (Tuscaloosa: Alabama Historical Society, 1898), pp. 17-18 and in the *Report of William F. Perry, 1857*, p. 18. Similar comments were made in Iowa, according to Clarence Ray Aurner's *History of Education in Iowa*, vol. 2 (Iowa City: State Historical Society of Iowa, 1914), p. 21.

Steven Mintz has noticed that the champions of public schools generally tended to overstate deficiencies in education and commented on this inclination in *Moralists and Modernizers: America's Pre-Civil War Reformers* (Baltimore: Johns Hopkins University Press, 1995), p. 109.

[16]   Prescott A. Parker, *Story of the Tensaw* (Montrose, Ala.: P. A. Parker, 1922), p. 11.

[17]   Washington Bryan Crumpton, *A Book of Memories, 1842-1920* (Montgomery: Baptist Mission Board, 1921), p. 17 and John Massey, *Reminiscences: Giving Sketches of Scenes through which the Author Has Passed and Pen Portraits of People Who Have Modified His Life* (Nashville: Publishing House of the M. E. Church, South, 1916), p. 11.

[18]   All of John Massey's quotations came from his *Reminiscences*, pp. 47-53, 56-57, 77, 95, 131, 163, 165.

[19]   *Report of Gabriel B. DuVal, 1858*, p. 10; DeBow, *Statistical View of the United States;* and Ann Harwell Gay, *Choctaw Names and Notes: Alabama's Choctaw County* (Meridian, Miss: Brown Printing Company, 1993), pp. 32-33.

[20]   John G. Aikin, *Digest of the Laws of the State of Alabama: Containing All the Statutes of a Public and General Nature, in Force at the Close of the Session of the General Assembly, in January, 1833* (Philadelphia: Alexander Towar, 1833), § 30, § 31, § 35.

21 I am indebted to my colleagues at the Kettering Foundation—especially to Mary Hatwood Futrell, who made valuable suggestions, and to Estus Smith, who reviewed this section and provided a long list of publications to consult.

22 In a very useful Ph.D. dissertation by Christopher Andrew Nordmann, "Free Negroes in Mobile County, Alabama," done at the University of Alabama in 1990, there was an account on pages 209 and 210 of a controversy over children in two public schools who were said to be of "African descent," a matter that the board eventually tabled. Nordmann drew on this incident in concluding that "there is some indication that a few of the lighter skinned free persons of color found their way into all white schools." He also pointed out that under the law, at the time, anyone of less than one-eighth African descent was legally white. In addition, I used Horace Mann Bond's *Negro Education in Alabama: A Study in Cotton and Steel* (1969; reprint, Tuscaloosa: University of Alabama Press, 1994), p. 74, and James Benson Sellers's *Slavery in Alabama* (University: University of Alabama Press, 1950), p. 387.

23 All of the descriptions of the school in Greene County taught by Lucy Skipwith are from a collection of letters she wrote to John Cocke, which are reprinted in Randall M. Miller's *"Dear Master": Letters of a Slave Family* (Ithaca: Cornell University Press, 1978), pp. 19-20, 33-34, 184-185, 198-199, 224, 233.

24 Historians have confirmed other instances of free blacks developing schools for the free and enslaved community. Leroy Davis provided good examples in *A Clashing of the Soul: John Hope and the Dilemma of African American Leadership and Black Higher Education in the Early Twentieth Century* (Athens: University of Georgia Press, 1998), p. 7. Davis discussed schools in Charleston, South Carolina, and Augusta, Georgia.

25 *Impressions of America and the American Churches: From Journal of the Rev. G. Lewis* (1848; reprint, New York: Negro Universities Press, 1968), p. 159; Gordon Baylor Cleveland, "Social Conditions in Alabama as Seen by Travelers, 1840-1850, Part II," *Alabama Review* 2 (April 1949): 126-127; and Anne M. Boylan, *Sunday School: The Formation of an American Institution, 1790-1880* (New Haven: Yale University Press, 1988), pp. 26-29.

26 Wayne Flynt, *Alabama Baptists: Southern Baptists in the Heart of Dixie* (Tuscaloosa: University of Alabama Press, 1998), pp. 47-48.

27 John J. Ormond, who assisted in passing the bill that recognized the right of Creoles to an education, was an English immigrant whose family settled in Charlottesville, Virginia. Orphaned at an early age, he arrived in Alabama in 1827. When elected to the state supreme court in 1837, he moved to Tuscaloosa County, where he died in 1866. Ormond was a Whig and a member of the Methodist Episcopal church. Thomas McAdory Owen, *History of Alabama and Dictionary of Alabama Biography*, vol. 4 (Chicago: S. J. Clarke Publishing Company, 1921), p. 1303.
The account of passing the bill itself is in Alabama General Assembly, *House Journal*, 15th annual sess., 1833 (Tuscaloosa: May and Ferguson, 1833), pp. 3-4, 28, 39, 74, 122. The statute is found in Alabama General Assembly, *Acts*, 1833 (Tuscaloosa: May and Ferguson, 1834), p. 68.

28 John Hope Franklin directed me to the work of his student Loren Schweninger, whose book *Black Property Owners in the South: 1790-1915* (Urbana: University of Illinois Press, 1990), pp. 126-130 was an excellent source on Creoles. So was Gary B. Mills's *The Forgotten People: Cane River's Creoles of Color* (Baton Rouge: Louisiana State University Press, 1977).

29 James Benson Sellers wrote about literacy among Creoles in *Slavery in Alabama* (University: University of Alabama Press, 1950), pp. 386-387. The Mobile census is in *Population Schedules of the Seventh Census of the United States: 1850* (Washington, D.C.: National Archives Microfilm Publications, 1964), microfilm, roll 11. Be advised that the handscript is difficult to read and that the distinction between white, black, and mulatto (Creole) isn't always clear.

30 *Mobile Daily Advertiser*, 3 May 1849, and Nordmann, "Free Negroes in Mobile County, Alabama," pp. 201-202, quoting *Mobile Register and Journal*, 28 April 1849.

31 *Mobile Daily Register*, 17 January 1850; Nordmann, "Free Negroes in Mobile County, Alabama," p. 204, quoting *Mobile Daily Register*, 24 September 1850; and *Mobile Directory, Embracing Names of the Heads of Families and Persons in Business, Alphabetically Arranged, for 1837* (Mobile: H. M. McGuire and T. C. Fay, 1837), p. 18.

32 Mobile School Board Minutes, 1852-1857, 3 September 1856, p. 295; Harriet Amos, *Cotton City: Urban Development in Antebellum Mobile* (University: University of Alabama Press, 1985), p. 104; and Nordmann, "Free Negroes in Mobile County, Alabama," pp. 205-209.

[33] An account of Creole education was in Amos, *Cotton City,* p. 185.

[34] In 1955, the Clarke County Board of Education issued a report titled "A Brief History of the Development of Negro Schools of Clarke County, Alabama." Later, it appeared in the *Clarke County Historical Society Quarterly* 23 (fall 1998): 29-33, 36-37, 41-42.

[35] For more on the education of African-Americans after 1865, I recommend going back to Bond's *Negro Education in Alabama.*

I base my assumption that there is more to be learned about black Alabamians in education on what scholars studying other states have found. For instance, there was a school run by free blacks in antebellum Augusta where "a Negro named Ned Purdee . . . had a school for boys and girls going on in his back yard." Despite being a Methodist minister, he was imprisoned and lashed for his efforts. In Charleston, two white lawyers established a school "for the colored children of wealthy white men" and another was conducted "by a black woman—who, ironically, was also a slave owner." Leroy Davis, *A Clashing of the Soul: John Hope and the Dilemma of African America Leadership and Black Higher Education in the Early Twentieth Century* (Athens: University of Georgia Press, 1998), p. 7.

[36] John Graham's accounts of education are in his *History of Clarke County* (1923; reprint, Greenville, S.C.: Southern Historical Press, 1994), pp. 84, 147, 221-224, 229. A contemporary example of equating "public" and "tax supported" can be found in Don Eddins's *AEA: Head of the Class in Alabama Politics, A History of the Alabama Education Association* (Montgomery: AEA, 1997), p. 249.

[37] My grandfather made a series of recordings for his grandchildren in the 1970s, which include the story of the struggle to provide children in rural areas with the same nine months of schooling that children in the towns were receiving. These recordings and a transcript of them titled "Children's Stories" are at the Clarke County Historical Society in Grove Hill, Alabama.

[38] "Order of Court of County Commissioners," 11 August 1922, Clarke County, Alabama Courthouse.

Chapter 6

THE LEGISLATURE RESPONDS:
LOFTY IDEALS AND DIFFICULT CHOICES

C LARKE COUNTY'S superintendent of education, D. C. Mathews, was well aware of how long it had taken to get tax dollars from the state. Every time the antebellum legislature had been on the verge of acting, something seems to have interfered—an economic recession, problems in the state bank, or competition between friends of the state university and advocates of public schools. Alabamians also had to decide on the role they wanted the government to play in public education.

The state was faced with difficult choices among options that were all rooted in things people held dear. One was to keep control of education close to communities and make them responsible for providing schooling. It reflected the importance of self-reliance and autonomy. Another option was to make certain that all white children, whether or not they lived in a community that had resources to use for education, had the same opportunity to learn, even if that meant sharing resources. Feelings about fairness or equity came to the surface in this option. A third approach appealed to the ambitions that had brought settlers to Alabama—to perfect society and promote prosperity. Some believed the only way to do that was by using an activist state government not merely to encourage, but to guarantee, schooling.

The tensions among these imperatives were obvious: Was local responsibility and control more important than equity? Was economic prosperity and social well-being to be purchased at the price of a more active and expensive

It is useful to keep in mind that the first representatives may have had a somewhat different relationship with the public than many elected officials have today. Members of the general assembly liked attending to local matters; personal involvement translated into influence back home and helped build a constituency. Nothing new there. The difference is that in order to stay in tune with local sentiments, representatives appear to have been reluctant to strike out too far on their own. They were more inclined to respond to the voice of the electorate, and public meetings instructed them on how to vote.[1]

Citizens would secure pledges from candidates before sending them to the statehouse. In 1830, Philip Woodson, editor of the Huntsville *Democrat* and himself a candidate for the legislature, argued that citizens "have both the *right* and the *power,* to instruct their subordinate officers." Legislators had to know the will of the people and "*obey* their voice," even if it ran counter to their own wishes.[2]

To be sure, not all nineteenth-century politicians thought that the voice of the people was the voice of God. To the contrary, some felt duty bound to save the citizenry from itself. Nonetheless, the expectations were clear: a legislator was to be the literal representative of the people who elected him. That is, he was to represent their point of view faithfully, even if he disagreed.

state government? Every option required trade-offs.

Given what is known about the extent of public deliberations on important issues during the early nineteenth century, there is every reason to believe these options were discussed in wagon lots, camp meetings, and the Alhambra coffee shop. The official forum, of course, was the state legislature.

In order to make its decisions, the general assembly had to hammer out its own answers to "Why public schools?" Its reasons were somewhat different from those of communities. The most obvious difference was that the legislative rationale was expressed in ideals—abstract, universal notions about what the political, economic, and social order *should* be like, the sort of conceptualizations that "deep thinkers" enjoyed. Debates in the house and senate show what power these ideals had (and didn't have) in the rough-and-tumble of politics.[3]

FREEDOM AND PROSPERITY: POLITICAL RATIONALES FOR PUBLIC SCHOOLING

James Simmons argued logically and clearly in the *Southern Quarterly Review* that the state has no business in education because it is the parents' responsibility. Alabama law took just the opposite position: everybody has a stake in public schooling. Education is a family matter, though not solely a matter for families. Alabama's new constitution of 1819 made a simple pledge: "Schools and the means of education shall forever be encouraged in this state." The wording was taken from the Northwest Ordinance passed by the Continental Congress in 1787: "Religion, morality, and knowledge being necessary to good government and the happiness of mankind, schools and the means of education shall forever be encouraged." (Legislation in North Carolina and Georgia had said essentially the same thing a decade earlier.)[4]

This provision reflected the conviction that a government that places power in the hands of the people has to have an educated citizenry. Thomas Jefferson had explained why: Freedom can only be protected if people govern themselves; otherwise, some individual or faction may seize power. Citizens can rule wisely if they are educated, but expecting them to be both ignorant and free is expecting the impossible. Here was a powerful rationale for public schools—a public reason. This logic led Alabama's political leaders to decree that schools had to be available to all citizens. They weren't just mouthing Jeffersonian rhetoric. The president of the constitutional convention, John Williams Walker, wanted a school in every neighborhood. In time, the scope of the state's responsibility would grow as the definition of "all citizens" changed, yet the principle was in place from the beginning.[5]

Jeffersonian ideals weren't the only political force at work, however. The southwestern counties and the whole of the state depended on economic development, which required a physical infrastructure of roads, bridges, canals,

Jefferson had laid out the rationale for public education in a "Bill for the More General Diffusion of Knowledge" in 1779: "Whereas it appeareth that however certain forms of government are better calculated than others to protect individuals in the free exercise of their natural rights, and are at the same time themselves better guarded against degeneracy, yet experience hath shewn, that even under the best forms, those entrusted with power have, in time, and by slow operations, perverted it into tyranny; and it is believed that the most effectual means of preventing this would be, to illuminate, as far as practicable, the minds of the people at large."[6]

and the like. That created political pressure in the legislature to finance these internal improvements, such as a ship channel in Mobile Bay. Seeing a bandwagon to jump aboard, the champions of education recast schools as another internal improvement. Consequently, public education drew considerable support from the ambition to turn a wilderness into a new Rome on the Gulf of Mexico—or the Tennessee River, depending on which part of the state the representatives were from.[7]

This line of reasoning applied to rich and poor alike. No one could prosper where ignorance flourished; even the well-to-do had a stake in common schooling though they might not have needed public support to educate their own children. The wealthy have had the reputation of opposing the general diffusion of knowledge but, if they accepted this logic, they had to recognize their self-interest in education for all. Friedrich List, the economist who said that the ability to produce wealth is more important than wealth per se, warned slaveholders that treating bodily labor as the key to prosperity, while neglecting the productive forces of future generations, was the height of folly.[9]

Linking education to the enthusiasm for financing internal improvements was a smart legislative strategy. But there was more to the notion that schooling was linked to economic development than just political expediency. Remember the arguments about the importance of "mental capital" that appeared in the *South Western Baptist*. The economic theory of the time held that public schooling was "the connecting link between labor and capital"; it made labor productive and laborers enterprising. Some political economists argued that the power to produce wealth came from the benefits of public education—the intelligence to look to the future, an enterprising spirit, and freedom from false ideas or superstitions.[8]

The Federal Government: A Factor from the Beginning

The political rationale for public schooling was attractive to both state and national governments. To supplement tuition and money raised locally, Alabama looked to a federal ordinance passed in 1785 that provided grants for education. That legislation, which governed the sale of large tracts of land on the frontier, designated the revenue from the sixteenth section in each township to be used for schools. Later, the federal government made these land grants to state governments. In Alabama, however, the grants were made to the townships, a distinction that would have important consequences.[10]

Relying on federal land grants to support good causes in education soon became a habit, but one that brought out the tension between state and local authority. Clarke County's representative, William Mobley, wanted Congress to give the state (not the townships) four quarter sections of unsold land to create more schools for young women. Prominent representatives like General Enoch Parsons, a native of Tennessee who had served with Andrew Jackson and earned his military title, endorsed Mobley's proposal. (The basis for this alliance is unclear; perhaps it was nothing more than the fact that Parsons was

Mobley's neighbor in Monroe County.)[11]

Mobley's bill met considerable opposition from a review committee chaired by David G. Ligon, an affluent legislator who had moved from Virginia to Lawrence County to plant cotton and practice law. Giving federal lands to the state rather than local governments was unacceptable. Thomas Fearn, from Madison County, moved that the grants go to the counties. Overriding Mobley's objection, the general assembly adopted the substitute motion. The dispute was a harbinger of things to come.

NORTH

6	5	4	3	2	1
7	8	9	10	11	12
18	17	16	15	14	13
19	20	21	22	23	24
30	29	28	27	26	25
31	32	33	34	35	36

WEST ... **EAST**

SOUTH

A Township with the Sixteenth Section Shaded

LOCAL CUSTODIANS FOR A SACRED TRUST

Even though public schooling served a wide range of state interests—education for women, education for prosperity, education for self-rule—Alabamians didn't want the state government to manage their schools. Perhaps not even William Mobley did. That would have been inconsistent with the prevailing political sentiment, which favored a limited central government. Communities were supposed to operate the schools.

Local responsibility was married to local control in a precedent dating back to the colonial period, when towns employed schoolmasters or legislative bodies required communities to offer public or free schooling (both terms were used) at the expense of householders (parents, masters of apprentices, or inhabitants in general). Community responsibility and control were later central tenets of Jeffersonian democracy; the work of providing education in the "small republics" was work that would turn private individuals into public citizens.[12]

Consistent with the terms of the federal land grants, Alabama's general assembly followed the constitutional convention with legislation that put the primary authority for schooling in the most local unit of government, the townships within each county. Under a statute passed in December 1819, chief justices of the county courts were to arrange elections so that citizens in each township could select three trustees as their agents to lease the sixteenth sections. These three officials made up Alabama's first school boards long before there were county boards. Revenue generated by the leases was to be used for buildings and teachers' salaries. Township trustees had to construct schoolhouses, select instructors, set the terms of their employment, and direct the organization of the schools.[13]

In 1823, the general assembly passed a law that began to involve county governments and authorized even more community control by creating school districts within townships. Thereafter, the county court, not the township voters, would select three householders as school commissioners for each township. (The court was composed of a judge and the commissioners of revenue and roads.) Township trustees, however, retained control of the sixteenth sections as well as the authority to allocate the revenue and to license teachers. But now the county clerk had to consolidate annual reports from township commissioners and give the general assembly an account of teachers employed, students enrolled, money received, and debts incurred. This began the practice of reporting to the state government.

The new legislation required township officials to take a census of prospective pupils and then divide their area into districts that would serve thirty students apiece. Three or more householders in these districts could elect what amounted to boards for every school, which brought these institutions closer in law to what they were in fact—the public's schools. Every school in Alabama would have a body of citizens pledged to hold their school's best interest as a sacred trust. Together, the district boards made up an army of public support for public education.

District trustees received the sixteenth-section income, but since that didn't provide enough money, they had to raise additional funds from their communities. And these trustees, not the township officials, did everything that schools required. They put up the buildings, employed teachers (who were still licensed by the township), purchased books and stationery, set fees, and waived tuition for students unable to pay.

THE CHALLENGES OF EQUITY

Local control didn't mean leaving every community to fend for itself. Alabamians seem to have understood that the benefits of education serve the political system as a whole, the economy as a whole, and society as a whole. For example, it made no sense to have part of the electorate informed and leave the rest uninformed. Obviously, "the rest" could still vote. Given that understanding, local control had to be reconciled with an equally powerful imperative—the equitable distribution of resources for education. How to do that was one of the most difficult issues before the general assembly.

Even though the state legislature had discharged its duty by passing along the federal land grants to the townships and district schools, much more had to be done to make instruction available to all. One of the first challenges was to provide schooling for children whose parents couldn't pay the tuition that nearly all schools charged. The 1823 law had attempted to solve the problem by waiving tuition for parents who would testify that they had no money. But that required some Alabamians to, in effect, declare themselves paupers in order for their children to go to school. I can't imagine anything more offensive to the sensitivities of proud farmers like the Masseys, who had little cash, or genuinely poor squatters in the pine barrens. Many probably would rather have had their children go without an education than make such a declaration.

Equally serious, the value of the sixteenth sections varied considerably, leaving some communities with little or no federal revenue to use for schooling. Counties with the richest land, which were usually the wealthiest counties, naturally had the most valuable sections. Land in the poorest counties tended to be the least valuable. Disparities were extreme. Counties such as Greene, Sumter, and Dallas, with valuable cotton-producing land, realized from ten to one hundred times more from their federal grants than others; some, like Mobile and Baldwin, showed no revenue in 1850. To make matters worse, sixteenth-section income had no relationship to population; Dallas County had only half as many children to educate as Mobile. Land-grant values in all the southwestern counties were below the state average, though Monroe and Clarke were better off than Washington and Choctaw.[14]

The legislature responded differently to these two kinds of inequity. Waiving tuition probably seemed a sensible and unexceptional policy since the practice was widespread nationally. Yet Alabama, you may recall, had not done what states like Georgia had, which was to designate all of its revenue for education as a poor-school fund. The Alabama policy suggests that its legislators thought of public schools as common rather than as charity schools. Yet this distinction wasn't always clear, as illustrated in proposals made by Representative Pleasant H. May, who attacked the unequal distribution of funds from the federal grants but saw nothing wrong with giving the poor priority in distributing the available funds.[15]

May was a Jacksonian Democrat and newspaper editor (*Flag of the Union*) representing Tuscaloosa County. Like many politicians of his generation, he found justification for his positions in examples from classical antiquity. He elaborated on the arguments for universal education that Ephraim Kirby had used in the Tensaw country, such as the necessity for public virtue—for citizens who would act in the best interest of their communities more than for personal gain. The state needed people of such character, and the schools had to see that virtue was instilled in the next generation. The policy implications were clear: education had to be available to all, though not necessarily without making distinctions among students in distributing funds.[16]

Despite this logic and pleas by legislators like May, the general assembly didn't address the sixteenth-section disparities for some time. When representatives looked at the land grant funds, they were inclined to see a tempting source of badly needed capital for economic development. Merchants and planters wanted loans, and the legislature obliged. It capitalized the Bank of the State of Alabama with "such public funds as may now or hereafter be in the possession of the State." Now the fate of the public schools was inextricably tied to the fate of the state bank.[17]

In order to get its hands on the land grants, the general assembly had to have congressional permission for townships to sell their sixteenth sections rather than merely leasing them. With this authorization in hand in 1828, the legislature directed township commissioners to hold elections to determine whether citizens wanted to sell their school property. If they did, the money paid by the highest bidders would be deposited in the state bank and immediately frozen as capital assets. In return, the bank would issue stock paying 6 percent interest quarterly. The state pledged its good faith and credit to guarantee both payment of the interest and redemption of the principal.[18]

THE STATE ACTS

Between 1819 and 1839, the democratic ideals of Jefferson, pressure for economic growth, and conservative worries about the lack of public virtue served as rallying themes for successive generations of legislative champions of public education. A number of these political leaders came from the southwestern counties, and they undoubtedly knew how important free schooling was to such people as Henry Hitchcock and his colleagues on the Mobile board as well as to the coalitions of citizens building community schools largely with their own resources.

Boosting the efforts in Alabama, a public school crusade was gaining momentum in legislatures across America. In 1837, Massachusetts selected Horace Mann, a leading voice in this effort, as secretary of its state board of education. At the same time, a broad coalition in support of public education was taking shape in the Alabama general assembly. The southwest was represented by Arthur Bagby, a lawyer and Jacksonian Democrat who had walked, bundle in hand, from Virginia to south Alabama.

Bagby rose from the legislative ranks to replace Hugh McVay as governor in 1837, defeating Samuel W. Oliver of Conecuh County. He came to office as a strong champion of internal improvements, penal reforms, and closer supervision of the state banking system. The new governor wanted greater oversight of the banks because favoritism in the form of loans to legislators had

Amassing capital for development had been a legislative priority for some time. In 1820, the general assembly had invited people to subscribe or invest their savings in a state bank. Few responded. The next plan, offered by friends of private banks, was to make these private institutions branches of a state bank. Although the legislature voted in favor, the governor vetoed the bill, fearing that the system would place the credit of the state in the hands of a small group of wealthy men. That set the stage for chartering a state bank.[19]

Arthur Pendleton Bagby

Although based in Monroe County, the future governor practiced in the courts of the area, which is probably what took him to Tom Brown's hotel in Grove Hill. In his travels, Bagby had opportunities to become well acquainted with the first settlers—men like Sam Dale and Tom Woodward. He was particularly indebted to Dale because of what happened after a night of drinking and political debating in Claiborne turned violent. The fight started when Bagby threw a decanter at a dinner companion who criticized Henry Clay, someone Bagby admired at the time. Dale saved his life.[20]

led to more than six million dollars in bad debts, forcing the state government to issue bonds to cover the deficit. Alabama had also been affected by a financial panic precipitated by President Jackson's refusal to accept anything other than gold or silver as payment in land sales. That had caused a run on the state bank. The recession also stopped legislators from using state funds to offset the disparities in the value of the sixteenth sections. (This was the Panic of 1837 that cost Henry Hitchcock his fortune.)[21]

Though taking office during a serious economic crisis, Bagby advocated state support of education. He used an economic argument to make his case, reasoning that, just as the state needed a transportation system, it also needed a network of schools, which Bagby insisted were more important than a rail line "from Louisiana to the Lakes." They were as essential to the social, intellectual, and political infrastructures as trade routes were to the economic infrastructure.[22]

Advocates of public schooling didn't confine themselves to one theme, and the governor also stressed the schools' ability to promote moral and intellectual virtues, which was a way of making the case for universal education. From Bagby's point of view, the primary obstacle to education for all was not disagreement over ideals but demographics. Families lived too far apart in many sections of the state to generate enough money for schools. They needed extra assistance; all Alabamians would have to make sacrifices to help them. And Bagby predicted that a free people would willingly respond.

They did. In 1839, the legislature made its first appropriation for public schools. The cause of education undoubtedly benefited by a windfall of federal money from a surplus in the national treasury, which Congress approved for distribution to the states in 1837. Initially, Alabama's share ($669,087) went to the state bank to provide operating capital. With the bank back on sound footing, the general assembly compensated townships with valueless sixteenth sections by allocating one hundred thousand acres set aside for internal improvements and by authorizing yearly payments of $150,000 dollars to the schools on January 31, 1839. Every township was to have a minimum of two hundred dollars annually, with state money used to supplement land-grant income if it was less than that minimum. One of the equity challenges was met. This appropriation suggests that public education was accepted as a common good entitled to common support.[23]

Legislators addressed, in part, the other equity problem: people who couldn't pay the fees that public schools charged. They stipulated that state funds were to be "applied for the purpose of tuition," which was a way to reduce the costs to families.

To ensure local responsibility, which was the corollary of local control, the 1839 law stipulated that the total drawn from the state bank in any year couldn't exceed the amount subscribed by school patrons the previous year. Unfortunately, this provision would have nullified the attempt to get more money to the poorer and less densely populated townships. In order to prevent that from happening, the legislature waived the subscription requirement for the less-affluent townships. In calculating local support, their commissioners could proceed as if poor students had each paid ten dollars. All officials had to do was certify that the children's parents lived in the township, that they wanted their youngsters to go to school, that the prospective students were between eight and eighteen, and *that the family was indigent.* The total allowed for the poor couldn't exceed half of the amount used to match the two hundred dollar commitment, and the funds allotted for those unable to pay fees had to be used exclusively for their benefit.[24]

At this point, legislators had accepted the principle of equity among counties but still didn't see any problem with what they apparently regarded as a generous policy toward the poor. The new law was much like the 1823 statute. Yet in making certain that the families to be assisted by the state got the funds provided for them, the Alabama legislation may have prompted something like the reaction in Georgia, where people objected to taking what amounted to a poverty oath. It is unlikely that those feelings stopped at the state line.

In 1840, education profited again from a second act increasing the state's appropriation to two hundred thousand dollars. Under the revised law, townships could receive up to twelve dollars for each pupil, for a total of four hundred dollars rather than two hundred dollars. (This was an early version of the per-pupil method for allocating state funds.) The act also reduced the amount local patrons had to subscribe, to one-third of the state's grant. This meant that the less prosperous townships would receive even larger compensatory appropriations. The new law suggests that the value placed on equity was increasingly important in educational legislation.[25]

As in 1839, local responsibility remained the bedrock of educational policy in the 1840 act. Before they could qualify for state funds, communities continued to have to raise enough money to build schoolhouses, employ teachers, and operate schools. The state government was now more than a pass-through agency, yet it was still only an ally and not the main actor.

REFORM IDEALS AND ECONOMIC REALITIES

Around the time of the Bagby administration, Alabama and other states were caught up in social and religious causes that reinforced the public school movement and likely influenced the 1839-1840 legislation. As I mentioned, the causes included temperance, humanitarian reform of prisons and hospitals, and women's rights. About the only initiative Alabamians didn't embrace in great numbers was the effort to abolish slavery. Reformers called into question society's values and institutions, and they held out the hope of a cleansed and perfected civilization. Simultaneously benevolent and coercive, they were willing to use both moral suasion and the force of government to achieve their ends.

These reformers brought an elevated rationale and a more impassioned rhetoric to the public school argument. Education didn't just serve political purposes; *it was politics in another form.* That idea enlivened the public school movement sweeping through legislatures. The schools took on another meaning as public institutions. They were public, not just because the citizenry created them, but because they were instruments for perfecting society in the "public interest." Reformers believed that education could not only inform, it could transform. To instill temperance, educate the people. To develop a peace-loving country, educate the people. To create an entirely new social order on a national scale, educate the people. Some enthusiasts dared hope that schooling would eventually replace legislation as the principal means for bringing about change.[26]

Benjamin Porter, the South Carolinian who described working on public roads, was Alabama's quintessential reformer. In 1833, as a legislator from Monroe County, he offered his first proposal on education. Later, he moved to Tuscaloosa County, where he was elected one of its representatives. Porter redirected the debate in the general assembly, focusing it not so much on the role of schools as on that of the central government. It was an important shift in politics given William Mobley's defeat at the hands of David Ligon a little over a decade earlier.[27]

As a young man in South Carolina, Porter had struggled to support a widowed mother and two sisters as he moved through a series of jobs before becoming an attorney. Restless to learn and to succeed, he left his post as a clerk in a countinghouse (at age fourteen) in order to study pharmacy and medicine. A biographer describes him as fond of the dramatic and eager for public recognition, traits that convinced him a lawyer's life had more to offer than a physician's. After clerking in a Charleston law office, Porter moved to Alabama in search of a more lucrative practice. Initially a partner with James Dellett, an anti-Jacksonian attorney of some political standing, Porter settled in Tuscaloosa because he wanted to meet people of influence. He quickly became an ally of planters, merchants, and other professionals who shared his lack of concern about the power of elites.[28]

Hardworking, though somewhat mercurial, Porter won a seat in the legislature just two years after arriving in Tuscaloosa (1837). There he showed himself to be a man with warm, humane impulses as well as a spirited interest in the material development of the state. An accomplished legal scholar, he introduced bills to amend the penal code

Benjamin Faneuil Porter

and abolish punishment by death. He was much like his counterparts who were developing model penitentiaries in New York and Pennsylvania and making inroads against capital punishment in Maine and Vermont. Philosophically he was a Whig, a party that wanted to cross the nation with canals and railroads and give new industries every possible legal advantage. The only characteristic he might not have shared with some of his Northern contemporaries was his states' rights leanings.[29]

Porter's educational arguments were soon tested by another economic downturn that resulted in the repeal of the 1839-1840 legislation. Despite prosperity in 1840, this depression was more than a fleeting panic; it held on until 1845. Falling cotton prices resulted in the complete failure of the already troubled state bank in 1843, which robbed the government of income and the schools of appropriations. The bank, where the sixteenth-section funds had been deposited in 1828, lost its reserves. Making a bad situation worse, the crisis diverted the attention of Alabama's leaders to economic matters, with the result that education lost political as well as monetary support.

Compounding the problem, the state university and public school partisans clashed in an unfortunate battle over appropriations, splitting potential allies in the cause of education. The University took the position that Alabama needed a leadership of merit. Champions of public schools, on the other hand, wrapped themselves in the mantle of egalitarianism, arguing that the state needed able citizens, not just leaders.

Benjamin Porter had a plan to resolve the funding crisis that shows a new rationale for education was evolving, one with significant implications for the role of state government. Porter placed the state at the center of the educational universe. The original intent of the federal grants, he argued, required the trustee of the funds (which he saw as the state government) to make good on the money lost by the state bank. He pointed out that the legislature had banked the school funds and then liquidated the banks; to him that meant the general assembly had a clear duty to redeem what it had lost. The goal, he insists, was "not the education of a few and the denial of education to many; but Education, in the most comprehensive expression of the term."[30]

Consistent with this view and in order to replace the lost fund, the Tuscaloosa reformer proposed a general state tax, a rather bold idea under the circumstances. Opposition to taxation was so strong that all taxes had been abolished from 1836 to 1843. And, when the legislature was forced to reinstate taxation in 1843 because the state was suffering serious economic reversals, revenue went exclusively to operate the government and pay off bank debt.

As bold as his tax plan was, Porter's conviction that the state government was primarily responsible for education was even bolder for Alabama: He proposed that a state superintendent be appointed to oversee education. Other Southern states had already taken this step: Tennessee had created a state superintendency in 1835 and Kentucky in 1838. Porter's proposal wasn't novel in calling for a chief state school officer: it was significant because

House of Representatives Chamber at the State Capitol in Tuscaloosa

it opened a debate over the role of state government in Alabama and marked the beginning of a trend to equate public schools with state tax-supported institutions.

No reformer had a clearer sense of the public's interest than Benjamin Porter, and none took greater political risks to back his ideals with a concrete plan of action. Yet few had less faith in the public. Porter didn't trust his fellow citizens, even though everything he did was done in their name and for their benefit. Appealing to a like-minded elite, he asked them to join him in "leading, rather than being led by the people." It was a telling statement made in the name of Christianity, law, and liberty but not of democracy, not of self-rule. For all that he did to promote a state system of education, Porter's attitude toward other Alabamians placed a small stone into what would eventually become a large wall separating the public from the public schools. Fearful that the people wouldn't embrace his reforms, Porter fed a distrust that came to characterize many of Alabama's educational leaders.

WHAT MIGHT HAVE BEEN:
THE LAST STAND FOR COMMUNITY RESPONSIBILITY

While the house was rejecting Porter's tax proposal, concern for public education prompted the senate to come up with other options for solving the problem created by the failed bank. Senator Benjamin Hudson of Franklin wanted each township to take its own sixteenth-section fund out of the bank, the ultimate in local autonomy. Senator Solomon C. Smith, representing De Kalb and Cherokee, favored investing the proceeds from the sale of federal lands in state stock and "apportioning the interest arising therefrom among the several townships." This was a device for equalizing resources, which would have helped poorer counties like De Kalb and Cherokee (and, interestingly, also Hudson's county, Franklin). Smith proposed that the sale proceeds become a common fund for schools, and he wanted congressional assistance to compensate for worthless sixteenth sections.[31]

Governor Benjamin Fitzpatrick (a Democrat from Wetumpka who went on to the United States Senate) favored issuing state stock, too—but for the varying amounts on deposit in the bank, with the interest on the deposits going to the townships (presumably not reapportioned). This and the Smith proposal, rather than Hudson's, attracted the most legislative attention.

Recognizing that the land-grant income was inadequate, the senators on the sixteenth-section committee shared the conviction that the schools weren't sufficiently common or free. They even agreed that poor townships should be compensated in some way. But agreement stopped there. Committee members opposed consolidating all the township funds into a common fund because they considered it wrong to deprive "one portion of our citizens of the sacred rights of property, [and] to bestow them on another class." At the same time, they thought the federal act limiting the use of the grants to townships violated the principle that educational funds were "for the common benefit" of all citizens.[32]

Unable to find a way around this impasse in the 1845-1846 session, the next assembly considered what could have been the answer: a policy of joint state and local funding. In the house, Leroy Pope Walker, a man of considerable political influence, reopened the education debate by proposing a state tax and an appropriation of the sixteenth-section funds "to equalize as near as may be" the resources available for education. (Son of John W. Walker, who presided over the state's constitutional convention, Leroy Walker represented Lauderdale County. He later served as a cabinet member and brigadier general in the Confederacy.)[33]

While committed to equal funding, Walker was convinced that the localities, not the state, should have primary responsibility for education. He wanted "a board of Educational Superintendents for each county in this State." In making this proposal, he was unwilling to sacrifice the autonomy that goes with home rule but was willing to move the authority for education one step away from the townships and to vest it in the counties. Walker used the usual rhetoric in support of his plan: republican governments controlled by popular will must provide "facilities for the improvement of the moral and intellectual condition of the masses."

Members of the house education committee (which included Peter Hamilton of Mobile) responded by saying that intelligent statesmen had long been familiar with these ideals, a response that suggests Walker's colleagues may have bridled at his preaching or that Jeffersonian arguments were getting shopworn. Taxes were another matter: the committee was alarmed by the financial implications of state responsibility for education. Assuming that there would be either one school per township or one school for every thirty students, that teachers could be hired for five hundred dollars, and that the sixteenth-section income would be used to supplement tax revenue, the state would have to raise between three hundred thousand and five hundred thousand dollars every year. The committee balked at these amounts, fearing that they were more than the government could collect. Instead, this group of legislators proposed that the state pay half of the school expenses (primarily teachers' salaries) and the townships pay the other half. Members had heard that this system worked well in New England and believed that it would require only two hundred thousand dollars of state revenue. But, given the financial situation in Alabama, the general assembly wasn't ready to risk appropriations, even at that level. Representatives did, however, acknowledge the importance of community support, which was in the 1839 statute.[34]

Later, in 1848, the general assembly settled the most immediate issue, which was where to put the land-grant endowments that had been in the state bank. Representatives did as Governor Fitzpatrick had recommended in 1845: they made the federal funds part of the state treasury, issued certificates attesting to the amounts belonging to each township, and promised every county 6 percent interest. In effect, the townships held onto their grants, though not control of the principal. But the problem of inequities remained unsolved.[35]

Had the house committee acted on the proposal for joint state-local responsibility, the state would have gone in a different direction than the one Benjamin Porter proposed, yet without neglecting the maldistribution of resources. Alabama might have escaped some of the centralization that later resulted from the landmark school act passed in 1854. Community responsibility was quite strong in the 1840s: citizens in townships, not federal funds, provided most school revenue. Joint funding was a viable option.

EDUCATION AS AN AGENCY OF GOVERNMENT

By the late 1840s, the state began to recover from the depression. With a rally in the cotton market, Alabamians regained their economic confidence, and legislators once again boasted of "fields white with cotton" and "rivers burdened with freight and travel." As the economy improved, the state bank yielded to reform and finally to liquidation. Sensing a more favorable political climate, ever-persistent enthusiasts of internal improvements and public schooling redoubled their efforts.[36]

Porter had opened a door that would never be closed. The state government was about to take on fiscal and administrative responsibility for schools, although with no thought of doing away with local responsibility. Porter was soon to have political allies and, more important, a new argument—that education served state government, not just communities.

Before Alabama could concentrate on the role of the government in the state's development, however, conflict with the North over slavery and states' rights grabbed the headlines. During the late 1840s and increasingly thereafter, lofty ideals about education and even practical arguments about economic development had to compete with emotions aroused by a growing sectional rivalry. State issues didn't return to the top of the political agenda until around 1853, when sectionalism waned, at least temporarily. Once again, politicians began to take sides on social reforms and economic improvements proposed during the administration of a new governor, Henry W. Collier, an eminent jurist from Tuscaloosa.

In his messages to the legislature on education, Collier added a new theme to the rhetoric when he said that "among the paramount objectives of government" was the "promotion of individual happiness . . . [and] the improvement of society." He believed that education is the perfect means for a state to use in achieving these objectives. The governor was saying that the purpose of education is the same as the purpose of the government: government is the primary mechanism for fostering social well-being, the schools are the state's means to that end, and the welfare of individuals is the measure of progress. These notions were quite different from what had been the prevailing view—that government should be limited, that schools are the public's agent, that local control is better than central, and that the measure of progress is the well-being of society as a whole.[38]

Preoccupation with sectional issues didn't completely eclipse all else. While this controversy raged, the Alabama legislature listened to national reform leader Dorothea Dix and responded favorably to her 1849 report on the deplorable lot of the mentally ill. The state chartered an asylum for the insane in 1851. Members of the assembly also answered the demands of temperance advocates by passing antiliquor legislation. And lawmakers worked on developing a better transportation system by encouraging eight different railroad schemes.[37]

Consistent with his belief that government and education have the same objectives, the governor saw no reason that the public schools shouldn't have an office in the capital. Like Benjamin Porter, he wanted a state superintendent and proposed that judges of the county courts be county superintendents. Collier urged public school proponents to shift their attention from the inequities stemming from variations in the value of sixteenth-section grants to the potential of an effectively administered state system of schools in the service of government. Presumably, this system would eliminate the problem of the inequitable distribution of resources.[39]

At first, the legislature rejected the governor's advice. The majority of representatives interested in educational progress weren't willing to give up their frontal attack on the land grants. Inequities produced by the variations in the value of the lands were obvious, and efforts to consolidate the funds had become a habit. Legislators called a referendum on a plan to consolidate the sixteenth-section revenue into a single education fund. The proposal actually won by a three-to-one margin. Voting for a central fund were 852 townships, while only 264 opposed it. Yet the referendum failed because an additional 456 townships didn't vote; and those, along with the townships voting "no," represented nearly half the state. Governor Collier might have said, "I told you so."[40]

The governor wasn't alone in believing that Alabama had to revise its 1823 policy on education; a number of legislators saw a popular tide pressing for some kind of state aid. Much of the initiative came from the lower chamber's 1851 committee on education, chaired by a Mobilian, C. P. Robinson. In their recommendations, members of the committee joined Collier in advising school enthusiasts to be wary of concentrating solely on the sixteenth-section problem. Decrying the injustices of the land-grant system and promoting the consolidation of township funds had become sterile habits, they charged. By framing the education issue this way, the general assembly had painted itself into a corner. To get out, the committee also endorsed Collier's proposal to have a chief state school officer.[41]

Their report explained the recommendations. Members acknowledged two of the traditional ideals that argued for popularizing knowledge. It is an ancient and undeniable truth, they said, that education is necessary for the good life, adding that the "conservative elements of a popular education" are particularly effective in ensuring a stable government that would prevent a return to the "mad liberty of an ancient democracy." Then they added their assessment of the political sentiment in the state, which was apparent in community after community: "It cannot be disguised," they observed, "that the people are fast becoming restless under the present condition of things. They are alive to the importance of education. They appreciate its advantages to their children, as fully as any other people. They are as willing to contribute freely and generously for its encouragement. They recognise the duty of the State to do something in this nature." More persuasive than all the ideals, an insistent public demanded action.[42]

The report of the Robinson committee is also noteworthy because it makes one of the first legislative references to children. (Governor Collier had also mentioned them.) The recognition seems to have been the logical corollary of a political philosophy that placed a premium on individual well-being.

THE PUBLIC'S SCHOOLS AND A PUBLIC SCHOOL SYSTEM

Two forces now came together in Alabama even more powerfully than they had in 1839. Citizens had not only established schools but also had decided that public education meant "free" or commonly accessible. Communities had no doubt that local schools were essential to the way of life they wanted, one where lawfulness, learning, and social responsibility would flourish. And members of the general assembly had moved from the view that they had only to encourage education to the conclusion that they had to appropriate funds. Furthermore, providing state money paved the way for giving the central government a role in managing instruction. Alabamians were working their way through the options confronting them, and a new sense of direction was emerging.

While these two forces (one coming from the general assembly and the other from the communities) reinforced one another, they weren't the same. The public had established schools that attempted to be free and common. And the legislature had developed a rhetoric that celebrated free and common schooling as an ideal. But the *public's schools* should not be confused with the legislature's concept of a *public school*. As events after 1854 would show, differences between the two would create serious tensions in educational politics.

People certainly wanted more funds for local schools and hoped the state would resume its appropriations, but it isn't clear how many appreciated the consequences of the system that Porter and Collier had in mind. Support for schools free to all and support for state control were different. Yet the Robinson committee didn't acknowledge any potential side-effects from a more centralized system. Alabama had a model to follow in states that had already established superintendencies, and the national public school movement was in full force. And, not incidentally, citizens in the southwestern counties and elsewhere were impatient for the legislature to act.

NOTES TO CHAPTER 6

[1] J. Mills Thornton III discussed the responsiveness of antebellum legislators in *Politics and Power in a Slave Society: Alabama, 1800-1860* (Baton Rouge: Louisiana State University Press, 1978), pp. 85-86, 98, 116-117, 148, 201.

[2] The editor of the Huntsville *Democrat,* Philip Woodson, championed literal representation in the June 17 and 24, 1830, issues of the newspaper.

[3] When I refer to ideals and idealistic political rhetoric, I mean statements about what a perfect society should do and be. Sometimes several of these ideals are grouped together and given names like "Jeffersonianism." That political philosophy joined a series of propositions into a logical argument: "We want to be free; to be free, we have to rule ourselves; in order to rule ourselves we have to have an educated citizenry." Educational historians concern themselves with such ideals or ideologies. For a brief overview on what is going on in this field, I suggest Carl F. Kaestle's "Ideology and American Educational History," *History of Education Quarterly* 23 (summer 1982): 123-137.

[4] Harry Toulmin, *Digest of the Laws of the State of Alabama: Containing the Statutes and Resolutions in Force at the End of the General Assembly in January, 1823* (Cahawba: Ginn and Curtis, 1823), p. 529.

Early federal policy on education was in documents of the Confederate Congress. They can be found in a compilation prepared by Benjamin Perley Poore, *The Federal and State Constitutions, Colonial Charters, and Other Organic Laws of the United States,* part 1, 2d ed. (Washington, D.C.: Government Printing Office, 1878). The documents I cite were in "The Northwest Territorial Government, 1787," specifically p. 431. The quotation from the Northwest Ordinance was in Edgar W. Knight, ed., *A Documentary History of Education in the South before 1860,* vol. 2 (Chapel Hill: University of North Carolina Press, 1950), p. 136.

[5] John Williams Walker, "Celebrating Fourth Hundred Years Ago: Masterly Oration Delivered on July 4, 1811, by John W. Walker at 'Twickenham, Mississippi Territory,'" *Birmingham News,* 4 July 1915.

[6] "A Bill for the More General Diffusion of Knowledge," in *The Papers of Thomas Jefferson,* ed. Julian P. Boyd, vol. 2 (Princeton: Princeton University Press, 1950), p. 526.

[7] Alexander Hamilton, Jefferson's nemesis, was credited with advancing a federal policy to promote manufacturing in the East. After the War of 1812, Henry Clay from Kentucky took up the cause. Hamilton had emphasized the benefits to industry; Clay broadened the appeal to western farmers by proposing a plan to have the government pay for internal improvements. It was very attractive to some Alabamians.

[8] "Popular Education—No. 2, Utility of the Measure," *South Western Baptist,* 16 February 1854.

Douglass North laid out the assumptions affecting investments in public education. He contended that plantation societies saw little reason to invest in mental capital. But Alabamians like Arthur Bagby, James DeVotie, and the editors of the *South Western Baptist* made it clear they thought an investment in education had broad social, political, and economic benefits that justified a broad investment. Douglass C. North, *Economic Growth of the United States, 1790-1860* (New York: W. W. Norton, 1966), p. 9.

[9] Friedrich List explained his ideas in *The National System of Political Economy* (1885; reprint, New York: A. M. Kelley, 1966), p. 138. If not List himself, those who did convince Americans that public education and national prosperity were linked had their arguments vindicated in the twentieth century. The United States was an industrial giant by 1900, economic historians have shown, because of its unique approach to public schooling. At the beginning of the century, this country alone had more than a fraction of its young people in upper-level secondary institutions. The result was that America outstripped everyone else in the development of mental or human capital. Despite the introduction of systems, nineteenth-century schools in most states remained small, secular, relatively independent, financed by locally generated income, open, academically "forgiving," and the objects of considerable public support. Some economists now worry these "virtues" are increasingly seen as vices. For evidence of the impact of these schools on the national economy, see Claudia Goldin, "The Human-Capital Century and American Leadership: Virtues of the Past," *Journal of Economic History* 61 (June 2001): 263-292.

[10] Toulmin, *Digest of the Laws of the State of Alabama,* pp. 539-540.

[11] Mobley's proposal for women's education and the response were recorded in Alabama General Assembly, *House Journal,* 11th annual sess., 1829 (Tuscaloosa: McGuire,

Henry and Walker, 1830), pp. 158-159, 163. Also read Willis Brewer's *Alabama: Her History, Resources, War Record and Public Men, from 1540 to 1872* (1872; reprint, Spartanburg, S.C.: Reprint Company, 1975), pp. 308, 442-443.

[12]   Lawrence A. Cremin described the colonial practices of providing school in *American Education: The Colonial Experience, 1607-1783* (New York: Harper and Row, 1970), pp. 167-195. He noted that "free" could mean free to the children of people who subscribed (made donations), free to the poor, or free to all. He also discussed local responsibility in *American Education: The National Experience, 1783-1876* (New York: Harper and Row, 1980), pp. 112-113.

[13]   Legislation on the organization of schools was in Toulmin's *Digest of the Laws of the State of Alabama*, pp. 544-547, 568-573.

The act of 1823 was explained in Jay Emmett Thomason's "The Development of the Administrative Organization of the Public School System of Alabama" (Ph.D. diss., University of Alabama, 1959), pp. 14-19.

[14]   The Alabama House of Representatives issued a *Report from the Committee on Education, on the Subject of Public Schools* (Montgomery: Brittan and De Wolf, 1852), pp. 4-5, 11-12, which dealt with inequities in sixteenth-section funding.

[15]   Pleasant May's argument for public schools appeared in the November 8, 1837, issue of the *Flag of the Union* (Tuscaloosa).

[16]   For a discussion of public virtue, look at the sections on civic humanism and republican values in Gordon S. Wood's books *The Creation of the American Republic, 1776-1787* (Chapel Hill: University of North Carolina Press, 1998) and *The Radicalism of the American Revolution* (New York: Alfred A. Knopf, 1992). Also read descriptions of these concepts in J. G. A. Pocock's *The Machiavellian Moment: Florentine Political Thought and the Atlantic Republican Tradition* (Princeton: Princeton University Press, 1975). Also see Garrett, *Reminiscences,* p. 156.

[17]   The state bank was authorized by the Alabama General Assembly, *Acts,* 5th annual sess., 1823 (Cahawba: William B. Allen, 1824), p. 3.

[18]   Unfortunately, school property was sold at less than market value, and some purchasers failed to pay debts. This mismanagement of the land grants is one of the subjects of

Ira W. Harvey's *A History of Educational Finance in Alabama, 1819-1986* (Auburn, Ala.: Truman Pierce Institute for the Advancement of Teacher Education, 1989), pp. 13-15, 23-24. Fraud or abuse are also discussed in *An Educational Study of Alabama* published by the Bureau of Education in the Department of the Interior (Washington, D. C.: Government Printing Office, 1919), p. 36. While no one denies that these abuses existed, in other states such as Iowa, officials did not always assume that the problem was a result of inadequate local control.

John G. Aikin, *Digest of the Laws of the State of Alabama: Containing All the Statutes of a Public and General Nature, in Force at the Close of the Session of the General Assembly, in January, 1833* (Philadelphia: Alexander Towar, 1833), § 33, § 34, § 35.

[19]   Albert Burton Moore, *History of Alabama* (1934; reprint, Tuscaloosa: Alabama Book Store, 1951), p. 213.

[20]   Thomas S. Woodward tells the story of Governor Bagby's youthful escapades in *Woodward's Reminiscences of the Creek, or Muscogee Indians, Contained in Letters to Friends in Georgia and Alabama* (Montgomery: Barrett and Wimbish, 1859), pp. 104-105.

[21]   William Garrett described Governor Bagby's political position in *Reminiscences of Public Men in Alabama, for Thirty Years* (Atlanta: Plantation Publishing Company, 1872), p. 206. Bagby's support of internal improvements, penal reforms, and temperance is evident in his remarks to the state senate in 1838. Alabama General Assembly, *Senate Journal,* annual sess., 1838 (Tuscaloosa: Hale and Eaton, 1838), p. 13.

I located the information I needed on the economic situation in 1837 in Emory Q. Hawk's *Economic History of the South,* Prentice-Hall History Series, ed. Carl Wittke (New York: Prentice-Hall, 1934), p. 358. For a broader account of the Southern economy, I used Douglass C. North's *Economic Growth of the United States, 1790-1860* (New York: W. W. Norton, 1966).

[22]   Bagby's arguments for public education appeared in the *Senate Journal* of the Alabama General Assembly, annual sess., 1840 (Tuscaloosa: Hale and Phelan, 1841), pp. 14-15.

[23]   Alabama General Assembly, *Acts,* annual sess., 1838 (Tuscaloosa: Hale and Eaton, 1838), pp. 65-66.

[24]   Alabama, *Acts,* annual sess., 1838, pp. 65-66.

[25]   The statistics on the per-pupil expenditures envisioned in

the 1840 law came from Alabama General Assembly, *Acts,* annual sess., 1839 (Tuscaloosa: Hale and Eaton, 1840), pp. 49-50 and Stephen B. Weeks, *History of Public School Education in Alabama,* U.S. Bureau of Education Bulletin, 1915, no. 12 (Washington, D.C.: Government Printing Office, 1915), p. 49.

[26] Rush Welter presented evidence that education became a form of politics in America in *Popular Education and Democratic Thought in America* (New York: Columbia University Press, 1962). Also see Alice Felt Tyler's *Freedom's Ferment: Phases of American Social History from the Colonial Period to the Outbreak of the Civil War* (1944; reprint, New York: Harper and Row, 1976). John W. Quist described the reform movement in Alabama in *Restless Visionaries: The Social Roots of Antebellum Reform in Alabama and Michigan* (Baton Rouge: Louisiana State University Press, 1998).

[27] Benjamin Faneuil Porter wrote an autobiography entitled *Reminiscences of Men and Things in Alabama,* which was later edited by a relative, Sara Walls (Tuscaloosa: Portals Press, 1983), pp. 85-86. John Buckner Little also wrote about Porter's career in *The History of Butler County, Alabama 1815 to 1885* (1875; reprint, Cincinnati: Elm Street Printing Company, 1972), pp. 114-117. Other sources were Garrett, *Reminiscences,* pp. 310-319 and Brewer, *Alabama: Her History,* p. 148.

[28] Paul M. Pruitt, Jr., wrote the most useful article on Porter for my purposes, "An Antebellum Law Reformer: Passages in the Life of Benjamin F. Porter," which appeared in the *Gulf Coast Historical Review* 11 (fall 1995): 23-58.

[29] Porter's burst of reform proposals was recorded in the Alabama General Assembly, *House Journal,* annual sess., 1845 (Tuscaloosa: John McCormick, 1846), pp. 25, 30.

I intentionally said that Northern reformers may or may not have shared Porter's feelings about states' rights. As Forrest McDonald explained, the doctrine of states' rights, though associated with the practice of slavery by the mid-nineteenth century, actually developed in the early years of the country and was fiercely championed in the North, particularly during the War of 1812. Consequently, to say that Southern reformers differed from their Northern counterparts in their allegiance to this doctrine would not necessarily be accurate. The rights of states or local jurisdiction vis-à-vis the rights of central government rests on the proposition that sovereignty in the United States is divided; on some matters, states are the final authority, while on others,

the central government is supreme. Even a champion of the Union like Daniel Webster argued at one point in his career that state governments have obligations that "bind them to the preservation of their own rights and the liberties of their people." See McDonald's *States' Rights and the Union: Imperium in Imperio, 1776-1876* (Lawrence: University Press of Kansas, 2000), p. 69. Eugene D. Genovese supported McDonald's conclusions in "Getting States' Rights Right" in the March 2001 *Atlantic Monthly,* pp. 82-89.

[30] With legal thoroughness, Porter spelled out his plan for education in *Argument of Benjamin F. Porter, in Support of a Bill Introduced by Him into the House of Representatives* (Tuscaloosa: n.p., 1848). All statements attributed to Porter were in this paper. The quotations are on pp. 3-4.

[31] Alabama General Assembly, *Senate Journal,* annual sess., 1845 (Tuscaloosa: John McCormick, 1846), pp. 3-4, 12, 125-127.

Governor Fitzpatrick's career was chronicled in Thomas McAdory Owen's *History of Alabama and Dictionary of Alabama Biography,* vol. 3 (Chicago: S. J. Clarke Publishing Company, 1921), pp. 582-583.

[32] Alabama, *Senate Journal,* annual sess, 1845, pp. 126-127.

[33] In addition to Leroy Walker's reputation as a Confederate general and Secretary of War in Jefferson Davis's cabinet, he was remembered by his contemporaries as a great champion of state aid for internal improvements, as in his proposal to build a railroad from Mobile Bay to the Tennessee River (presented in 1853). Garrett, *Reminiscences,* pp. 507-509 and Brewer, *Alabama: Her History,* pp. 354-355.

Although the *Sumter County Whig* of October 18, 1854, included Walker on its list of possible Whig candidates to run for governor in 1855, he had been a Cass elector in 1848 and was more identified with the states' rights Democrats (*Southern Advocate,* 16 January 1856). Lewy Dorman, *Party Politics in Alabama from 1850 through 1860* (1935; reprint, Tuscaloosa: University of Alabama Press, 1995), pp. 104, 129.

The full text of Walker's proposal was recorded in the Alabama General Assembly, *House Journal,* 1st biennial sess., 1847-1848 (Montgomery: McCormick and Walshe, 1848), p. 147.

[34] The members of the committee that favored joint state and local funding were P. Hamilton (Mobile), Robert T. Johnson (Pickens), John Edmund Moore (Lauderdale), Felix G. Norman (Franklin), L. S. Smith (Barbour), Ashley W.

Spaight (Dallas), James A. Stallworth (Conecuh), and Joseph W. Taylor (Greene). Alabama, *House Journal,* 1st biennial sess., 1847-1848, pp. 3-4, 31, 375-376.

[35] Ira Harvey described the act placing the sixteenth-section funds in the state treasury in *History of Educational Finance,* p. 41.

[36] *Report from the Committee on Education,* p. 6.

[37] Several years prior to her legislative visit, Dix had toured Alabama while gathering data on the care of the insane. During her stay in Tuscaloosa, she was the guest of Judge Collier. Garrett, *Reminiscences,* p. 521.

The Sons of Temperance asked the legislature for a local option or prohibition law. According to Dorman, *Party Politics,* p. 83, this group met in Selma in 1852 to draft its demands into a bill. However, according to Garrett, *Reminiscences,* p. 577, this same or an identical meeting was held in Selma in the spring of 1853.

The eight railroads encouraged by the legislature were "the Mobile and Ohio Railroad, the Memphis and Charleston Railroad, the Selma and Rome Railroad, the Alabama and Mississippi Rivers Railroad (from Selma westward), the Montgomery and Pensacola Railroad, the Mobile and Girard Railroad, the Alabama and Chattanooga Railroad, and the Columbus branch of the Montgomery and West Point Railroad." Brewer, *Alabama: Her History,* p. 59.

[38] Alabama General Assembly, *Senate Journal,* 2d biennial sess., 1849-1850 (Montgomery: Brittan and DeWolf, 1850), p. 203.

[39] Governor Collier's education reform proposal was first presented in 1849; Alabama, *Senate Journal,* 2d biennial sess., 1849-1850, p. 205. He repeated it in 1851; Alabama General Assembly, *Senate Journal,* 3d biennial sess., 1851-1852 (Montgomery: Brittan and DeWolf, 1852), pp. 29-30.

Illustrative of the sixteenth-section problem, the combined value of the school land in 12 counties (Autauga, Chambers, Dallas, Greene, Limestone, Lowndes, Madison, Montgomery, Perry, Pickens, Sumter, and Tuscaloosa) was five-sixths, or "one-third more than half," of the total value of all sixteenth sections in the state. These same 12 counties had only one-fourth of the white population. *Report from the Committee on Education,* pp. 4-5.

[40] Weeks, *History of Public School Education,* p. 34.

[41] Robinson's committee consisted of Representatives Marion Banks (Tuscaloosa), William W. Byrd (Marengo), George W. Hendree (Chambers), Porter King (Perry), O. H. Oates (Lauderdale), George Shelly (Talladega), S. A. Tarrant (Jefferson), and O. B. Walton (Russell). Alabama General Assembly, *House Journal,* 3d biennial sess., 1851-1852 (Montgomery: Brittan and DeWolf, 1852), p. 54 and Garrett, *Reminiscences,* pp. 745, 753-754, 758, 763-764, 766, 768. In all but three of these counties (Marengo, Perry, and Russell), the white population outnumbered the slave population in 1851. *Report from the Committee on Education,* pp. 6-7.

[42] *Report from the Committee on Education,* pp. 5, 10.

Chapter 7

The Restless Citizenry
behind the Scenes

T HE LEGISLATURE WAS on the verge of implementing the Porter-Collier proposal. Although the house education committee had read the mood of the public correctly in 1851, its recommendations didn't become law, which made public education a major issue in the next session. Leadership for a new round of political battles wouldn't come so much from Collier's successor as governor as from a group of reform-minded legislators. While representatives prepared for their next assembly, communities put more and more of their resources into building schools, which put more and more pressure on the legislature to do its part. Communities were rallying places for "restless" citizens, and they influenced lawmakers not by lobbying but by the political climate they developed in the state.

The Commercial Republic on the Gulf

Hard-hit by the depression of the 1840s, Mobile began to recover in the 1850s. A federal land grant, plus generous subscriptions, community fund-raising events, and backing from the city government, got the Mobile and Ohio Railroad moving toward Cairo, Illinois. In 1851, citizens supplemented voluntary contributions by approving a 2 percent property tax for the project. In a parallel effort to strengthen the institutions of public life, Mobilians built new homes for civic associations like the Temperance Society and the Odd Fellows, as well as for a number of churches. Yet not all was well in the city.[1]

Mobile was racked by increasingly bitter disputes among the political parties. Standard-bearers for the Whigs included the mayor, Charles C. Langdon, the Hamilton brothers (Peter and Thomas), most city officials, and the legislative delegation. Langdon was also editor of the *Mobile Daily Advertiser* (and later an Auburn trustee). In an age when newspapers were openly allied with political parties, the mayor/editor was a fierce partisan. He was locked in a conflict with his nemesis, Hamilton Ballentyne, who pushed the states' rights cause at rival papers. Antagonism turned violent; at one point, Langdon fought a duel with one of his critics (fortunately, no one was killed).

Democrats looked to John A. Campbell, law partner of Daniel Chandler and a good friend of John C. Calhoun. Other party leaders included Thaddeus Sanford, a merchant from Connecticut who became editor of the *Register,* and Joseph Sewell (Seawell), judge of the county court and one-term mayor. Sanford was allied with the co-owner of his newspaper,

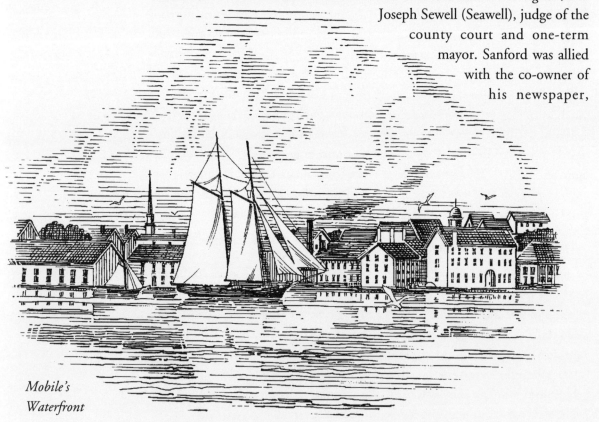

*Mobile's
Waterfront*

Alexander Meek, and another business partner, C. A. Bradford.

Disagreements over slavery and state sovereignty, followed by attacks on foreigners and Catholics (a large part of Mobile's population), charged the political atmosphere. The Whig paper, the *Advertiser,* was soon trading editorial insults with the Democrats' *Register.*

As the states' rights cause gained influence, Whigs began to lose their hold on city offices, and Democrats elected Joseph Sewell mayor in 1851. Politics got even nastier. The Southern Rights Association urged a boycott of Langdon and all merchants with Union sympathies. The Whigs held on in 1853 by merging with the Know-Nothing Party and regained seats on the city council. The partisan zealotry strained the civic fiber of Mobile. And, when the Know-Nothing campaign against foreigners and Catholics lost steam, antiabolitionist hysteria took its place. A local bookstore owner was run out of town simply because he had two books by Frederick Douglass on his shelves. As unlikely as it may seem, the cause of public education flourished while all of this was going on, even overcoming intense partisan rivalry.

A Community Takes Back Its Schools

Recall that after 1843, Mobilians lost the right to elect their school commissioners, making the board what one critic called a "close corporation." Responding in a forceful display of political will, the public challenged the board in 1851, and a reorganized body of commissioners rode to power on the shoulders of a frustrated citizenry. The public for the public schools reasserted itself in this and other ways, making it clear that free public education did not mean exclusively "for the poor" (a qualification the board had put on its free schools in 1839 as a response to limited resources).[2]

Provocation for a Revolt: Sell Barton Academy?

Born out of a public meeting, the school board was the agent of its creators in the first years. From that beginning, and throughout the first half of the nineteenth century, individual members usually took their trusteeship seriously; most were the city's elite, prominent in various civic enterprises. As a group, however, they became caught up in their own internal maneuvering, particularly in the 1840s, when they were unable to muster a quorum. In the

1850s, they met their legal responsibilities but failed in their civic role. The board lost touch with the people.

Throughout Samuel Fisher's tenure in the 1840s, meetings dealt with routine business—raising revenue, paying off debts, repairing Barton's cupola, and electing new members. In 1845, a veteran commissioner, Samuel Bullard, persuaded the board to lease the entire Barton building (not just classrooms) and half of the square. Leaseholders could use the property only for educational purposes, and their contracts with the board had to be renewed yearly. William Merrill rented the building to operate a free school of his own and renewed his lease several years running. Except for approving leases and disbursing small amounts to free schools operated by churches, the public's agent—the school commission—wasn't a significant force in education during the decade. Indebtedness immobilized the board to the point that it declined to provide even modest scholarships; as late as 1849, commissioners rejected an appeal to support children who couldn't pay tuition at a small school near Spring Hill because they feared the precedent it would set.[3]

In December of that year, the board was asked to make Barton available to house the state capitol, replacing the building in Montgomery recently destroyed by fire. Commissioners authorized a committee to answer the mayor "forthwith," yet there are no records for the next seven months to show what must have been a negative response. In August of 1850, however, in reply to an offer from the county board of revenue, the school board passed a resolution opposing the sale of any part of the Barton Academy square.[4]

The presidency of the commission then fell to Peter Hamilton, who had sponsored the resolution. A lawyer practicing with John Campbell and Daniel Chandler, he was the son of Mobile's popular Presbyterian minister, William Thomas Hamilton. Being raised in a family of Scottish Jacobites may have had something to do with Hamilton's independent cast of mind on school matters. He may also have been reflecting the philosophy of Henry Hitchcock, with whom he had a close association.[5]

Authorized to select its own members, the board chose new commissioners, including General Walter Smith. Probably no one realized it at the time, but the issues and the personalities that would shake the board to its foundations were in place.

One of the most powerful of the new board members, General Smith wore many hats. He seems to have been the officer who built the Mount Vernon Arsenal in 1830, later rising to high rank in the militia. He was also coeditor with Charles Langdon at the Whig paper, the *Advertiser*. The Democrats charged that, as city recorder, Smith had used municipal wharves without paying rent. Doubtless scarred but unbowed, the general was still a force to be reckoned with.[6]

After assuming the chair in 1850, Hamilton began to agitate for change. He appointed committees to look into paying off the debt (which appears to have been less than the balance in the treasury) and to recommend a suitable plan for the "extension of public free schools." Nothing indicated that these institutions were to be exclusively for the poor.[7]

Walter Smith served on both committees and likely had a great deal to do with reintroducing the idea proposed by the county revenue board—and rejected by Hamilton four months earlier—which was to sell (by means of renewable ninety-nine-year leases) school property. This proposal had a long history; as early as 1838, the board had determined the sale value of the portion of the Barton square fronting Conti Street, apparently without stirring up a controversy. Smith had his eye on the same land, which was prime real estate in the center of the city. The committee dealing with the debt agreed the site was ideal for two-story brick homes; selling it would give the board more money for schools. Without additional revenue, all commissioners could do was to distribute their three thousand-dollar appropriation more equitably among the existing schools, which meant allocating two thousand dollars to those in the city and one thousand dollars for instruction in the county.

Under these conditions, the committee favored deferring a permanent system until further study could be done. Board members didn't voice any reservations about public, common, free schools (all these terms were used), though no one said exactly what "suitable" meant. The committee did encourage opening more county schools and told outlying communities that the board would welcome their interest and would work with local trustees.[8]

Two members evidently believed the commissioners needed to do more—and quickly. William Redwood proposed creating a new school committee at the next meeting, and Peter Hamilton supported him. But they were alone.

A champion of reform for many years, Redwood wasn't a typical board member. He was a commission merchant, meaning that he sold "bagging and rope, whiskey, flour, . . . [and] bacon," primarily to upriver planters. He had additional business interests, including the Point Clear Hotel and the Mobile and Ohio Railroad. A Whig, Redwood also served on the city council.[9]

One month after Redwood and Hamilton objected to Smith's plan to sell the Barton property, the firm of John Campbell and Daniel Chandler (both former school commissioners) notified the board that it had been retained to secure a restraining order preventing real estate development on the school site. (Remember that Chandler was one of the Mobilians who had reclaimed Barton Academy when it was sold in 1840.) "We find," the lawyers wrote, "that a portion of the community are not satisfied with the proposed disposition of the property. . . . If your plan was modified and the public enlightened as to what you proposed to do, their views might be changed." This last sentence shows that selling the Barton land was only one issue; the board's relationship to the public was equally important. Apparently, a number of citizens weren't sure what their agent was up to.[10]

General Smith, who had no qualms about defending his plan, responded by urging that the board have an explanation printed in the newspapers. However, his colleague on the committee, Daniel Wheeler (a merchant who traded largely in British accounts), beat a strategic retreat and got the commissioners to postpone the matter until the legal problems were resolved. William Redwood still wasn't satisfied; he wanted more than a delay, and he wanted the records of the board moved to the probate judge's office where they would be open for inspection. The commission's venerable secretary, Henry Stickney, took Redwood's proposal as a personal affront and threatened to resign. Personalities clashed, a serious problem on a board where so many of the same people kept reappearing that it looked like a private club.[11]

THE INFLUENCE OF WORKING PEOPLE

In April 1851, seven new members, with some repeats from previous boards, took office and a new president, C. C. Hazzard, was named. Redwood and Smith retained their seats. The board approved the annual lease of Barton (this time to Daniel Merrill, not William, who made a more attractive offer of one thousand dollars). It also received requests to support instruction in the county and continued the three thousand-dollar appropriation to existing schools. Then, routine business out of the way, Hazzard suggested that a committee be appointed to move ahead with "a plan for public education for the satisfaction of the public." Debt was no longer a barrier, having been liquidated in November. Hazzard wanted the plan to deal, as well, with the question of board governance, which had become a major issue. The five members appointed to carry out these responsibilities included the two long-time adversaries, Redwood and Smith (the general was now board vice president).[12]

Who exactly needed to be "satisfied" by the plan? Not only the business and civic elite, who saw good schools as an advantage in Mobile's competition with other cities, but also the working people of the community. While some Mobilians were genuinely destitute, the workforce doesn't appear to have been impoverished ("labor in general is as well rewarded . . . as in any community in the country"). Still, working families couldn't afford the tuition of the existing schools, including Barton Academy. Even night schools offering practical and academic subjects (bookkeeping, mathematics, and French) charged from four to five dollars a month. Barton's fees, at five to six dollars, were higher and, if French and Spanish were included, could go up to seven dollars. The board committee acknowledged that these prices "required more than the ordinary income of the laboring man to keep one child at a good school, much less could he educate several." A family whose income came from one of the trades and had several children of school age might have to spend a third of its annual income on tuition, clearly an impossibility.[13]

The workforce was sizable. Mobile had laborers, artisans, and clerks employed in such occupations as dressmaking, shipbuilding, and metalwork-ing. These people weren't voiceless; they spoke out in the newspapers about children who weren't able to get into the limited number of free schools, which had the reputation of being institutions of charity. Low-wage earners weren't paupers and didn't want to be treated as such. Their complaint suggests that they saw education as a public necessity and an obligation that had to be met without creating a distinction among citizens.[14]

Home of a Working Family in Mobile. Smaller and without the ornamentation of the Creole cottages, this working-class home was nonetheless a substantial structure. The architecture dates back to the time French styles influenced buildings; the same type of house is found in other areas in the Caribbean.

GOOD INTENTIONS AND AN AMBITIOUS PLAN

The board's committee agreed with the criticism, reporting that "almost one-half of the children in this favored land and wealthy community are growing up without a knowledge of the simplest rudiments of an education." Even though a majority of Mobile's children were in school (2,040 out of 3,524), which was quite good for the time, more than a thousand were getting no instruction. Of the 1,653 school-age youngsters in the outlying county, probably fewer than half were in classes.[15]

The needs of the city and county were so different, the committee observed, it might be better "to separate them in the end." This point of view suggests a tension between city and county interests, which may account for some of the criticism later directed at the Hazzard board.[16]

The committee's plan envisioned a countywide array of elementary and secondary schools, not unlike the arrangement the board's critics would eventually put in place. The report was quite clear about the committee's objective, which was not to perpetuate schools exclusively for the indigent but to place "the means of a suitable education within the reach of all." Public schooling continued to be seen as essential to Mobile's economy and as a means of making a diverse society more cohesive. As one newspaper article explained, the city needed public schools to encourage "social intercourse and individual friendship among the different classes of the community." That implied common schools—certainly not schools solely for the poor.[17]

The committee proposed high schools for both boys and girls "in the city or some eligible point in the county, say Spring Hill, Cottage Hill, or Citronelle." These four-year schools would prepare young men for college or "mercantile pursuits" and provide young women with instruction in "all the branches necessary for a finished formal education." In addition, the city would have primary schools in every ward, and there would be other schools throughout the county, "as the wants of the population should be thought to require." Commissioners would select suitable teachers to be accountable to the board, suggesting that they would be employees rather than independent instructors tied to the school board by leases. All of this would be done at public expense, estimated at twenty thousand dollars a year, a sum much greater than had been spent on education in the past. The plan had all the marks of providing truly public education. As the committee pointed out, it was proposing what older cities in the North and East were already doing and similar to what New Orleans, "our sister city" (that is, the competition) had in operation.[18]

Walter Smith used the twenty thousand-dollar price tag to justify an even more ambitious scheme—to sell not only Barton but also the sixteenth sections throughout the county. Estimating the academy's value at forty thousand dollars, he said the interest on that amount, plus the taxes, tuition, and other income, would produce eleven thousand dollars, leaving nine thousand dollars to be raised. The committee laid out several options for doing that: taxing only parents of school-age children, doubling the board's share of county taxes, or adding a new education tax. Since these measures would require legislative approval, the board asked Smith to prepare a request.[19]

Reasoning that taxing only parents would be unfair since education was a communitywide obligation and "would leave a large portion of the wealthy in the county untaxed," the committee decided on a property tax "as being the most equitable mode of distributing the burden." In addition, the petition asked the legislature for half of the county tax revenue and for authorization "to sell the building known as the Barton Academy in the City of Mobile with the entire square of ground on which it stands, and also all the sixteenth sections of land lying in the County of Mobile." Everything the commission owned was to go on the market, and the board would have the right to acquire and sell any future property. Mindful of being criticized for keeping the public in the dark, commissioners called a public meeting in Franklin Hall to explain their decisions.

Though critics would charge that the Hazzard board wanted to continue the practice of distributing funds only "among the schools patronized by the board," the criticism doesn't seem justified. Continuing to support existing schools would have cost less than twenty thousand dollars. The proposed plan suggests that the commissioners actually had a progressive understanding of public education. Taxing everyone indicated that the board thought school-ing benefited the public, not just those with school-age children. Commission members gave other indications that they saw a close tie between education and the community. For instance, rather than claiming that half of the school-age population was without an education because families were indifferent, the board said this was a reflection on the "fair city" as a whole.[20]

AN ISSUE THAT STIRRED THE POPULAR MIND

Walter Smith was confident his plan reflected the wishes of the citizens. He was dead wrong. Reaction to the board's decision to sell Barton and all school property was instant and dramatic; the issue "stirred the popular mind as no other local subject had affected it for many years." Special associations formed either to support or oppose the sale, and they held rallies. Public meetings generated a counterproposal, and disaffected Mobilians endorsed a "no sale" slate of candidates for the board. Perhaps anticipating the reaction, the general assembly had stipulated that the electorate vote on the proposed sale in August of 1852. (The board doesn't appear to have asked for the referendum.) The legislation also required electing a new group of commissioners.[21]

Why so strong an outcry? Why the disparagement, even the distortion of the board's intentions? Possibly education was a surrogate for other issues. Take the proposal to locate the high schools outside the city. Mobile's commercial and professional leaders favored the downtown area for obvious reasons: that is where they had their homes and offices. Citronelle, one of the proposed locations, may have seemed a world away, even though it was just north of the city. Furthermore, the Barton building was more than a school-house; it was a symbol that gave Mobile the image its leadership wanted. Downtown interests couldn't have been pleased by the prospect of losing what they had worked so hard to create.

Given the rivalries in Mobile, opposition to the sale appears to have been amazingly bipartisan. Whigs were represented by people like Willis G. Clark, who was an editor of the party's journal, the *Mobile Daily Advertiser*. (He was a lawyer in the firm of Campbell and Chandler and, later, a University of Alabama trustee.) Clark, then a young man in his twenties from New York, where he had taught school, was a stand-in for Charles Langdon. Langdon, from Connecticut, had also been a teacher earlier in his career. That experience may have influenced both men's position on the issue. In a show of unity, the *Mobile Register,* under editor and proprietor Thaddeus Sanford, also opposed selling Barton. Sanford was joined in the reform group by his business partner, C. A. Bradford. (The stand taken by the two newspapers illustrates the strong support most of the press gave public education.)[22]

Although Willis Clark insisted that the opposition was nonpartisan, later accounts indicate party politics may have been a factor. Ralph Poore's analysis of those for and against the sale suggests that Whigs like Langdon and Clark were joining with regular Democrats like Sanford to keep the states' rights forces from overwhelming them both. States' righters, according to this interpretation, dominated the board of commissioners and favored the property sale in order to fund free schools for working people. Hamilton Ballentyne, by then editor of a third paper, *The Herald and Tribune,* spoke for this faction. He argued that Barton was too expensive and drained resources from children who would be better off attending a school under trees than having no instruction at all. To thwart the states' rights enthusiasts, Whigs and regular Democrats are said to have put together a slate of four candidates from each of the two major parties to run against incumbent commissioners. The nonelected status of the board also figured in the controversy. In requiring incumbent commissioners to stand for reelection, the legislative delegation was evidently aware that the community was exercised about a self-appointed board.[23]

Walter Smith, a strong proponent of the sale, debated Kiah B. Sewall, a lawyer who just as vigorously opposed it. Their exchange appeared in a July 1852 edition of the *Advertiser*. Smith, departing from the views of the board committee on which he served, wanted to use public money only for "plain" schools offering instruction in the basic subjects to all children, "without distinction." He believed that public schooling should be limited to the primary grades (that was apparently how he understood what the board had called "suitable" education). In an argument compatible with though somewhat different from Ballentyne's, Smith reasoned that the Barton property, with a market value of thirty thousand to forty thousand dollars, was inappropriate for an institution operating at citizens' expense. He didn't want to restrict public education to the poor, yet he didn't think the public's obligation went beyond the three Rs—even though his committee had clearly opted for public high schools.[24]

The citizenry evidently didn't see public education as the general did: most people thought they should have an opportunity to learn as much as they could and that everyone should have access to instruction in the "higher" subjects. Sewall spoke directly to this matter, explaining that many states had three types of institutions in their public systems: primary, grammar, and high schools. Furthermore, he said, selling a debt-free building, which could easily house a diversified educational program, would be foolish. Predictably, the *Advertiser* endorsed Sewall's position, observing (perhaps unfairly) that, if the commissioners had pursued educational improvements as vigorously as they had the sale of Barton, the entire county would already have schools second to none.

Opponents of the sale saw it as an attempt to abandon the very idea of public education. They charged that the commissioners's practice of subcontracting some instruction to churches was a violation of the 1826 act directing them to operate public schools.[25]

AND THE WINNER WAS . . .

The fight over selling Barton ended in a resounding 2,225 to 224 victory for the antisale faction and a return to public election of the school board. Mobilians chose a new group of commissioners, who selected Thaddeus Sanford as president. The winning slate included C. A. Bradford and Willis Clark. William Redwood, a candidate for reelection, returned in triumph. His victory may have had something to do with Henry Stickney's decision not to accept reappointment as secretary. As the law prescribed—and in what was surely an effort to bring some harmony to the board—the eight new members selected four from the old board to join them. Not surprisingly, Walter Smith wasn't chosen. One of them, Gustavus Horton, later to be mayor, was selected vice president.[26]

THE FIRST PUBLIC SCHOOLS?

The new board endorsed a tax-subsidized (though still tuition-supported) constellation (system) made up of a high school, grammar school, and primary school, all of which opened in the Barton building in November 1852. Four hundred students enrolled, a number that more than doubled by February of the following year. Mobilians demonstrated their support for the commissioners' actions in August of 1853, when they defeated opponents of the new board by an overwhelming 1,597 to 869 majority.[28]

By August 1854, the board had divided the city and county into school districts and reduced tuition. Perhaps to make up for a decrease in income from lowering fees, the commission sought and received legislative approval in 1856 for a local property tax. The board also appointed the first county superintendent

*Originally from Boston, **Gustavus Horton** was a leading cotton merchant and active in the city's civic associations, including the Samaritan Society. As a staunch supporter of the Union, he was politically acceptable to the anti-states' rights coalition. Although his views would land him in prison during the Civil War, Horton's reputation was such in the community and with the federal government that he went from jail to the mayor's office in 1867. Erwin Craighead tells the touching story of Horton coming out of prison in chains to greet his son marching by to join the Confederate forces. He was prepared to make great personal sacrifices to stand by his political convictions, a quality of character he surely brought to the school board.[27]*

of schools, an office soon abolished (in 1859) because it was felt that the principal of the boys' high school could do the job. The commissioners' reason for wanting an administrator is significant: they thought there were too many schools for them to oversee personally—without compensation.[29]

On the whole, the system that Willis Clark and his fellow commissioners adopted was quite similar to the one the previous board had in mind. Walter Smith to the contrary notwithstanding, both groups assumed that the objective of public schools was to educate the greatest number in the best manner and at the lowest cost. The new board was legitimate as well as effective, although there were differences among members from time to time, as in the dispute over the Creole public school. When Willis Clark tried to close the institution (or discontinue funding), Thaddeus Sanford rallied the board to defeat his recommendation.[30]

Members of the Creole Community (Probably from the Chastang Family)

Having faced determined opposition in two elections, the new commissioners were probably eager to demonstrate progress. As early as 1854, Willis Clark reported that the "means of acquiring a good education were brought, for the first time . . . within reach of all classes in the community." He was understandably proud, yet to date public education from the election of the new board in 1852 wouldn't be fully justifiable. Mobile had schools supported by the public long before then. The new board continued funding these schools, provided they would consent to supervision by the commissioners. As a matter of fact, when Barton Academy opened in 1852, William Merrill, the schoolmaster under the old regime, was there to greet the students.[31]

The new board's perception of its relationship to the public is reflected in an 1856 report on its organization and regulations. In publishing the report as well as a detailed schedule of when and where they would meet, the commissioners showed the community that they got the message about keeping the public informed. Board members continued visiting each school once every three months, and they began putting a notice in the newspapers before selecting principals. The commission also authorized communities outside the city to elect their own school boards annually.[32]

In response to the demand for access, primary and intermediate classes were free, though tuition at the grammar and high schools remained two dollars and four dollars a month, respectively. Public examinations were mandatory.

THE END OF PUBLIC EDUCATION BY FAITH-BASED INSTITUTIONS

The most significant difference between the Hazzard and Sanford boards was the elimination of subsidies for the public schools maintained by churches. Catholics objected most, sending a petition for continued funding to the board on October 30, 1852. The clergy was joined by one hundred and thirty-one citizens. They made an eloquent argument, pointing out that the church had organized and operated "Public Free Schools for both sexes" for seven years. For an appropriation of twelve hundred dollars per year, in addition to their own contributions, Catholics provided schools that enrolled six hundred students and instructed them "in the elements and the ordinary and most useful branches of a good practical English education." Two of the departments were for "the Creole or free colored children of both sexes." The church also sponsored "Orphan Schools," which had an average attendance of one hundred and thirty pupils.[33]

Catholics pointed out that all of these institutions were "free of expense to all who choose to attend them," which suggests that parents weren't required to prove they were poor and that the instruction wasn't intended exclusively for the indigent. Children being educated either by the church or under its sponsorship, including Creole children, studied side-by-side in the same school building—a new brick structure on the corner of Franklin and Conti Streets.

The petitioners claimed a portion of the education funds on the grounds that Catholics were taxpayers. They made up the bulk of Mobile's large Irish and German population and were well represented among the families of the original French and Spanish colonists.

School commissioners didn't agree with the petitioners' argument. They contended that the Catholic schools weren't subject to their supervision, which was the deciding factor in denying the request for funding. "Public" had come to mean "under the direction of an elected board of citizens." In 1854, the legislature adopted the same policy, perhaps influenced by events in Mobile. Public money could no longer be used to support schools under sectarian control.[34]

Mobile commission rules further discouraged instructors from teaching in private schools or tutoring by requiring approval from both the principal and the school board. These restrictions made a distinction between types of schools that hadn't been made as sharply before. Without support from the city, the free schools of the Protestant churches began to close, and enrollments in the Catholic institutions declined.[35]

Educational controversies are often masks for political disputes. In Mobile and elsewhere in the country, people were struggling with how citizenship should be understood. Were Americans to be defined by their religion or some other distinctive identity, as in some European countries? Or was citizenship to be based on what people had in common? Should there be Catholic citizens and Protestant citizens or just citizens? Americans, even those of the Catholic faith, eventually favored defining citizens simply as citizens—period. For instance, Catholics in Mobile took pains to present themselves, first and foremost, as citizens when petitioning the school board.

That stance was difficult to maintain at times because of prejudice and denominational rivalry. While the commission was deciding the fate of the church-based schools, the country, in general, and Mobile, in particular, were awash in a reaction against foreigners, especially Catholics. In that atmosphere, the city overturned a decision to have the Sisters of Charity manage the city-owned hospital.[36]

This bitter sectarian conflict was erupting across Alabama. Competition among the numerous church-sponsored institutions of higher education, as well as between these denominational colleges and the nonsectarian state university, was fierce. When the Baptist president of the University of

Alabama, Basil Manly, resigned, he charged his Methodist successor and the faculty with refusing to hire Baptists. Religious controversies were extremely divisive because the rhetoric was so intemperate. For instance, Presbyterians claimed that Baptists favored polygamy, and Baptists responded by criticizing churches that practiced infant baptism on the grounds that babies can't possibly be aware of their sins, much less repent or make professions of faith. No wonder some ministers began preaching tolerance![37]

As these controversies swirled around them, Mobile's school commissioners faced serious financial pressures without the resources of the churches. Even when revenue increased to $17,658, they weren't able to provide fully free instruction. Expenses totaled $32,429, so tuition, though much lower than before, had to make up most of the difference. Still, the board appears to have been making progress toward its goal of providing the best possible instruction with the most prudent use of public funds.

Willis Clark reported that the quality of education in the public schools was such that the "rich soon sought them for their children." And declining enrollments in the expensive private schools gave the public institutions a more economically diverse constituency. Still, the legacy of "for the poor exclusively" continued to haunt public education. Critics assumed that instruction in what they stigmatized as charity institutions

Writing about a controversy in antebellum New York that was similar to the one that erupted in Mobile, Diane Ravitch says that two definitions of public schools were at issue in the dispute over control, which was larger than the question of religious instruction. One side argued that the common school "should be whatever the community around it wanted it to be." In other words, if a community, through its school board, decided that all children should learn the tenets of a particular denomination, so be it. If Protestants or Catholics were in the majority, then they had the right to set the policy. The other side held that the school is the instrument of the state and "should neither suppress opinions nor hold any of its own." In other words, the church and state must be absolutely separate; the state must be neutral and free from any partisanship.[38]

I would add that different concepts of democracy were also at stake in New York and Mobile. As Ravitch noted, one notion is that the majority rules and the minority must defer. But another concept of democracy is based on the principle that majority rule must never be total; minority rights have to be respected. Everyone has to have a place at the table. According to the first view, it is perfectly acceptable to have either nonsectarian or faith-based public schools, whichever, as long as the majority agrees. According to the second, even if a community were to choose nonsectarian schools, a minority, say Catholics, would have a right to their own schools—perhaps even to public funding. That seems to be what Mobile Catholics were advocating, without success.

would necessarily be inferior, an assumption that dogged the public schools even as they multiplied. Reversing it became central to the agenda of a new group of educational leaders in Alabama who began to emerge in the 1850s, Clark among them.[39]

IN COMPARISON

Mobile is usually cited as the place where public education began, but without detracting from what happened there, it is important to note that similar efforts had been under way for some time in other cities—Montgomery, for instance. An 1821 editorial in the Montgomery *Republican* pointed with pride to the number of homes and places of business being built, as well as to the efforts being made to provide for public worship and schooling. Actually, instruction had been available even earlier. The William Ashley family and their friends employed Neil Blue to open a school; he located it in 1819 across from the jail and added to his income by serving as warden. Professionals also did some teaching in order to supplement their regular fees. Dr. Samuel W. Patterson, because his medical practice had failed to attract enough patients, began teaching in 1818.[40]

Mathew P. Blue's papers testify to the importance of education after 1821. He reported more than a dozen school openings, announcements of lotteries for education, advertisements of scholars offering to teach various subjects, and lists of schoolbooks for sale. As in Mobile, entrepreneurial teachers apparently weren't enough to meet the demand, so the town council took a hand by employing Jonathan Mayhew to open a school in 1821. That same year, the state legislature authorized Clement Freeny, William Graham, and Ebenezer Washburn to conduct a lottery to pay for a school building. The lottery may not have been successful, but in 1827, the Milton Academy opened in the Masonic Hall, with Mayhew as the teacher. It appears to have been the community's principal school until succeeded by the Franklin Institute, which was organized by Professor A. S. Vigus (who moved to Mobile in 1836 to teach at Barton Academy).

Montgomery citizens continued to press for a school building large enough to accommodate both male and female departments, and the township school commissioners (Neil Blue, Wade Allen, and Charles L. Gilmer) eventually succeeded in erecting one in 1840 at the corner of Montgomery and Molton Streets. It was called the Montgomery Academy and was later referred to as a public free school. By 1852, Montgomery had experienced a groundswell of support for more public education. Within two years, a free school supported by sixteenth-section funds and local revenue opened. And, in 1856, the county selected A. B. McWhorter as its first superintendent of public schools.

NOTES TO CHAPTER 7

[1] In addition to the sources on Mobile's history already cited, for Mobile's economic and political climate in the 1850s, I used Alan Smith Thompson's "Mobile, Alabama, 1850-1861: Economic, Political, Physical, and Population Characteristics" (Ph.D. diss., University of Alabama, 1979), pp. 84-87, 115, 127-172 and Ralph E. Poore, Jr.'s *Alabama's Enterprising Newspaper: The Mobile Press Register and Its Forebears, 1813-1991* (Mobile Municipal Archives, Mobile, Alabama, photocopy, 1992), pp. 44-45, 55-56, 59-61. William Garrett's *Reminiscences of Public Men in Alabama, for Thirty Years* (Atlanta: Plantation Publishing Company, 1872), p. 408 was the best source for biographies.

[2] Willis G. Clark, *History of Education in Alabama, 1702-1889,* Contributions to American Educational History, no. 8 (Washington, D.C.: Government Printing Office, 1889), p. 221.

[3] Mobile School Board Minutes, 1845-1852, 17 June 1845, pp. 3-4. The conversation about the financial crisis was reported in the minutes through page 44. The rejection of the Spring Hill appeal is on page 37.

[4] Mobile School Board Minutes, 1845-1852, 15 December 1849 and 29 August 1850, pp. 45-46.

[5] Thomas McAdory Owen reported on Peter Hamilton's career in *History of Alabama and Dictionary of Alabama Biography,* vol. 3 (Chicago: S. J. Clarke Publishing Company, 1921), pp. 734-735.

[6] A number of sources mentioned Walter Smith: R. P. Vail, *Mobile Directory, or Strangers' Guide, for 1842* (Mobile: Dade and Thompson, 1842), p. 53; Poore, *Alabama's Enterprising Newspaper,* p. 38; and Caldwell Delaney, ed., *Craighead's Mobile: Being the Fugitive Writings of Erwin S. Craighead and Frank Craighead* (Mobile: Haunted Bookshop, 1968), p. 188.

[7] Peter Hamilton's vision of public education and Walter Smith's plan to finance the schools with proceeds from selling board property were in the book of the school board minutes for 1845 to 1852, 4 September 1850, 14 December 1850, 6 January 1851, and 13 January 1851, pp. 48, 52-53, 56.

[8] Mobile School Board Minutes, 1845-1852, 6 January 1851 and 13 January 1851, pp. 53, 55-56.

[9] Richard B. Redwood, Jr., *The Redwood Family of Mobile* (Mobile: Willowbrook Press, 1993), pp. 20-28.

[10] Mobile School Board Minutes, 1845-1852, 19 February 1851, p. 61.

[11] Mobile School Board Minutes, 1845-1852, 19 February 1851 and 26 February 1851, pp. 61-63.

[12] The work of the Mobile school board under C. C. Hazzard was covered in the minute book of 1845-1852, 2 April 1851, 23 April 1851, 16 July 1851, 8 October 1851, and 6 November 1851, pp. 64-66, 69-73.

[13] *Mobile Daily Advertiser,* 4 December 1851 and Mobile School Board Minutes, 1845-1852, 6 November 1851, p. 75.

Monthly tuition of $5 was typical in Mobile for a school term of 10 months (the length of the Barton term). That amounted to $50 for each child per year. Since families of working people usually had several children, the cost could have been $100 or more. Not surprisingly, income to pay this expense varied by occupation. Men and women producing turpentine earned about $200 per year; machinists averaged around $600. The two men who distilled liquor divided $2,400 in expenditures for labor. Even with these differences, the conclusion is the same: education would have taken an unacceptably large percentage of the income of hundreds of families.

The data on the workforce comes from *Manufactures of the United States in 1860; Compiled from the Original Returns of the Eighth Census, under the Direction of the Secretary of the Interior* (Washington, D.C.: Government Printing Office, 1865), pp. 8-9; from Thompson, "Mobile, Alabama, 1850-1861," particularly Chapters 6-8; and from Harriet Amos, *Cotton City: Urban Development in Antebellum Mobile* (University: University of Alabama Press, 1985), pp. 80-85.

[14] A member of the workforce wrote in the *Alabama Planter* that children were poorly served by "the little charity schools in the city." Harriet Amos, *Cotton City: Urban Development in Antebellum Mobile* (University: University of Alabama Press, 1985), p. 186 quoting the *Alabama Planter,* 18 August 1851.

[15] Mobile School Board Minutes, 1845-1852, 6 November 1851, pp. 75-76.

[16] Mobile School Board Minutes, 1845-1852, 6 November 1851, p. 76.

[17] Mobile School Board Minutes, 1845-1852, 6 November

1851, p. 75 and Amos, *Cotton City,* p. 186 quoting the *Mobile Advertiser,* 15 August 1852.

18 Mobile School Board Minutes, 1845-1852, 6 November 1851, pp. 76-77.

19 Mobile School Board Minutes, 1845-1852, 6 November 1851 and 19 November 1851, pp. 77-81.

20 Clark, *History of Education,* p. 221.

21 The account of the dispute over the proposal to sell Barton Academy was taken from Clark, *History of Education,* p. 221; Nita Katharine Pyburn, "Mobile Public Schools before 1860," *Alabama Review* 11 (July 1958): 185; and Alabama General Assembly, *Acts,* 3d biennial sess., 1851-1852 (Montgomery: Brittan and DeWolf, 1852), pp. 463-464.

22 More on the controversy and the combatants is in Willis Brewer, *Alabama: Her History, Resources, War Record and Public Men, from 1540 to 1872* (1872; reprint, Spartanburg, S.C.: Reprint Company, 1975), pp. 397-399; Owen, *History of Alabama,* pp. 336, 339; Peter J. Hamilton, *Mobile of the Five Flags: The Story of the River Basin and Coast about Mobile from the Earliest Times to the Present* (Mobile: Gill Printing Company, 1913), pp. 229, 266; and Poore, *Alabama's Enterprising Newspaper,* p. 61.

23 Poore, *Alabama's Enterprising Newspaper,* pp. 60-61.

24 Weeks included a detailed description of the 1852 debate in *History of Public School Education in Alabama,* U.S. Bureau of Education Bulletin, 1915, no. 12 (Washington, D.C.: Government Printing Office, 1915), p. 44. Unfortunately, the microfilm copies of the *Advertiser* for July 1852 at the Mobile Public Library are illegible.

25 Stephen Weeks said that the proponents of selling Barton were charged with violating the 1826 school law in his *History of Public School Education,* pp. 44-45. Legislation setting out the mission of the Mobile schools is in Alabama General Assembly, *Acts,* 7th annual sess., 1825 (Cahawba: William B. Allen, 1826), pp. 35-36 and Alabama, *Acts,* 3d biennial sess., 1851-1852, pp. 463-464.

26 Other new members of the school board were Sidney E. Collins, C. LeBaron, R. L. Watkins, and J. M. Withers. Those held over from the old board, in addition to Horton, were Jacob Magee, D. C. Sampson, and M. R. Evans. Mobile School Board Minutes, 1845-1852, 6 September 1852, pp. 94-96 and Clark, *History of Education,* p. 223.

27 Erwin Craighead, *From Mobile's Past: Sketches of Memorable People and Events* (Mobile: Powers Printing Company, 1925), p. 253 and Delaney, *Craighead's Mobile,* p. 109.

28 Clark, *History of Education,* pp. 224-225.

29 The new board's concept of public education was reflected in Mobile School Board Minutes, 1845-1852, 26 October 1852, pp. 120-126. Willis Clark, a member of that board, put his recollections in his *History of Education,* p. 225. Weeks's *History of Public School Education,* pp. 46-47 and Amos's *Cotton City,* pp. 190-191 also commented on the new commissioners.

30 Board minutes from late 1855 to early 1856 recorded the controversy over the education of Creoles and its eventual resolution. Interestingly, during this same period, the board approved a Creole school for the Chastang's Bluff community. (This was the school where Zeno Chastang, Jr., was a trustee.) Christopher Andrew Nordmann, "Free Negroes in Mobile County, Alabama" (Ph.D. diss., University of Alabama, 1990), pp. 208-209 and Amos, *Cotton City,* pp. 189-190.

At roughly the same time that Willis Clark was trying to discontinue the Creole school in Mobile, other areas of the country were also debating the education of African Americans. In Iowa, with only 271 people of African descent, the state superintendent of education said that "'colored persons have no claims whatever to any part of the School Fund' because they 'are not and cannot become citizens of the state under the existing laws.'" Advocates of education for black Iowans and Native Americans did succeed in leaving this issue to the discretion of local school boards. Part of the political pressure came from the states first "colored convention" in 1857. Carroll Engelhardt, "The Ideology and Politics of Iowa Common School Reform, 1854-1860," *The Annals of Iowa* 56 (summer 1997): 219.

31 Mobile School Board Minutes, 1845-1852, 4 October 1852 and 9 October 1852, pp. 104-106. (Daniel F. Merrill was first offered the schoolmaster's job but declined.) Clark, *History of Education,* p. 226.

32 *Organization of the Board of Mobile School Commissioners, and Regulations of the Public Schools, for the City and County of Mobile* (Mobile: Farrow, Stokes and Dennett, 1856).

33 Mobile School Board Minutes, 1845-1852, 30 October 1852, p. 126. A typed copy of the Catholics' petition to restore public funding to their schools is included between

pages 126 and 127 of the board minutes.

The petition of the Catholic Church on behalf of its Free Public Schools was one of the subjects in Oscar Hugh Lipscomb's "The Administration of Michael Portier, Vicar Apostolic of Alabama and the Floridas, 1825-1829, and First Bishop of Mobile, 1829-1859" (Ph.D. diss., Catholic University of America, 1963), pp. 232, 234-236. Alan Smith Thompson described the Catholics of Mobile in "Mobile, Alabama, 1850-1861," pp. 153-158.

Catholic schools had a legitimate claim to serving the public interest because they taught "the moral values incumbent on Republican citizens," according to Nikola Baumgarten, who wrote about "Education and Democracy in Frontier St. Louis: The Society of the Sacred Heart," which appeared in the *History of Education Quarterly* 34 (summer 1994): 172-173. St. Louis needed free schools in 1823 for its growing population, and the Society of the Sacred Heart was the first to respond, long before the first public schools were established in 1838.

[34] The controversy over the Catholics' Free Public Schools was spread over the school board minutes from August 2, 1852, to August 31, 1857.

[35] Amos, *Cotton City,* p. 191.

[36] Thompson, "Mobile, Alabama, 1850-1861," pp. 159-160.

[37] Sectarian rivalry may have influenced the prohibition against public money going to church-sponsored schools. Minnie Boyd described this conflict in her study of Alabama in the 1850s, and Wayne Flynt discussed it from the perspective of the Baptist Church, where theological differences actually split the denomination. Wayne Flynt, *Alabama Baptists: Southern Baptists in the Heart of Dixie* (Tuscaloosa: University of Alabama Press, 1998), pp. 76-85 and Minnie

Clare Boyd, *Alabama in the Fifties: A Social Study* (New York: Columbia University Press, 1931), pp. 138-139.

[38] Diane Ravitch, *The Great School Wars: A History of the New York City Public Schools* (New York: Basic Books, 1988), pp. 61-62.

[39] Amos, *Cotton City,* p. 191 and Clark, *History of Education,* pp. 225-226.

[40] On pages 36-37 of his papers, Mathew P. Blue quoted the *Montgomery Republican,* 17 February 1821. Mathew P. Blue, "History of Montgomery" in Papers, 1824-1884, Alabama Department of Archives and History, Montgomery, Ala.

The legislation authorizing the Montgomery town council to establish an academy appeared in Alabama General Assembly, *Acts,* 3d annual sess., 1821 (Cahawba: William B. Allen, 1822), p. 76 and Alabama General Assembly, *Acts,* 7th annual sess., 1825 (Cahawba: William B. Allen, 1826), p. 60. Also see Annie Beatrice Barnett's "A History of Education in the City of Montgomery, Alabama, from 1818 to 1860" (master's thesis, Alabama Polytechnic Institute, 1949), pp. 26-27, 74-76, 79, 81.

Teachers in Montgomery were listed in Mathew P. Blue's "A Brief History of Montgomery," in *City Directory and History of Montgomery, Alabama, with a Summary of Events in that History, Calendarically Arranged, besides Other Valuable and Useful Information* (Montgomery: T. C. Bingham, 1878), pp. 10, 22, 29, 41.

Clanton Ware Williams wrote about public education in Montgomery in his book *The Early History of Montgomery and Incidentally of the State of Alabama* (University: Confederate Publishing Company, 1979), pp. 47, 59-62, 65, 87-88.

Chapter 8

THE PEOPLE'S VICTORY:
THE FREE PUBLIC SCHOOL ACT OF 1854

I N 1854, ALABAMA'S general assembly was poised to enact its first major piece of school legislation since 1840. Governor Collier had made the case, and the Robinson committees had endorsed it. Citizens hoped to have the funds needed to make schooling free, or at least more accessible. Reformers expected to put the state government in the educational driver's seat.

THE GENERAL ASSEMBLY RESPONDS

Implications of the votes of Mobile citizens in 1852 and 1853 surely weren't lost on the capital. The legislature of 1853 to 1854 asked the house education committee to draft a bill for a comprehensive public school system and selected the coeditor of the *Mobile Daily Register,* Alexander Meek (now in the Mobile County legislative delegation), to head the group. Meek was a man of considerable accomplishment. A powerful orator, he was also physically imposing (six feet four inches and two hundred and forty pounds). By the time he took on the legislative assignment, he had practiced law, volunteered for the war against the Seminole Indians, served briefly as probate judge in Tuscaloosa and as attorney general of the state (both appointed positions), edited a newspaper (*Flag of the Union*) as well as a literary magazine (the *Southron*), and held the position of assistant secretary of the treasury during the Polk administration. He went from that post to become federal attorney for the southern district of Alabama, which induced him to move to Mobile. Yet the work Meek probably thought defined him best was his poetry. He made something of a literary splash in 1855 by telling one of the defining stories of southwestern Alabama—about William Weatherford of Tensaw, the "Red Eagle." He had Jacksonian and, later, states' rights leanings. And, although not a parent, he was one of the community leaders who had championed public education locally.[1]

The legislative battle was, for the most part, over when Meek's committee began to draft its bill; the people were impatient and representatives knew it. Finding the right rationale and the rhetoric to use wouldn't be a problem; it had been rehearsed for decades.[2]

The genius of the Meek bill was in resolving financial disputes that had plagued the legislature since 1823. It bridged the gap between those who favored consolidation of the sixteenth-section funds and those who opposed by compensating townships with valueless land from a separate education account. Meek's committee estimated that this would require only $148,000 more than the $80,000 of the land-grant income already in hand. The amount was considerably less than the $300,000 to $500,000 the senate's education committee had projected in 1847. Meek pointed out that the proposal was quite reasonable (some might have called it parsimonious) compared to school budgets of $2 million in New York, $1.5 million in Massachusetts, $1 million in Pennsylvania, and $450,000 in Louisiana.[3]

Avoiding controversy over a new tax, the committee recommended three sources of funds: a direct appropriation from the state treasury of $100,000, interest on both a federal refund in 1836 and a land grant in 1848, plus tax revenue from banks and railroads. Even though the legislators anticipated that this income would provide a free primary education for every child, the proposal stipulated that, when absolutely necessary, students could be charged a modest tuition. The plan wasn't based on the proposition that parents were fully responsible for education or that state resources were only for the poor. It simply assumed that schools

Alexander Beaufort Meek

receiving parental support were no less public than those that didn't.

Counties could supplement their portions of the state fund with their own school taxes. (It is clear that many did this since county expenditures increased significantly after 1854.) Unlike previous laws, however, the Meek bill did not require matching local funds. It authorized a one-mill property tax for education but regulated the way citizens could spend their own local funds. The bill stipulated that at least 50 percent of the county tax revenue had to be used for teachers' salaries. Since state funds were also earmarked for salaries, counties had to build schools, furnish libraries, and meet all remaining expenses with only half of their revenue. State control had arrived.[4]

Centralized direction implied centralized administration. Following the advice of Porter and Collier, the committee proposed that the general assembly appoint a state superintendent—though not a state school board made up of citizens as some other legislatures were requiring. While the Meek plan shifted some authority from the townships to the counties, communities remained in charge of the day-to-day operation of their schools through local trustees.

VOTES FOR AND AGAINST

Both chambers passed the free school bill by large majorities, prompting Meek to say that it was favored by "the great body of the people," not by a particular faction. The extent and diversity of the support was reflected in the house, where the bill was approved by an overwhelming seventy-one to twelve majority. In the senate, the victory was twenty-two to eight. Most of the opponents were from counties dominated by planters and located in either the Black Belt or the Tennessee Valley. Their schools were already relatively well financed.[5]

Votes for the free school bill came from legislators representing the hill counties of northern Alabama and the counties of the southeastern Wiregrass. People in these areas tended to be yeoman farmers rather than affluent planters, and they had championed public education for some time. These counties typically had few schools, meager sixteenth-section resources, and very little taxable wealth. They needed state revenue. Most delegations from the southwestern counties also voted for the bill.

SOUTHWEST LEGISLATIVE VOTES ON THE FREE PUBLIC SCHOOL BILL		
Legislator	District	Vote
In the House of Representatives		
William Wilkins	Baldwin	Did not vote
Edward McCall	Choctaw	Yes
E. S. Thornton	Clarke	Yes
J. Bell, Jr.	Mobile	Yes
A. B. Meek	Mobile	Yes
R. B. Owen	Mobile	Did not vote
Percy Walker	Mobile	Yes
Noah A. Agee	Monroe	Yes
G. W. Gordy	Washington	Did not vote
In the Senate		
James S. Dickinson	Baldwin, Clarke, Monroe	Yes
William Woodward	Choctaw, Sumter, Washington	Yes
T. B. Bethea	Mobile	Yes

Because some wealthy planters objected to the act while less affluent farmers generally endorsed it, it is tempting to conclude that the political alignment was based on economic interests. But while legislators opposing the school bill came from counties with favorable ratios between students and school revenue, the fact is that the overwhelming majority of those for the Meek bill represented counties that already had substantial income for their schools, even more than the state average. Though the new legislation protected property owners by capping tax rates, support of the 1854 act suggests that they were not unwilling to help the poorer counties.[6]

With this vote, Alabamians were saying that they saw education as a public good which shouldn't be less available to those who had fewer dollars. The reasoning went like this: if a county had more money to spend on law enforcement or the courts, should its people have greater legal protection or surer justice than those in a poor county? No! Public goods have to be equally available to all, regardless of economic happenstance. And institutions that serve the commonweal are entitled to equal levels of support.

Why did Alabamians come to this conclusion? Why care about the education of someone they may not even know in a community not their own? Why do public goods have to be equally available to everyone? The answer was that a democratic society has a vested interest in the well-being of every citizen because every citizen is, in some way, dependent on every other citizen. Champions of free public schooling used a story from antiquity to make this point. No one knows, they argued, when a citizen, like Cincinnatus of Roman legend, may be called to leave the plow and save the republic. Educators added a corollary: parents who fail to educate their children fail the community, not just their families.[7]

I don't imagine that every Alabamian went through such elaborate reasoning in deciding that education was important. Yet many who may not have known about Cincinnatus had some appreciation of the extent to which they were dependent on each other.

Alexis de Tocqueville explained this sense of interdependence as self-interest rightly or well understood. Americans, he observed, "almost always know how to combine their own well-being" with the well-being of others. Knowing how "to combine" doesn't require people to go so far as making the interests of others their own or sacrificing unselfishly for the benefit of all. It just means that citizens have to see the relationship between their concerns and those of others. That was possible in America, even though people sometimes abandoned themselves, Tocqueville also noted, "to the disinterested and unreflective sparks that are natural to man."[8]

A NETWORK OF STRANGE BEDFELLOWS

Perhaps because it was self-interest rightly understood, the public school movement benefited from converging purposes and was relatively immune to political rivalries that divided the state on other matters. Except when public schools and the state university competed for scarce resources, the legislative advocates of free schooling had different though complementary attitudes and objectives. Optimists believed that a democracy had to have—and could have—informed citizens. Pessimists felt threatened by the masses and feared that disorder and lawlessness would undermine moral standards. (Actually, most representatives were probably both optimistic and pessimistic.) A good many legislators may simply have wanted better schools for their communities. Others were probably less interested in education than in economic development. Nonetheless, all of these concerns led to one goal—expansion of free schooling.

Significantly, the cause of public education doesn't appear to have been affected by competition between different sections of Alabama. Northern and southern counties that vied for railroads and manufacturing facilities joined forces on public education. Similarly, planters and farmers were both represented in the free school camp, evidence that planters were no more unanimous in their thinking about education than farmers were.

Political parties had another kind of rivalry, fierce at times. Yet it didn't necessarily dictate the alignments on education. The state legislature could be a hotbed of partisan politics, with Whigs on one side and Democrats on the other (nothing new there). Whigs were quite visible on committees dealing with education and other social reforms, perhaps, as Mills Thornton explained, because of a fear of the unlettered—or because Democrats saw to it that Whigs were placed on committees where their elitist views would be exposed to an anti-elite electorate. Yet some Whigs vigorously opposed public education, just as some Democrats often led the reforms. Most of the senators who voted against the Free Public School Act of 1854 were, in fact, Whigs, while its author, Meek, was a states' rights Democrat.[9]

THE POWER OF AN ENGAGED PUBLIC

Though difficult to document, I think the major reason the cause of public education succeeded in the legislature was its resonance with the day-to-day concerns, hopes, and fears of people. I don't believe Alabamians were persuaded to work for free schools by their leaders; they came to the conclusion that education was a means to the end they held dear as they deliberated among themselves in the ordinary places where people normally congregated and in formal meetings like those in Mobile's Franklin Hall. The people in the southwest (and Alabamians generally) supported the cause of education because it was their cause. And it was their cause because the schools were their schools, serving their purposes. I infer that from the breadth of support citizens gave public education. This broad commitment was unmistakable in 1854.

It would be understandable to assume that the public schools were born of grand ideals because, as I have noted, education is bound up with the sacred values of democracy—equity, justice, freedom. This might encourage people to try to rally support for schools today by repeating time-honored arguments about how much our way of life depends on public education. While true, that probably won't be an effective strategy now; I don't think it ever was. Certainly people in the nineteenth century responded to democratic values; legislators were particularly fond of talking about them. The ideals had considerable political magnetism and, like flags, attracted politicians. The citizenry as a whole, however, may not have been drawn together primarily by lofty precepts; everyday imperatives were more basic, more immediate and, possibly, more influential. That said, commonplace concerns and grand visions often complemented each other; for instance, the principle of equity is rooted in the ordinary desire to be treated fairly. Ideals are most powerful when they reinforce, and are reinforced by, public imperatives.

SUMMING UP THE REASONS

Broad support for free schools, evident in both the 1854 law and in the growth of these schools before then, mirrored the wide range of reasons for treating these public-serving institutions as a public responsibility. The rationale can be broken down into the usual moral, social, economic, and political components used to categorize nearly everything that happens in society. The reasons can also be divided into those that appealed to communities and those that were important to legislators—provided no one lost sight of how much the logic of public education flowed from many streams into a mighty river.

Settlements and towns wanted schools because they were concerned about their way of life and eager to gain a competitive advantage over other communities. Add to that the need to prepare a new generation of local leaders. Frontier society lacked law and order, and was prone to violence. Settlers hoped to curb vice by promoting what Ephraim Kirby called moral and political virtues. This trend suggests that *a community wasn't just a place for schools, it was a reason.*

Virtue had a particular meaning for people like Kirby. It had less to do with desirable personal traits, like prudence and frugality (which served people's individual interests), than with traits that made for responsible members of a democratic society. Public virtue meant concern for the well-being of the community and willingness to participate in public life—to do one's civic duty without gaining anything personally.[10]

Public virtue was closely associated with another prized trait—benevolence. This shouldn't be confused with what we call "charity," which prompts gratitude and, in some cases, breeds dependence. Benevolence is not helping the less fortunate; it is being answerable for our conduct toward others. Nineteenth-century America assumed that everyone has the capacity to share the feelings of others, a capacity embedded in human nature. The social reciprocity that results from benevolence was thought to be the force that held democratic society together, replacing the raw power that monarchies use to unite their subjects.

The opposite of virtue and benevolence is criminality. In antebellum Alabama, civic leaders and ministers alike made the case that ignorance leads to crime as surely as education leads to virtue. Editorials drove the point home by comparing the high number of convictions in Spain, where "not more than one in thirty can even read," with the low number in Scotland, "celebrated for learning and religion." Legislators like Pleasant May had a great deal to say about public education as an antidote to vice. Schools had both a progressive mandate to promote virtue and a conservative mandate to guard against its absence.[11]

Social reasons for having public schools included an aversion to the English class system, a fear of any kind of privilege that could give some people power over others, and an instinctive sense that antagonism between different segments of white society would mean trouble. Recall the argument in Mobile that common schooling was needed to create friendly relationships among the different classes of the community. Some journals, like the *Southern Free Press* in 1830, went so far as to promote public education on the grounds that it would have a leveling effect—that it would break down barriers between ordinary folk and would-be aristocrats.

The Alabama general assembly doesn't appear to have shared community concerns about social relationships as much as those about sixteenth-section disparities. Even so, the 1854 law

Public relations campaigns promoted free common schools and, in New York, advocates sang about equal opportunity, as in this stanza:

Then free as air should knowledge be —
    And open wisdom's portal,
To every thirsty, earnest soul,
    Who longs to be immortal.
Here rich and poor stand side by side,
    To quaff life's purest chalice,
And never dream that deathless names
    Belong to cot or palace.[12]

made clear that public schools weren't exclusively for the poor, though the need for tuition meant that there had to be a policy for those who couldn't pay.

Many legislators thought that popular education was key to the state's economic development. That was clear in references to schools as a form of internal improvement, as essential as a rail line to the Great Lakes. From the perspective of communities, public schools served the economy by increasing real estate values. Property owners, large and small, benefited.

I have already commented on the principal political argument legislators used in advocating support for public education: Free people intent on governing themselves had to be educated in order to carry out the responsibilities of citizenship. Communities took a similar position; they had to have citizens willing and able to maintain the local institutions that provided structure and order—schools, churches, civic associations, courts, municipal governments.

Finally, no summary of why Alabamians established schools is complete without accounting for what is less a reason than an impulse—a humanitarian bent to perfect society. This gave rise to the belief that all people have to have schools that will promote their moral and intellectual development, so they can reach their highest destiny as human beings. From this perspective, education is a right—one that the state has to see is exercised because its own well-being depends on it. (Editors of the *South Western Baptist* were especially eloquent on this point.) Only a few disagreed with these objectives; the most difficult challenge was to decide on the best means to diffuse knowledge.[13]

Recall the history of the effort to diffuse learning. In the colonial era and through Jefferson's time, many thought that the proper use of scarce resources was to aid the indigent. Free schools meant schools primarily for the poor. Later, citizens and local governments established schools they intended to be common but provided tuition subsidies for those who needed them. (That practice was something like "means testing" today, which is basing government benefits on the income level of recipients in order to ensure that money goes to those most in need.)

Alabama didn't create a state school fund exclusively for the poor, though in 1838 Mobile had set aside a school for children whose parents couldn't pay tuition. However practical and well intentioned, giving priority to the poor conflicted with democratic sensibilities. With pressures likely coming from farmers and other working folk, Alabamians decided that public schools had to be available to all citizens on the same basis and that the charity stereotype would prevent these institutions from ever being good schools. They made a conscious trade-off in having schools free to all because they worried that students wouldn't value what they had not paid for. Alabamians chose to take the risk.

How much instruction the public should pay for was another thorny issue. Almost everyone agreed that citizens should have access to the three Rs, but the final decision, which could be seen developing in the Mobile controversy of 1851 to 1852, was that everyone should be able to learn as much as they were capable of learning.

Alabamians also had to decide who would fund and control their schools. If education was for the benefit of individuals, it made perfectly good sense for parents to pay. If education was to benefit a community or a state as a whole, everyone should pay. Weighing the alternatives, Alabamians opted for having the public bear the costs. There was a particularly strong feeling that the wealthy should not be excused on the grounds that they would educate their own children—nor should members of denominations that had their own schools. This principle was adopted both in communities and in the legislature.

Using tax revenue raised still another issue: Should income be taken from the haves and given to the have-nots? Abrogating the "sacred rights" of property ownership was unacceptable, so the township revenue couldn't be redistributed. But using county taxes and state revenues (which came largely from the rich) was apparently accepted without much fuss, despite taxation being unpopular. The legislature ended up reducing a county's state revenue by the amount of its land-grant income; that was actually a way of equalizing resources.

All in all, Alabamians in the first half of the nineteenth century appear to have understood public education much as it was understood in other states.

NOTES TO CHAPTER 8

[1] A. B. Meek had quite a varied career. Sources on his life included Herman Clarence Nixon, *Alexander Beaufort Meek, Poet, Orator, Journalist, Historian, Statesman*, Alabama Polytechnic Institute History Series (Auburn: Alabama Polytechnic Institute, 1910), pp. 1-53; Margaret Gillis Figh, "Alexander Beaufort Meek: Pioneer Man of Letters," *Alabama Historical Quarterly* (summer 1940): 127-151; and Thomas McAdory Owen, *History of Alabama and Dictionary of Alabama Biography*, vol. 4 (Chicago: S. J. Clarke Publishing Company, 1921), pp. 1183-1184. George G. Smith's *The History of Georgia Methodism from 1786 to 1866* (Atlanta: A. B. Caldwell, 1913), pp. 113, 287 described the influence of Meek's father and of Meek's childhood experiences.

[2] The Free Public School bill was drafted in the house's committee on education (1853-1854); it consisted of Representatives Walter Cook (Lowndes), Daniel J. Fox (Wilcox), James M. Greene (Jackson), Bolling Hall (Autauga), Thomas P. Lawrence (Shelby), R. B. Lindsey (Franklin), A. B. Meek (Mobile), H. C. Sanford (Cherokee), and N. G. Shelly (Talladega). Alabama General Assembly, *House Journal*, 4th biennial sess., 1853-1854 (Montgomery: Brittan and Blue, 1854), pp. 3-4, 57, 93.

[3] In his proposal for a system of public education in Alabama, A. B. Meek wanted public schools to have at least 4 grades, beginning with the primary level, which would teach children between the ages of 5 and 18. His plan to use a special fund to deal with sixteenth-section inequities was similar to the solution approved in the appropriation bills of 1839 and 1840 (though never implemented). Compensation through a state fund was a popular remedy in other states (Ohio, Indiana, and Illinois) that had sixteenth sections given directly to their townships. Alabama, *House Journal*, 4th biennial sess., 1853-1854, pp. 307, 309-310 and Alabama General Assembly, *Acts*, 4th biennial sess., 1853-1854 (Montgomery: Brittan and Blue, 1854), pp. 8-9, 16-17.

[4] Alabama, *Acts*, 4th biennial sess., 1853-1854, pp. 9-12, 17-18.

[5] Alabama, *House Journal*, 4th biennial sess., 1853-1854, pp. 3-4, 444-445 and Alabama General Assembly, *Senate Journal*, 4th biennial sess., 1853-1854 (Montgomery: Brittan and Blue, 1854), pp. 3-4, 301-302.

[6] To see if the vote reflected opposition to education per se in or to public schools in particular, my colleagues (April Lanzilotti and Melinda Gilmore) and I, with considerable help from the foundation's economic historian, Randy Nielsen, selected 19 counties to represent those with considerable wealth from agriculture. We used several criteria to select these counties: terrain and soil type, the cash value of the agricultural land, and distribution of slaves. Admittedly, the designations we made are somewhat arbitrary. Counties had both plantation owners and farmers who lived side by side. Even counties with more farmers had some sections that favored large plantations (broad plains of fertile soil) while the terrain and soil fertility in the other parts would only support small farms. Clarke County, for example, tended to have its plantations in river bottom lands, especially along the Alabama River, while the southwestern pinelands were settled by yeoman farmers. The 19 counties were in the center of the state in what is called the Black Belt and in the fertile valley of the Tennessee River to the north. The information used in selecting this group came primarily from Neal G. Lineback, ed., *Atlas of Alabama* (University: University of Alabama Press, 1973), pp. 5-6, 9, 17, 26 and Lewy Dorman, *Party Politics in Alabama from 1850 through 1860* (1935; reprint, Tuscaloosa: University of Alabama Press, 1995), pp. 215-126, 222.

Conclusions about support for the 1854 law are based on analyses that compared the voting by county with 1) the value of sixteenth-section endowments in 1851 (per school-age whites), 2) the percentage of students enrolled, 3) the total number of schools of all types, and 4) the number of public schools. Several counties with the largest endowments (Limestone, Lawrence, and Morgan) in the Tennessee Valley and a number in the Black Belt (Autauga, Dallas, Montgomery, Russell, and Wilcox) voted solidly for the public school appropriations even though their schools were better financed than most. These were all counties with a large number of plantations. Lauderdale, which was in this group but had the smallest endowment, also voted "yes." Seven other plantation counties split their votes (Barbour, Franklin, Lowndes, Macon, Marengo, Perry, and Sumter). Only 2 out of this group of 19 totally opposed the bill: Butler and Greene. Apparently voting against their self-interest, Barbour and Franklin had endowments below the state averages. Three other counties with even smaller endowments (Bibb, Jackson, and Shelby) had at least one legislator who opposed the obvious advantage of state funding. The assumption that counties just voted their pocketbooks is difficult to accept at face value.

Of this group of 19, 2 counties voted against the public school legislation, 8 split their votes, and 9 gave the bill full support. We compared these votes with other 1850 county data showing the number and percentage enrolled in all schools as well as the percentage and number of public schools. Total enrollment suggests that planter counties voting against the public school legislation were as committed to educating their children as those that voted for the 1854 bill. And the overwhelming majority of these youngsters attended public, not private, institutions. The opposing counties had no more land-grant income to support their instruction than others in this group. The two solidly against the 1854 law actually had a higher percentage of children enrolled than the other planter counties, though they had a slightly smaller percentage in public schools.

Sources were Alabama, *House Journal,* 4th biennial sess., 1853-1854, pp. 3-4, 444-445; Alabama, *Senate Journal,* 4th biennial sess., 1853-1854, pp. 3-4, 301-302; Alabama General Assembly, *Acts,* 4th biennial sess., 1853-1854 (Montgomery: Brittan and Blue, 1854), p. 17 and Stephen B. Weeks, *History of Public School Education in Alabama,* U.S. Bureau of Education Bulletin, 1915, no. 12 (Washington, D.C.: Government Printing Office, 1915), p. 41. Of the 38 counties fully supporting the Meek bill, some had representatives or senators who did not vote. Of the opposing counties, Madison had one representative in this category.

[7] *Report of William F. Perry, Superintendent of Education, of the State of Alabama, Made to the Governor, for the Year 1857* (Montgomery: N. B. Cloud, 1858), p. 11 and *Report of Gabriel B. DuVal, Superintendent of Education, of the State of Alabama, Made to the Governor, for the Year 1858* (Montgomery: Shorter and Reid, 1859), p. 6.

[8] Alexis de Tocqueville, *Democracy in America,* trans. Harvey C. Mansfield and Delba Winthrop (Chicago: University of Chicago Press: 2000), pp. 359, 501-502.

[9] J. Mills Thornton III, *Politics and Power in a Slave Society: Alabama, 1800-1860* (Baton Rouge: Louisiana State University Press, 1978), pp. 294-295.

Other studies have concluded that support for popular education did reflect political, economic, and social divisions. In the case of Virginia, for instance, Thomas Hunt argues that there was a close tie between attitudes on slavery and Southern rights, on the one hand, and opposition to public schooling, on the other: "Public education was overshadowed by, yet inextricably intertwined with, the debate over slavery after 1825." He had good evidence to back up his conclusion. Western Virginia, where there were few slaves, was much stronger in support of free schools than in the East. Farmers particularly objected to any system of schooling that made a distinction between the instruction of poor and rich children. The state's school fund was stigmatized as for the poor exclusively. Thomas C. Hunt, "Sectionalism, Slavery, and Schooling in Antebellum Virginia," *West Virginia History* 46 (1985-1986): 125-136.

[10]   Gordon S. Wood, *The Radicalism of the American Revolution* (New York: Alfred A. Knopf, 1992), pp. 104-105, 217-218, 239-240.

[11]   "Popular Education, No. 4: Moral Education," *South Western Baptist,* 9 March 1854.

[12]   Alice Felt Tyler found the campaign song for equal access to education in E. P. Cubberley's *Public Education in the United States: A Study and Interpretation of American Educational History* (Boston: Houghton Mifflin, 1947), p. 201. She quotes it in *Freedom's Ferment: Phases of American Social History from the Colonial Period to the Outbreak of the Civil War* (1944; reprint, New York: Harper and Row, 1976), p. 241. Though a bit dated, her book is still a very informative history of antebellum reforms.

[13]   "Popular Education, No. 3: Moral Dignity of the Enterprize," *South Western Baptist,* 23 February 1854.

Chapter 9

A State System—
and Unintended Consequences

O NCE THE MEEK BILL had become law, educational policy in
Alabama was shaped to a large extent by new leaders, particularly
William Flake Perry of Talladega and Gabriel B. DuVal of Montgomery, the first two state superintendents. Central direction of education
and a state system were synonymous in their minds—regardless of whether all
legislators had seen them as the same in 1854. The influence of the state capital
began to grow and, with the exception of Mobile, counties in the southwest
felt the impact. Arguing that it already had a plan for its public schools,
Mobile's legislative delegation succeeded in getting an exemption that kept
them outside the state system the county had had such a strong hand in
creating. Mobile did, however, accept state funds.[1]

Why a State System?

Surely Mobilians didn't want to lose community control again after a long
battle to regain it, and citizens in other counties probably only wanted the
state money. So why did Alabama establish a system to oversee its schools? Part
of the answer is that the general assembly was simply copying other states.
Systems were a legislative favorite throughout the country, and they took on
a political meaning quite different from what the word had initially implied.
Originally, a "system" meant little more than a comprehensive array of
schools, from the primary to the college level and extending across a city or

state. A "school system" was like a "railroad system," which was simply a network of train tracks spanning the state—not a central agency for transportation. When Mobile's school commissioners talked about a "system" early on, they probably had this definition in mind.

Reformers in state assemblies around the country, before and during the 1850s, advocated another kind of system, one that was synonymous with centralized administration. They complained about independent schools, which they criticized for being governed by their "own habits, traditions, and local customs." The public's schools had "no common, superintending power over them; . . . no bond of brotherhood or family between them," or so the reformers argued.[2]

I recognize that the mechanisms for central administration in the mid-1800s hadn't developed to the point of being able to overwhelm the authority vested in counties, townships, and districts. Yet state education officials chipped away at local control and devoted a great deal of their time to persuading community folk that they had new, scientifically valid truths about improving teaching and administration. Schools needed a "superintending power" to be certain they had access to this wisdom. Otherwise, left to their own devices, a handful of independent institutions might discover these truths—if they were exceptionally alert, or just lucky.

Systems supervised by chief state school officers arose nationally for several reasons. Some scholars have seen the public school movement as evidence of the power of democratic ideals, but more recent interpretations suggest the opposite—elite concerns about people's lack of civic virtue and intelligence. In weighing the promise of democracy against the worry that the masses wouldn't be up to its demands, these elites listened more to their fears. They decided that states had to fund schools and control what they taught. Leaving the fate of the nation in the hands of independent schools was too risky.[3]

State control ushered in a centrally prescribed

William F. Perry at Seventy

curriculum, which some historians argue was intended to instill the dominant values of American Protestantism and capitalism, an objective that took on greater importance because of concerns about foreign values that new immigrants were bringing with them. Responding to this supposed threat, educators are said to have imposed a cultural uniformity on public schools. Indoctrination in these values is said to have been in response to the perceived threat of social disorder coming from new immigrants. Reformers are charged with having imposed a cultural hegemony on the public schools.[4]

Did Alabamians worry that social disorder would result from foreign influences? Even though the state's Know-Nothing Party was hostile to immigrants and attracted some following, only about 2 percent of antebellum Alabamians were foreign-born, and those lived largely in Mobile. The state's schools did have a course of study dictated from the capital after 1854, though perhaps for other reasons.

Those reasons included the necessity for state action to overcome the inequitable distribution of land-grant income. Recall that, although most townships favored sharing these funds, many hadn't voted at all on consolidation, which made some form of state intervention imperative. Yet even the redistribution of sixteenth-section revenue didn't necessarily require a "superintending power" over local schools. What did? Reformers in Alabama justified a state system primarily with the argument that the public schools were inferior. Believing they had to convert Alabamians to their way of thinking, Perry and his successor, DuVal, began reshaping the relationship between the people and the schools. Their watchword was "excellence."

Reform and Central Supervision

Convinced that the public's schools weren't good schools, William Perry came to an unshakable conclusion: the absolute necessity of state control. It would be impossible to improve instruction school by school. Only comprehensive reform would do, and it required a unified system of institutions under the direction of a central administration. Perry argued that the free school law was not "self-executing" and that outside intervention was needed in order to hold local officials to a "strict accountability."[5]

Not everyone agreed. None of the reasons convinced everyone in Alabama or in northern states such as New York that all forms of state intervention were justified. In fact, Carl Kaestle, David Tyack, and Elisabeth Hansot have found widespread conflict between local and state forces after 1830. That tension was particularly evident in Alabama.[6]

Battle lines became clear when members of the legislature raised the banner of home rule to contest state control. A minority of the senate education committee insisted that "no officer with such arbitrary power [as a superintendent] should be placed over a free people"; no one should tell citizens or school trustees how to educate their children. Even county supervision was too much. Some legislators wanted to remove any official who refused to license a teacher selected by local trustees. From this perspective, citizens would properly object to any state action that interfered "with personal duties and rights" or threatened to absorb individuals into a body politic making them subject to the state. The issue wasn't public education as such but the role of government.[7]

The Origins of Standardization: Pedagogical Science as Politics

State superintendents couldn't have disagreed more with the minority in the senate education committee. They considered the state's first school boards (the township boards) the most serious obstacle to gaining the control they wanted. In their view, local officials were "plain unlettered men," incapable of selecting qualified teachers, given to favoritism in dispersing funds and, in some cases, prone to confuse public money with their own. Since the local trustees served without bond, the state had no effective way to punish them for any misdeeds. Sanctions applied only to the townships themselves, not to their officials, so penalties would have hurt innocent teachers and students. Perry's remedy was to install county superintendents to deal with the township trustees. The legislature agreed in 1856, and counties began choosing superintendents shortly after.[8]

As the state attempted to assert its power at the expense of local officials, communities resisted. Many were less than cooperative, and that rankled the new educational leadership, sparking a confrontation that would have broad ramifications not only for Alabama's schools but also for its public. Reform-minded educators were soon drawn into conflict with citizens who were still the primary source of political support for public education, the very people who had created the first schools.

While there is no mistaking their distrust of local authority, the chief state school officers didn't intend to undercut community responsibility for education, only to constrain the power of township officials. Initially, Perry wanted school trustees to be missionaries who would "create a correct public opinion" on the proper way to go about schooling. The implication for the public was that it would become a body of support for decisions that professionals had already made. That was a far cry from being a body that created and managed schools.[9]

At the same time, Perry worked quite hard (though unsuccessfully) to counter what he regarded as a dangerous perception—that there was to be a "mammoth system of schools wholly supported by the State." Not wanting to "suppress . . . the spirit of self-help in the people," he may have eventually been surprised by the unintended consequences of some of his reforms.[10]

Intentions to the contrary notwithstanding, Perry and DuVal employed strategies that led to greater centralization. Although presented as apolitical or purely educational, these measures had profound political consequences. The superintendents introduced a new pedagogy, one that mirrored a theory in vogue at the time—education should reflect the "natural order in which the human faculties are developed in childhood." In other words, if mental development followed a natural order, then there had to be a corresponding order to the way children were taught. That logic would lead to a centrally prescribed curriculum and centrally selected textbooks.[11]

The new pedagogy treated educational issues as technical matters best left to the control of those who understood the natural order of child development. In so doing, it removed from public consideration a good many concerns of citizens.

The 1854 law directed the state superintendent to instruct teachers in their duties. That requirement became the basis for a plan to weed out the unfit, whom Perry believed to be another blight on education in Alabama. The chief state school officer couldn't hire teachers (that was still done by local trustees), so he had to find other means of exercising control. Perry decided to get rid of the incompetents through constant "supervision and inspection" by county superintendents.[12]

Reporting requirements were another means of centralization. County superintendents, who were to judge competence of a host of teachers, faced quite a challenge: How could they determine the true quality of instruction? Perry's answer was in a twenty-eight-page document that asked county officials numerous questions and provided paragraph after paragraph of information and instruction. The questions dealt primarily with those things that could be counted—the number of pupils in each class, the number of days the school was open, the average daily attendance, the salary paid to teachers. How could the state superintendent tell from all this information if the natural order of a child's development had been disregarded? That remains a mystery to me. To be fair, Perry wasn't trying to be nosy; the law required him to report on the extent of public education.[13]

The state superintendents' authority to prescribe the best methods for management, or "methods of government," gave them additional power over local schools. Perry was particularly fond of mechanical metaphors when he talked about administration. He and other reformers (going back to Pleasant May) admired Prussia for the machinelike order of its schools, which they believed were first-rate. The use of mechanical analogies may have been prompted by fascination with new inventions like the steam locomotive and the telegraph. And it probably reflected a widespread belief that the universe operates in a precise order set in motion by a wise God. That notion began to take shape in the minds of Francis Bacon and Isaac Newton and had moved from science into the general culture by the 1800s. Many assumed that, just as the physical world is governed by laws like the law of gravity, so are the social, political, and economic worlds. Being rational, intelligent people can understand these principles and use them to engineer the best of all possible societies. The key to doing that is to standardize and systematize human activity—to bureaucratize it.[14]

Bureaucracy's Values

Bureaucratization was yet another reform introduced as a mechanism for centralization. According to Robert Hunt, the state system laid the foundation for a new way of organizing work that brought with it a new set of political values—along with a different concept of society. Though the educational leadership may have envisioned an Alabama of independent, self-directing individuals whose energy and creativity would sustain the state, the system they were creating did not. The system treated teachers as functionaries performing specialized tasks, which necessarily required integration by a central coordinating authority. The nature of the system the reformers were "selling" required that they be in positions of authority. The system was like an old-fashioned elevator that had to have an operator on duty at all times.[15]

Modern bureaucracies draw their authority from administrative expertise. And like specialized pedagogical know-how, management expertise can be used to keep citizens at arm's length. Educators (so inclined) are then able to decide important questions themselves, having removed them from the public agenda on the grounds that citizens are incompetent amateurs. Community politics had taken antebellum Alabama in one direction; bureaucratic politics began moving it in another.

These political proclivities are inherent in all bureaucratic systems; they aren't peculiar to Alabama. Furthermore, Perry and DuVal didn't set out to undermine democracy. As best as I can judge, they were simply carrying out their legal obligations in a state where lack of sound administration had already wrecked the central bank. And their concerns about the quality of education, which prompted their reforms, weren't without some basis.

Not all states that had superintendents had centralized control. Iowa's schools began as Alabama's did, through community initiatives. That grassroots support contributed to dismantling a centralized system of the type that Horace Mann recommended. Decentralization continued in 1872, accelerated by a law that permitted districts to become independent if a majority of township voters wanted to. Many did; "the rapid expansion of independent districts quickly followed." (Apparently, even township control was too centralized for Iowans.)[16]

Decentralization doesn't appear to have interfered with the growth of public schools or locally generated revenue. By 1863, Iowa was enrolling 71 percent of its school-age children.

EDUCATORS VERSUS THE PUBLIC

Superintendent Perry started out as public education's evangelist, addressing himself directly to "the Citizens of Alabama" in an avalanche of circulars and tracts. In appealing for the "encouragement and fostering care" of a system of free schools, he described himself as the public's agent. The law of 1854 directed him to disseminate information, and he warmed to the task, so much so that critics angrily attacked him for spending three thousand dollars to "educate" the citizenry. They saw this early version of a public relations campaign as a waste of money better used to instruct children.[17]

Perry acknowledged the power of the public, and in his 1856 report he continued to credit citizens with passage of the free school bill. Yet he distinguished between their support for schools and backing for his reforms, which he found lacking. Not everyone shared Perry's enthusiasm for what he considered improvements. So, in the tradition of the state's reform leadership, he and DuVal came to distrust the public even as they sought to serve its best interests.[18]

In time, the disappointments of frustrated superintendents would convince them that they were dealing with a benighted citizenry. Perry decided that most people couldn't educate themselves without material assistance and guidance from outside their communities. He saw public needs, not capacities.

These perceptions were reflected in the tone of a new publication, the *Alabama Educational Journal,* where Perry was proprietor and first editor. The *Journal* began to run articles blaming the deficiencies of the schools on the public. By 1857, Perry was quite ambivalent about his fellow citizens. In the June 1 issue, he writes about "the deep hold which the cause of popular education had taken upon the affections of the great mass of the people," and then lambastes Alabamians for being "listless and indifferent" to the same cause. On one hand, he acknowledged the power of public opinion, and on the other criticized it as "despotic" and in much need of "enlightenment." Following his lead, the *Journal* charged citizens with building "commodious jails" while leaving school buildings in disrepair ("the most uninviting houses" in any area). Not merely derelict in their duty, citizens were apathetic. Rather than living up to their constitutional pledge to foster schooling, people were said to be doing everything they could to discourage it. Educators had come to define their job, in Robert Hunt's words, "as one of convincing the hostile and the unenlightened," and so they attempted to lay a guilt trip on citizens.[19]

The most unfortunate effect of the 1854 reform movement may be a lingering tendency to see Alabamians as uninterested in education and incapable of understanding what makes for good schooling. The habit of blaming the public for the schools' deficiencies (or blaming citizens for resisting reform) not only continued but also spread into the twentieth century.

NOTES TO CHAPTER 9

[1] The duties of the state superintendent of education and the way the first two men who held that office understood their duties—along with the reforms they proposed—were described in the following documents: William F. Perry, *Report of the Superintendent of Education of the State of Alabama, to the Governor* (Montgomery: Brittan and Blue, 1855); *Annual Report of William F. Perry, Superintendent of Education, of the State of Alabama, Made to the Governor, for the Year 1856* (Montgomery: Smith and Hughes, 1857); *Report of William F. Perry, Superintendent of Education, of the State of Alabama, Made to the Governor, for the Year 1857* (Montgomery: N. B. Cloud, 1858); William F. Perry, "The Genesis of Public Education in Alabama," in *Transactions of the Alabama Historical Society: 1897-1898*, ed. Thomas McAdory Owen, vol. 2 (Tuscaloosa: Alabama Historical Society, 1898); and *Report of Gabriel B. DuVal, Superintendent of Education, of the State of Alabama, Made to the Governor, for the Year 1858* (Montgomery: Shorter and Reid, 1859).

[2] Lawrence A. Cremin, *American Education: The National Experience, 1783-1876* (New York: Harper and Row, 1980), p. 155 quoting Horace Mann's *Lectures on Education* (Boston: Ide and Dutton, 1855), p. 19.

[3] While some historians insist that school reformers were interested in exercising social control, others disagree. Read Lawrence Frederick Kohl's critique in "The Concept of Social Control and the History of Jacksonian America," *Journal of the Early Republic* 5 (spring 1985): 21-34.

[4] Again, for a review of educational historiography, see Diane Ravitch, *The Revisionists Revised: Studies in the Historiography of American Education* ([Stanford, Calif.]: National Academy of Education, 1977).

[5] *Annual Report of William F. Perry, 1856*, p. 13.

[6] Carl F. Kaestle, *Pillars of the Republic: Common Schools and American Society, 1780-1860* (New York: Hill and Wang, 1983) and David Tyack and Elisabeth Hansot, *Managers of Virtue: Public School Leadership in America, 1820-1980* (New York: Basic Books, 1982).

[7] Objections to the state school system were recorded in the Alabama General Assembly, *Senate Journal*, 6th biennial sess., 1857-1858 (Montgomery: N. B. Cloud, 1858), pp. 235-243. Superintendent DuVal understood these concerns and commented on them in *Report of Gabriel B. DuVal*, p. 5.

Although I don't think it dominated the effort to fund public schooling equitably, tension between rich and poor counties is evident in the senate protest against the public school legislation. Representatives from 15 wealthy counties continued to object to giving the poorer counties a larger share of state taxes in order to more nearly equalize the per-pupil expenditures. To buttress their case, the protesting senators provided a table showing that their counties paid the lion's share of taxes yet received far less in the state school appropriation.

[8] William F. Perry told of his efforts to deal with county and

township officials in "Genesis of Public Education," p. 20 and *Report of William F. Perry, 1857*, pp. 12-16. The amended school law was in Alabama General Assembly, *Acts*, 5th biennial sess., 1855-1856 (Montgomery: Bates and Lucas, 1856), pp. 33-48.

9 *Report of William F. Perry, 1857*, p. 13.

10 Perry, "Genesis of Public Education," pp. 22-23.

11 The notion of a "natural order" in education came from David P. Page's *Theory and Practice of Teaching or the Motives and Methods of Good School Keeping*, ed. E. C. Branson (New York: American Book Company, 1899), p. 46. Page's book was first published in 1845. His ideas were repeated by Perry in *Forms for the Officers of Free Public Schools, and an Abstract of the Laws Relating to the Sale of the School Lands of the State of Alabama* (Montgomery: Advertiser and Gazette Steam Power Press Book Office, 1854), p. 17.

12 Perry's letter (dated January 7, 1853) describing his plan to eliminate incompetent teachers was included in a manuscript collection of his writings, dating from April 9, 1857, to March 8, 1858, which were cited by Stephen B. Weeks, *History of Public School Education in Alabama*, U.S. Bureau of Education Bulletin, 1915, no. 12 (Washington, D.C.: Government Printing Office, 1915), pp. 72, 203. Also see Alabama General Assembly, *Acts*, 4th biennial sess., 1853-1854 (Montgomery: Brittan and Blue, 1854), pp. 9, 12.

13 Perry, *Forms for the Officers*, pp. 4-9 and Alabama, *Acts*,

4th biennial sess., 1853-1854, pp. 9-10.

14 Perry, "Genesis of Public Education," p. 17.

15 Robert Eno Hunt, "Organizing a New South: Education Reformers in Antebellum Alabama, 1840-1860" (Ph.D. diss., University of Missouri, 1988), pp. 308-309.

16 Iowa's experience with decentralization is reported by Carroll Engelhardt in "The Ideology and Politics of Iowa Common School Reform, 1854-1860," *Annals of Iowa* 56 (summer 1997): 201-232.

17 Legislative criticisms of Superintendent Perry and the circular that drew the criticisms were in William F. Perry, *Free School Law of the State of Alabama; Also a Circular of the Superintendent* (Montgomery: Advertiser and Gazette Job Office, 1854), pp. 3, 5 and Alabama General Assembly, *Senate Journal*, 4th biennial sess., 1853-1854 (Montgomery: Brittan and Blue, 1854), p. 323.

18 *Annual Report of William F. Perry, 1856*, pp. 29-31.

19 Much of the *Alabama Educational Journal* for 1857 is missing from the state archives and isn't in any of the other collections that my colleagues and I searched. Fortunately, we located a few pages photocopied from the April, June, and October issues and returned them to the Alabama Department of Archives and History. Weeks also quotes the *Journal* on pp. 70, 76 of his *History of Public School Education*. Robert Hunt described educators' attitude toward the public on p. 279 of "Organizing a New South."

Chapter 10

FROM COMMUNITY
TO STATE RESPONSIBILITY

FIFTY YEARS after the 1854 legislation, the very thing William Perry feared most had happened: many Alabamians thought that the state government rather than the local citizenry was responsible for education. Accounting for all that contributed to that change isn't the purpose here. But the condition of education at the turn of the twentieth century shows what can happen when schools slip away from their communities.

Alabama entered the new century facing a serious problem of illiteracy. State leaders said it was directly related to the lack of a community voice in matters of education. Their conclusion is a commentary on the significance of what had begun to occur between 1854 and 1860—discrediting local trustees, centralizing power through standardization, and demeaning the citizenry. While the Civil War, Reconstruction, and the reaction to Reconstruction shaped the political climate in the early 1900s, it is unlikely that waning community control of schools, even though it began a half-century before, wouldn't have contributed to the loss of public ownership that was apparent by 1904. A new state constitution in 1901 severely limited home rule, or local self-government, but progressive school reformers had started down that path much earlier.

READING, WRITING, AND DEMOCRACY

Although the state government was spending half of its revenue on schooling by 1900—not a mere $100,000—illiteracy in Alabama had precipitated a crisis. Alabamians paid more per capita for education than citizens in many other states. Still, illiteracy rates soared to the highest in the nation, even higher than in neighboring Mississippi. More than one hundred thousand white people ten years of age or older couldn't read or write in 1900. The only good news was that African-American illiteracy rates, though even higher, had fallen dramatically.[1]

The Constitution of 1901 made it difficult to respond to the problem because its one-mill restriction on property tax prevented counties from raising needed school revenue. Interestingly, this was the same amount specified in the 1854 school bill. Authors of the new constitution, intent on reversing the effects of Reconstruction, disfranchised black voters and limited the influence of poorer whites who had championed Populist challenges to the established order. A coalition of industrialists and planters centralized authority in order to thwart the ability of opponents to win local elections and control county governments.[2]

The centralization movement went beyond placing constitutional restrictions on local taxing authority. In 1903, the legislature abolished the township boards, which dated back to 1823. Townships retained ownership of their sixteenth sections but lost their authority in school matters to county boards and trustees of redrawn districts. Twentieth-century critics sounded much like those fifty years earlier when they charged township officials with inflating school censuses and misusing funds—failings that supposedly resulted from their inability to resist pressures from their communities.[3]

Townships were, in fact, an extra layer between the county and the district. But that wasn't the main argument made against local officials. Critics said these officers of the electorate were corrupt because they were too wedded to their friends and neighbors. These charges had implications for all citizen boards, which were under fire across the country in the early 1900s. Prominent figures like Nicholas Murray Butler, president of Columbia University, insisted that "the less the personal contact between the voter and public candidate, the greater the chance of an efficient appointed board" and that "the local-committee system of school government is the worst that has ever been invented by man." In what strikes me as strange logic, Butler argues that "a democracy is as much entitled as a monarchy to have its business well done." (Similar criticisms have been leveled recently in renewed attacks on local boards.)[4]

In 1904, a small group of Alabamians, including Edgar Gardner Murphy, Montgomery clergyman and executive secretary of the Southern Education Board, made the case for returning control to communities. John Herbert Phillips, superintendent of the Birmingham schools, documented the literacy problem and laid out a strategy for dealing with it; he believed the only remedy was to restore local ownership. Pride in the schools had faded away, Phillips argued, because citizens no longer had a voice in school matters. And, by reintroducing the restriction on local school taxation to one mill, the new constitution had left Alabamians with "shackled wills and fettered hands, powerless to help themselves" or their schools. The Birmingham superintendent was convinced that education would never improve until communities regained the power to act. He insisted that local control was the key to public responsibility.[5]

Impressive in its explicitly democratic tenor, the case for educational reform through home rule attracted distinguished advocates. John W. Abercrombie, former (and future) state superintendent and president of the University of Alabama, emphasized self-rule as a long-cherished tradition in the state. He was joined by C. C. Thach, president of Alabama Polytechnic Institute (now Auburn University), who criticized the new constitution for denying citizens the right to tax themselves. State Superintendent I. W. Hill pointed out that districts reserving the right of local taxation under the new constitution had already voted for school levies. And former governor W. C. Oates, a dissenting member of the 1901 constitutional convention, attacked the notion that the state should have primary responsibility for education.[6]

Phillips's most startling argument—given all the effort that had gone into winning state government support—was that while legislative attention is important, it is far more critical for the people to be interested in public education. Return local control, he predicted, and school funds would double as a result of taxes people imposed on themselves.[7]

Phillips, Murphy, and their friends based their reform strategy on two propositions. The first was that citizens have the ability to decide what is best for them. After all, they had maintained schools in their communities since the early 1800s. Although many of the state's elite distrusted the public, the Phillips-Murphy group wanted citizens to have a free hand in deciding how much to tax themselves. And unlike earlier reformers, who thought centralization ensured efficiency, the 1904 coalition believed that local control promoted the wisest use of resources.

The coalition's second assumption sprang from nineteenth-century ideals, specifically, the conviction that popular government can't be sustained without popular schooling. Alabamians were surely more passionate about self-determination after Reconstruction than they had been before 1860. Phillips especially liked the notion that local schools could do for Alabama what town meetings had done for colonial New England—create a citizenry capable of self-rule.

Illiteracy was the obvious issue, but the reformers' deeper concern was the deterioration of democracy in Alabama. Phillips didn't mince words: "The people are afraid of the taxing power [the state], and the taxing power is afraid of the people." The consequences of this mutual distrust were dramatic. In states like Massachusetts, where illiteracy rates were low and communities were still responsible for education, local support accounted for a large part of the revenue. "A democratic government pursues a suicidal policy," Phillips warned, "when it declares the people incompetent to decide for themselves."

Whatever Alabama has gained over the years through reforms—and some have unquestionably made life better for people—the state has sometimes paid for the progress with a reduced capacity for self-rule. That has often happened when changes have been imposed from the top down. In fighting for a greater public voice and stronger home rule, the 1904 coalition stands out as an effort to make democratic change democratically. The group addressed its argument *for* the people *to* the people and, in doing that, placed its faith in the ability of Alabamians to decide their future for themselves.

A DIFFERENT PUBLIC

Phillips, Murphy, and company weren't able to restore full home rule, but they weren't without some success. In 1916, the state raised the one-mill cap on county taxes to three and gave districts the option of adding three more mills.[8]

Despite these concessions, however, the legislature was becoming the principal source of revenue, which naturally gave it more power to direct what went on in the schools. That authority was reflected in the growth of a central bureaucracy. Officials in Montgomery made rules in the public's interest, yet for a public that was quite different from the one that got its hands dirty building the first schools. It isn't accurate to say that there was no place for the public in public education by the twentieth century, but there was another understanding of the citizenry. The "new public" was more of an abstraction, as in the phrase "public accountability." It didn't do any work, except perhaps as an electorate.

There were a number of reasons why state officials embraced bureaucracies as helpful reforms. They could create uniform standards that protected against mismanagement and corruption, protection that surely served the interest of all. The general assembly and governors also relied on the ability of bureaucracies to tell them, objectively, how much public schooling was actually available in the state. And reformers used bureaucratic controls as a strategy for improving the quality of instruction. All of this served the commonweal. Consequently, bureaucracies went about collecting data, promulgating regulations, and giving "the public" (in this case, a body of popular opinion) information intended to demonstrate that they, the overseers of instruction, were producing the results they had set out to produce. Bureaucrats considered these reports indications of their accountability. So accountability became more informational rather than relational as it had been when the schools and the working public were face-to-face.

Ironically, the very accountability that was supposed to serve the public interest kept the public that built the schools at arm's length. The bureaucracies that developed in the late nineteenth and early twentieth centuries were theoretically responsible to a public, but they weren't necessarily *responsive* to the citizenry. It is difficult to imagine a central administration being used to carry out mandates of a community, except in the broadest sense. While bureaucratic regulations are evenhanded, they don't vary, which makes it difficult to take into account unique factors that people might consider quite relevant in a particular setting. And while bureaucracies foster efficiency, they may not promote *effectiveness,* which reflects what citizens consider valuable. Furthermore, even though the objective data that a central agency provides is useful to citizens in understanding some of the things that are happening in their schools, people may not care for the relationship that a bureaucracy imposes on them in its pursuit of uniformity and efficiency. (Bureaucrats themselves—intelligent and well-intentioned—are sometimes frustrated by the restrictions on their ability to act as common sense dictates.)

Alabama's first superintendent, William Perry, had a very small bureaucracy, perhaps no more than a clerk in his office. But Perry's approach to organizing education took hold and grew to a point that it had spread down to the county level by the early 1900s.

By 1917, teachers in Clarke County had to register with the county office, show their state certificates, maintain daily records of pupils on forms furnished by the superintendent, follow the prescribed curriculum, and keep registers that were "neat and clean with pen and ink insertions." The state printed the required course of study, but teachers had to send for it—being sure to include postage of six cents. Instructors also had to complete monthly reports on the Friday before the last Saturday of the month, with all blanks filled in. If the required information was unavailable, teachers were to write "0." Annual reports had to be submitted in duplicate. All national holidays were to be observed; teachers could list them in the reports as workdays, but they had to be marked in *red* ink.[9]

Some rules were directed at county trustees. They had to continue the nineteenth-century practice of evaluating classroom instruction by visiting the schools once a month. During these visits, they were to encourage the students and sign teachers' reports. Besides answering to state superintendents, county board members also had to be sensitive to their communities and the citizens who elected them. Caught in the middle, they promulgated their own lists of rules for instructors—though to meet different expectations. The public that county officials served was still nearby and community-based—and their regulations reflected that political reality.

For monthly salaries that ranged from thirty-five to fifty dollars (five dollars were added for experience), teachers in Clarke County not only had to fill out the forms from Montgomery but also had to:

be in the school-room in time to have it properly heated and ventilated before school opens at 8 o'clock;

have a bountiful supply of fresh water, both to drink and to bathe with, and no child should be allowed to come into the school room with soiled body smelling like a rats-nest or the den of wild beasts;

remain at the school building throughout the entire day—no going home to dinner [i.e., lunch].[10]

Another county rule, directed largely at young women, probably played a role in keeping a number of them unmarried. The 1912 version reads:

Every teacher should be an example to the pupils and the community. To this end they must have a personal dignity commensurate with the moral training and rules for the government of their schools. For a young lady to sit out in a hammock, or swing, with a married man, is considered among nice people as very near the line of immoral. And if she takes walks down in the woods, alone with a young man, she has overstepped the line of what the Board considers decent. As she is an example in the community, the Board earnestly requests that she receive young men callers not later than ten o'clock. The young men should conform their habits to these rules as well.[11]

With the exception of a curious prohibition against fancy sewing, most other requirements were just common sense—be punctual, allow plenty of time for meals, try to enroll all school-age children in the community.

As the rules show, county boards encouraged good relationships between the schools and their communities. While teachers weren't allowed to work in their hometowns, they were expected to form close ties with the citizenry in the places where they taught. Instructors had to be in residence at least five days prior to the opening of school and "to study the character and needs" of the community. They were also expected to stay in the area on Saturdays and Sundays to do "community work" because the boards felt that such work had "a reflex action on the school" and both the school and the community were strengthened by the teacher's presence. Clarke County's board of education specifically asked faculty members to help form civic "improvement associations, to the end that the school grounds and buildings may be improved" and in order to build and maintain "common interest and good fellowship," wording that reflects a strong belief in the interdependence of school and community.[12]

County superintendents probably held views similar to those of their boards. Though ostensibly deputies of the chief state school officer, they had reason to be more responsive to their communities than to the capital. Also, twentieth-century superintendents were "descendents" of the first county officials, who appear to have been quite independent. In Clarke, local leaders like Stephen B. Cleveland and Isaac Grant, editor of the *Clarke County Democrat,* had held this post in the late 1850s. Prominent in their own right, they continued in their primary occupations and served only part-time, at least initially.[13]

To be sure, centralization was never absolute, and savvy county officials learned how to acquire power. Yet public ownership of the schools and the sense of local responsibility that went with it seems to have slowly eroded. By the early twentieth century, schools built by citizens were in danger of turning into schools they could scarcely affect. And the public that was once grounded in self-rule was at risk of becoming a public without the ground needed to rule itself.[14]

At the end of the twentieth century, the Alabama legislature began to try to check the forces that had been set in motion in 1854. In the spring of 2001, the senate approved and Governor Don Siegelman (a graduate of Mobile's Barton Academy) signed a bill to deal with the problems of "too much red tape, bureaucracy, and paperwork." It followed on the heels of a 1995 law passed for the same purpose. Teachers were finally given some voice in deciding what information was relevant.[15]

Notes to Chapter 10

[1] At the turn of the twentieth century, Mississippi had 35,432 white illiterates. In Iowa and Michigan, there were less than 13,000. Georgia, on the other hand, reported 99,948. Alabama wasn't the worst in the South, however. Tennessee had 156,342 people who were illiterate. This information can be found by using the United States Historical Census Data Browser, which includes statistical information for the United States from 1790 to 1960. The website address is http://fisher.lib.virginia.edu/census/.

[2] For a general history of the 1901 constitution, see William Warren Rogers et al., *Alabama: The History of a Deep South State* (Tuscaloosa: University of Alabama Press, 1994), pp. 351-354 and Albert Burton Moore, *History of Alabama* (1934; reprint, Tuscaloosa: Alabama Book Store, 1951), pp. 652-655.

[3] Ira W. Harvey gave an account of the declining powers of local school officials in *A History of Educational Finance in Alabama, 1819-1986* (Auburn, Ala.: Truman Pierce Institute for the Advancement of Teacher Education, 1989), pp. 89-90. Jay Emmett Thomason also deals with this subject in "The Development of the Administrative Organization of the Public School System of Alabama" (Ph.D. diss., The University of Alabama, 1959), pp. 39-42. Thomason notes that by 1907, the power of the district's trustees was considerably diminished, but the power of the county board had increased.

[4] Nicholas Murray Butler, "Remarks of Dr. Butler, President of Columbia University, before the Merchants' Club, on Saturday, December 8th, at the Auditorium," in *Public Schools and Their Administration: Addresses Delivered at the Fifty-Ninth Meeting of the Merchants' Club of Chicago* (Chicago: Merchants' Club, 1906), pp. 40, 42, 47. Jay Mathews reported on the current attack on local boards in "Are School Boards Really Necessary?" *Washington Post,* 10 April 2001, A19.

[5] Edgar Gardner Murphy, "A Personal Letter," in *Local Taxation for Schools in Alabama* (Montgomery: Phillips-Sheehan, n.d.), pp. 3-12.

All quotations of John Herbert Phillips on the lack of local control and responsibility and their effects on education can be found in "Local Taxation for Schools," in *Local Taxation for Schools in Alabama,* pp. 17-19.

Phillips's efforts in 1904 may have been a continuation of an Alabama Education Association campaign launched in 1896 to reverse the defeat of an 1894 amendment, which would have allowed districts to levy a 2.5 mill tax for public schools. See Moore, *History of Alabama*, p. 551 and Rogers et al., *Alabama: The History,* pp. 269, 324.

[6] Edgar Gardner Murphy, *Alabama's First Question: Local Support for Local Schools* (Montgomery: n.p., 1904), pp. 14-18.

[7] Phillips, "Local Taxation for Schools," pp. 15-16, 18-19.

8 The tortured ins and outs of school finance were skillfully tracked in Ira Harvey's *History of Educational Finance.* He discussed the constitutional amendment of 1915-1916 that allowed both counties and districts an extra 3 mills on pages 96-97, 461.

9 The 1917 requirements of the Clarke County Board of Education for teacher accountability were in the board minutes of 30 July 1917, pp. 105-107, which are available at the office of the superintendent of education for Clarke County in Grove Hill, Alabama.

10 Clarke County Board of Education Minutes, 30 July 1917, pp. 104-107.

11 Clarke County Board of Education Minutes, 11 October 1912 and 30 July 1917, pp. 105-106.

12 Clarke County Board of Education Minutes, 30 July 1917, pp. 106, 108-109.

13 Clarke County elected Stephen B. Cleveland its first superintendent in the spring of 1856. By August, he was traveling across the county to meet with school trustees and teachers. "County Superintendent of Education," *Clarke County Democrat,* 17 April 1856 and "To the Trustees and Teachers of Public Schools in Clarke County," *Clarke County Democrat,* 14 August 1856.

T. H. Ball described the "distinguished" Cleveland family on p. 489 of his book *A Glance into the Great South-East, or, Clarke County, Alabama, and Its Surroundings, from 1540 to 1877* (1879; reprint, Tuscaloosa: Willo Publishing Company, 1962). Isaac Grant replaced Cleveland by 1858. Cecilia A. R. Fuller, comp., "Articles from the Clarke County Democrat 1858," *Clarke County Historical Society Quarterly* 16 (spring 1992): 33. The role of these local officials is the subject of an article, "County Superintendents," which appeared in *The Southern Teacher* 2 (November 1860): 186.

14 A study of late nineteenth-, early twentieth-century schools in North Carolina showed the same shift from schools that had been the "crucible of community" to institutions that were seen as a "staging ground for the great race of life" and focused their attention more on individual achievement. While some North Carolinians fought the decline of "democratic localism," reform-minded educators favored efficiency over older values and sided with that state's post-Reconstruction "redeemers" who championed the same centralization as those who authored Alabama's 1901 constitution. James L. Leloudis, *Schooling the New South: Pedagogy, Self, and Society in North Carolina, 1880-1920* (Chapel Hill: University of North Carolina Press, 1996). Julia Walsh reviews this book in "Schooling the New South: Pedagogy, Self, and Society in North Carolina, 1880-1920," *Journal of Social History* 31 (summer 1998): 977-979.

15 "Paperwork Reduction Bill Becomes State Law," *Alabama School Journal* 118 (14 May 2001): 1.

Conclusion

THEN AND NOW

THIS BOOK BEGAN by arguing that the relationship between the public and the public schools is deeply troubled, that too many people doubt that the schools are really theirs. This lack of a sense of ownership plays out in a weakened sense of responsibility. It's not that Americans don't care—they do. They just don't see how to act on their concerns; they aren't sure they can ever have a constructive influence on the public schools.

If these perceptions are widespread, is there any reason to be hopeful about the future of public education? I think so, and I found hope in a closer reading of the story of the first schools. I ended my tour of Alabama convinced that the early schools belonged to the public because many of them began when people "sitting around a kitchen table" used their collective power to see that instruction was available in their communities. These small groups rallied citizens to build schoolhouses, hire teachers, and do whatever else it took to see that education was available. This was the public at work a long time ago. But I don't believe we have lost the capacity to join forces and tackle our common problems.

Of course, circumstances were different in the nineteenth century. Yet the basic principles of civic action are still valid and can be useful in efforts to put the public back into the public schools. Many communities are now trying to reengage their schools, and a number of schools are trying to reengage citizens. The key to success is the way these initiatives understand the public. Engagement campaigns that see the citizens as political actors exercising their collective powers are more likely to restore a sense of public responsibility than those that treat people as an audience to be "informed."

The challenge the public faces is to find meaningful work in today's highly bureaucratized school systems. For educators, the challenge grows out of the fact that it is impossible to rebuild a relationship by the unilateral action of one party. Engagement has to occur first among citizens and later between citizens and schools.

There is, however, a more immediate obstacle to public ownership. It was evident in a question I heard from one of the many south Alabamians who were good enough to review the first draft of this book. (They were the latter-day equivalents of Caleb Moncrief, Elizabeth Ball Woodard, Henry Hitchcock, and Lucy Skipwith.) *What difference would it make if the public regained ownership of the schools?* As long as the answer to that question isn't clear, "public engagement" will be little more than a sound bite.

WHAT A DEMOCRATIC PUBLIC PROVIDES

Is there really a role for the public in an age when teaching and administration require a good deal of professional expertise? To complicate matters, any projects have to pass through innumerable legal filters and comply with a multitude of regulations, some of them contradictory. What could citizens possibly do under these circumstances? Imagine what would happen if Clarke County's Union community tried to build a schoolhouse now.

No one knows exactly how to overcome these barriers. Still, while the precise role of the citizenry isn't as well defined as it should be, it's obvious that the schools still need things that only a democratic public can supply. A commitment to make public schooling good schooling remains indispensable, and constantly improving our schools requires vast amounts of political will. Parents alone can't meet the demand, especially since they make up a smaller proportion of the voting population today. Furthermore, voting represents just one form of civic action. Only the public firmly embedded in a community—a committed society of citizens—is likely to have the renewable resources required.

The need for a fully invested community is obvious when schools face a crisis. Educators across the country responded to the 1999 shootings at Columbine High School in Colorado with metal detectors and security guards. What else could they do? Yet they knew, better than most, that they wouldn't be able to solve this kind of problem on their own. Their communities had to come together and act on a number of fronts to deal with underlying social problems (which are easily misframed as school problems). That is far more likely if the public schools are seen as the public's schools.

In addition, there are academic reasons for putting the public, or the community, back into the schools. A community has a host of educating institutions that are the natural allies of schools. I'm not just talking about places to go on field trips. What about some of the original partners in public education? Churches, for example, are already showing their potential to contribute worthwhile after-school programs. A community is also a source of the social motivation that encourages young people to learn. In one state, schools actually began to improve *before* a reform campaign had succeeded in getting its new legislation in place. Perhaps the students began to do better when it became apparent that everyone wanted them to learn. The public no longer has to build schoolhouses, but it does have to bring all the educational resources of a community to bear on its concerns and to mobilize the social forces that prompt young people to learn. Organizing communities to do what they can do best is part of today's public work.[1]

I don't mean to imply that the public is merely a resource for schools. It is the other way around. Public schools are agents of a democratic citizenry; they exist for public purposes. The first schools weren't just *in* communities, they were *of* communities. What a difference it would make these days if schools were seen not only as professional institutions but also as examples of communities at work instructing their children.

Take away the public schools' mandate from citizens, and they become essentially private—just another kind of business. Even though I recognize that many of the early schoolmasters were quite entrepreneurial, I don't think the public's schools were intended to be public utilities. They had—and still have—responsibilities not merely to those who use their services but to all of us, to democracy.[2]

Restoring public ownership of schools may seem like an idealistic goal to some educators. What's in it for the schools? Nothing less than preserving their place in the never-ending effort of free people to govern themselves justly.

What If There Is No Public?

If these answers are persuasive, we are back to the challenges citizens and educators alike face in rebuilding their relationship. Teachers, administrators, school board members, and community leaders may agree that the public schools need to become more of the public's schools, yet fear there is not enough of a responsible public where they live. They could be right. Many of their neighbors could be sitting on their hands—uninvolved and unengaged with anything other than purely personal matters. What could get them connected and moving as a citizenry? Although the usual answer is "a crisis," I think people will come together under less dramatic circumstances.

People often get involved on problems close to home that affect them directly and that they can get their hands on. The spark could be finding drug paraphernalia in the neighborhood or seeing children with little to do after school. Civic activism can begin with nothing more than people making decisions with others about something they believe should or shouldn't be happening in the community. These are only the first steps, but they are essential. And they aren't impossible to take. There are few, if any, places where at least two or three people aren't talking about what should be. Their job is to find two or three more people to join the conversation.

Remember, too, the public isn't static; it is dynamic, people spurring others to action. That means developing the public sector in a community isn't like organizing an army, which involves recruiting and training before there is an effective force. We don't have to worry about creating a public—and then getting it to act. The public is in the acting. The public exists, at least embryonically, the minute people begin to consider their options and make decisions together. When these practices become customs, the public becomes deeply rooted in a community.

This way of understanding the public has implications for engagement campaigns. "Connecting to" the public or even "communicating with" it aren't quite the right images; they imply that the task is to link two fixed points. If the public is dynamic, then schools have to enter the dynamic—that is, they have to relate to a deciding and acting citizenry. For instance, schools might try putting themselves *inside* the deliberations that go on when people make collective decisions.

BEGINNING WITH THE COMMUNITY'S ISSUES

Harris Sokoloff, of the University of Pennsylvania's Graduate School of Education, conducts an annual summer institute on community decision-making. The objective is to add a genuine public voice to what are otherwise only the voices of special interests, each convinced that its concerns are distinct from those of others. Not unilaterally but in partnership with the Scouts, the public library, and the local newspaper, educators and school board members have participated—as citizens—in forums on critical community issues that are also school-related, for example, juvenile violence and economic development.[3]

By beginning with problems of interest to the community as a whole, these educators are reaching out to the public rather than attempting to bring the public to their school-based issues. For example, deciding on ways to prevent violence attracts people who probably wouldn't turn out to discuss class size.

The Pennsylvania forums are based on the assumption that community issues almost always have implications for schools and that no community can realize its objectives without an educational strategy. Tensaw couldn't in 1799; none can today. Here is what I mean by an educational strategy: When colonial workingmen wanted to prevent the English class system from spreading to America, they used a political/economic strategy; they opposed the creation of a national bank out of fear that it would give the wealthy undue influence. At the same time, these artisans and laborers organized libraries, lecture series, and other programs to diffuse knowledge, recognizing that, if access to knowledge was confined to the upper classes, these elites would easily dominate society. The working people had an educational strategy that complemented what they were doing politically and economically. Antebellum Alabamians used educational strategies for community-building. To attract new settlers, they sought out a good schoolmaster and added advanced courses to their academy's curriculum.[4]

PUBLIC ENGAGEMENT AND POLITICAL WILL

Educational strategies, however, are merely plans without a public to implement them, without a citizenry able to stay the course. The public is more likely to have this kind of commitment when citizens meet face-to-face to define problems in their own terms, exchange opinions, and fashion workable agreements that allow a diverse array of actors to contribute. That is what the Pennsylvania forums have been attempting and what happened in nineteenth-century Alabama to promote the growth of public schools.

Though from a different state and time, Glenn Frank describes citizens forming their own opinions in the local post office:

> [Though the people might wear] "hand-me-down" or ready-made suits, but not so their opinions; they, at least, are personally tailored. They do not surrender their day's opinion to the chance impression of head-lines. Each for himself . . . they mull over such head-line and hearsay information as may have come to them respecting the things that are holding the center of the stage in war, in diplomacy, in politics, and in industry; then later at the post-office they lay their minds alongside the minds of their neighbors, they pit their opinions against the opinions of their fellows, and before they get through they have made up the public opinion of the village.[5]

A public so engaged is more powerful than a persuaded population; a citizenry that makes up its own mind produces sustainable political will, not short bursts of enthusiasm. People rallied behind a charismatic leader, a catchy slogan, or a strategic plan that experts have devised typically don't have that kind of staying power. Collective decision-making generates lasting political energy because it promotes ownership. It is a principle of civic action: naturally we take more responsibility for what we have participated in choosing than for what is chosen for us.

Now, there isn't anything wrong with trying to persuade our fellow citizens. Educators have to do that constantly. Still, they can benefit from knowing what happens when people engage each other over community issues. Being in the room when citizens are struggling over their options allows professionals to see the public in a different light. Furthermore, this kind of collective decision-making produces information that professionals need— information about how people define the community's problems and about what they will and won't do to solve them.

THE SECRET OF ENGAGEMENT: A DIFFERENT WAY OF TALKING

The word most commonly used to describe citizens trying to make difficult decisions is "deliberation." Deliberation isn't the same as discussion or debate; it is choice work. As said earlier, it is weighing competing claims fairly, when all of them touch on things that are deeply valuable to people. These are the things we need for our collective well-being; they are different from our personal interests and beliefs. We all have our own points of view, which are often related to where we live and how we earn our livings. Yet, according to psychologists who have studied people's reactions to many issues over time, we have fundamental political needs that are as basic as our need for food and shelter. I have called them imperatives; fairness and freedom from coercion are examples.[6]

Different imperatives lead to different, often conflicting, approaches to solving problems. For instance, doing what allows us to be free and to seize opportunities may involve risks that threaten our collective security. So we have to make tough decisions; we have to struggle intellectually and emotion-ally in deciding on a course of action. Throughout the first half of the nineteenth century, the people of southwestern Alabama had to weigh competing concerns as they decided what kind of schooling was needed and who should be responsible for maintaining it. That required another type of public work—choice work.

Recall that Alabamians valued their independence, or autonomy, and they prized the means of ensuring it—local control. At the same time, people knew survival on the frontier required cooperation, that there was strength in unity. And this made them appreciate the things that promote unity, such as equitable distribution of resources. When it came to educating young people, however, these two imperatives clashed. Autonomy argued for keeping control of the schools strictly local. But some communities had far more money than others, and the value placed on cooperation and equity argued for sharing resources.

In the first decades of the nineteenth century, a deliberative citizenry in Alabama worked through such conflicts and, in this case, found a balance between cooperation and autonomy. Though never in complete agreement, Alabamians decided to compensate townships that had worthless land grants while keeping day-to-day control of the schools local. Like most decisions, however, this one didn't hold indefinitely. By 1854, the balance between autonomy and cooperation was unsettled by new forces that came into play as a result of efforts to organize the public's schools into a state system. Public issues are seldom resolved once and for all. Deliberation has to become a community habit.

In suggesting that deliberation can play an important role in public-building today, I am not romanticizing the past. When antebellum Alabamians deliberated, they didn't necessarily gather in formally organized forums, though there were plenty of those. Deliberative talk, then and now, is filled with uncertainty, doubt, and frustration, though it has moments of open, honest reflection. The struggle to make difficult choices becomes shared and less divisive when citizens recognize that they value many of the same things, even though they differ on their relative importance. That recognition doesn't eliminate conflict, yet it helps avoid paralyzing polarization. Choice work can connect people in a common moral struggle, even as they disagree. In fact, deliberation rarely ends with consensus on a single course of action; more often, it helps identify a number of complementary approaches to a problem.

To be sure, not all issues in Alabama were dealt with deliberatively. Meetings on education were relatively free of coercion, with people able to voice contrary opinions, but the discussion of slavery was not. Though remarkably open at first, according to Thomas Abernethy's research, the atmosphere changed as positions hardened and a growing orthodoxy shut down real deliberation. For instance, James G. Birney, mayor of Huntsville and a leading abolitionist, eventually had to leave the state. No wonder the public's ultimate decision was fatally flawed.[7]

Rechartering All the Public Schools

Public deliberation can build public legitimacy and support. The first schools enjoyed the confidence of the citizenry because they had implicit "charters" hammered out by their communities. These charters contained a number of mandates.

As the public's agents, the first schools balanced conflicting imperatives.

For instance, freedom was dear, but fear that it would turn into license was equally powerful. Alabama's schools couldn't fail to recognize their responsibility to striking the right balance, especially when it was spelled out in the 1851 report of the Robinson committee. Schools celebrated the patriotic virtues of self-rule yet had to warn against "popular despotism." (Seeing this tension has inspired historians to observe that Americans opted for the greatest of liberty but insisted on "schoolmasters" to tame any abuses.)[8]

Schools had additional mandates that grew out of other imperatives—for instance, developing the social morality that formed the basis for both the political and economic systems. While families had primary responsibility for shaping children's character, schools were to reinforce what parents taught. Although a few preachers in the early 1900s objected to public schooling on the grounds that moral training belongs in the church, they didn't attract a large following. Religious opposition to public education appears to have been less of a problem in Alabama than it had been in Puritan Massachusetts. Ministers of the Baptist churches joined Methodist and Presbyterian colleagues to promote the common school movement.

Some mandates were straightforward, though no less difficult to carry out. Alabamians worried about the coercion that might come from a privileged class; and, like the colonial workingmen, they recognized that controlling access to knowledge is a way of protecting privilege. So they insisted that their institutions of education, from primary schools to the state university, be highly accessible. The principle was unmistakable, though the effort to apply it would generate endless controversy.

Even though many nineteenth-century mandates are still in force, new ones have to be established to deal with today's imperatives. For this to happen, communities must provide places where people can work through difficult decisions about how to deal with competition among the many things they hold dear. We need the modern equivalents of wagon lots and camp meetings, and these must be continuously available. The reason is that citizens can't decide what kind of community they want all at once; it has to be done over time and issue by issue: What should we do about drug abuse and juvenile violence? How should we prepare the next generation for the new international economy? And, as always, what kind of life do we want to prevail in our community; what norms can we share without infringing on the conscience of others?[9]

Both citizens and educators can help provide this kind of public space, so that deliberation can become a habit—a habit that will serve them well when the next crisis erupts.

COMMUNITY BY COMMUNITY

I end where I began, with communities and what a few people sitting around a kitchen table can accomplish. The first public in southwestern Alabama formed in towns, often with distinctively American names like Monroeville and Jackson. The same thing can happen today. As Thomas Jefferson explained, people learn their citizenship in communities the only way that citizenship can be learned—from direct, personal experience.

Communities seldom act all together, however. They are more likely to operate through constellations of small groups. Little, independent initiatives accumulate and produce the larger defenses society uses against major threats to public life, such as violence, exploitation, and corruption.

The influence of small community groups isn't confined within town limits, as some critics charge. Without being united in any formal organization, "little republics" have affected entire states and even the country as a whole. Their larger impact has come, in part, from the resonance of similar purposes across political jurisdictions. Nineteenth-century Alabama demonstrates how this happened. Community after community built schools, largely with their own resources. These investments influenced the legislature, but the influence didn't come from the kind of special interest pressure we see today. It came from communities molding the political sentiment of the state, which was evident in the "restlessness" to promote the cause of public instruction. Perhaps Alexis de Tocqueville was thinking of this kind of influence when he observed that as soon as a group of Americans decided what they wanted and joined to bring it about, they became a political "power that speaks, and to which one listens." No longer an isolated phenomenon, people were united in their sentiments and became a force that had to be reckoned with. That is exactly what happened in Alabama in 1854.[10]

Communities can extend their reach by linking voluntary associations—

leadership organizations, historical societies, and the like. In the nineteenth century, these alliances began and remained local initiatives yet were also able to connect across economic, political, and geographic boundaries. The impetus for Alabama's statewide agricultural society, for instance, came from county associations, not the reverse.

Also consider the fact that a community-based public has an extra source of power because people don't have to meet the legal definitions of citizenship. Even though antebellum laws didn't recognize women or most black Alabamians as citizens, those restrictions didn't always keep them from having political influence. Citizens are people who act like citizens, that is, without asking permission.

Communities today have everything to do with whether we can maintain our country's tradition of public education. If there are ways to strengthen our schools—and I believe there are—then they will be found in our communities because local examples still offer the best models for state and national policy.

Of course, communities need help in educating the next generation. As in the past, some assistance has to come from state legislatures and the federal government. But the key to a good education for all may lie in an insight from a song of the civil rights movement: "We are the ones we have been waiting for." That should be every community's refrain.

NOTES TO CONCLUSION

1 In her dissertation, "How Three Governors Involved the Public in Passing Their Education Reform Programs," Jennie Vanetta Carter Thomas reported on the effect a political campaign to improve education in Tennessee had on school performance *before* the reforms themselves were fully implemented. (Ed.D. diss., George Peabody College for Teachers of Vanderbilt University, 1992), pp. 35-36.

The concept of public work came from Harry C. Boyte and Nancy N. Kari's *Building America: The Democratic Promise of Public Work* (Philadelphia: Temple University Press, 1996), pp. 11-12.

2 In saying that the public schools aren't the same as utility companies, I'm not necessarily saying that a community can't hire a private concern to operate its schools. I'm arguing that the relationship between a school and a community is more than a commercial relationship—it is fundamental to democratic public life.

3 Harris Sokoloff, "A Deliberative Model for Engaging the Community: Use of Community Forums Can Undercut Special-Interest Politics," *School Administrator* 53 (November 1996): 12-18.

4 Rush Welter, *Popular Education and Democratic Thought in America* (New York: Columbia University Press, 1962), pp. 45-59.

5 Glenn Frank, "The Parliament of the People," *Century Magazine* 98 (1919): 402.

6 Milton Rokeach and Sandra J. Ball-Rokeach, "Stability and Change in American Value Priorities, 1968-1981," *American Psychologist* 44 (May 1989): 775-784.

7 Thomas Perkins Abernethy, *The Formative Period in Alabama, 1815-1828,* 2d ed., Southern Historical Publications, no. 8 (University: University of Alabama Press, 1965), p. 167 and *The Heritage of Madison County, Alabama,* ed. John Rankin, Liz Langer, and Jim Zielinski (Clanton, Ala.: Alabama Heritage Publishing, 1998), p. 10.

8 Welter, *Popular Education,* pp. 58-59.

9 Philosophers have called the "space" that citizens create in order to deliberate or reason together a "public sphere." They argue that it's essential to political freedom because it allows citizens to promote their common welfare independent of and outside the control of the state. The freedom that the public sphere provides can be used to limit the power of official bodies (that happened when Mobilians turned out the school board). And the same freedom, in a positive sense, allows people to shape their collective future through collective decisions. (The 1825 meeting in Mobile to provide for public education is a case in point.)

For more on the importance of a public sphere to self-rule, I recommend Charles Taylor's *Philosophical Arguments* (Cambridge: Harvard University Press, 1995), especially Chapter 13.

10 Alexis de Tocqueville, *Democracy in America,* trans. Harvey C. Mansfield and Delba Winthrop (Chicago: University of Chicago Press, 2000), p. 492.

SOURCES OF ILLUSTRATIONS

Shell Banks School Construction, cover, Joy Callaway Buskens, *Well, I've Never Met a Native* (Columbus, Ga.: Quill Publications, 1986)

Southwestern Alabama, p. 14, The location of antebellum towns placed on contemporary county maps at the Alabama Department of Archives and History

The School at Tensaw, p. 18, Based on a sketch in the *Alabama School Journal* (n.d.)

Stairs from the Alabama River to Claiborne, p. 32, Mary E. Brantley, *Early Settlers along the Old Federal Road in Monroe and Conecuh Counties Alabama* (Baltimore: Gateway Press, 1976)

Josiah Mathews' Cabin in Clarke County, p. 33, An artist's reconstruction using the author's photograph of the remains of the cabin

A Mathews Home in Cahawba, Dallas County, p. 33, Virginia Pounds Brown and Helen Morgan Akens, *Alabama Heritage* (Huntsville: Strode Publishers, 1967)

Early Roads into Alabama, p. 41, Reproduction of a page in Brown and Akens, *Alabama Heritage*

The Greater Tensaw Area, p. 51, The location of family homes as recorded on a map made by a military explorer around 1815 and now at the National Archives, superimposed on modern maps of the waterways

John Green, Sr., Nancy Betts Jones Green, and Bettie Lanier O'Brien, p. 55, Mary E. Brantley, *Early Settlers*

A McGuffey Reader, p. 62, William H. McGuffey, *The Eclectic First Reader, for Young Children* (Cincinnati: Truman and Smith, 1836)

Women in the Typical Dress of the 1840s, p. 67, Joan Severa, *Dressed for the Photographer: Ordinary Americans & Fashion, 1840-1900* (Kent, Ohio: Kent State University Press, 1995)

Rebuilt Gainestown School, p. 71, "Old Gainestown Schoolhouse," *Clarke County Historical Society Quarterly* 15 (summer 1990)

Washington Firehouse in Mobile, p. 80, Caldwell Delaney, *Remember Mobile* (Mobile: Haunted Bookshop, 1969)

Henry Hitchcock, p. 85, William Garrott Brown, *A History of Alabama for Use in Schools: Based as to Its Earlier Parts on the Work of Albert J. Pickett*, State History Series (New York: University Publishing Company, 1906)

Barton Academy, p. 90, Bama Wathan Watson, *The History of Barton Academy* (Mobile: Haunted Book Shop, 1971)

Daniel Chandler and Sarah Campbell Chandler, p. 94,

Alabama Portraits Prior to 1870, comp. Historical Activities Committee for the National Society of the Colonial Dames of America in the State of Alabama (Mobile: Gill Printing Company, 1969)

The Skipwith School, p. 116, An artist's interpretation of photographs of clothing from the period and Lucy Skipwith's descriptions in Randall M. Miller, *"Dear Master": Letters of a Slave Family* (Ithaca: Cornell University Press, 1978)

State Street African Methodist Episcopal (AME) Church, p. 117, Robert Gamble, *The Alabama Catalog: Historic American Buildings Survey, A Guide to the Early Architecture of the State* (Tuscaloosa: University of Alabama Press, 1987)

Black Mobilians' Residences and Institutions, p. 120, Adapted from a map in Alan Smith Thompson's "Mobile, Alabama, 1850-1861: Economic, Political, Physical, and Population Characteristics" (Ph.D. diss., University of Alabama, 1979)

A Township with the Sixteenth Section Shaded, p. 133, Ira W. Harvey, *A History of Educational Finance in Alabama* (Auburn, Ala.: Truman Pierce Institute for the Advancement of Teacher Education, 1989)

Arthur Pendleton Bagby, p. 138, *Alabama Portraits Prior to 1870*

Benjamin F. Porter, p. 141, Alabama Department of Archives and History.

House of Representatives' Chamber at the State Capitol in Tuscaloosa, p. 143, Gamble, *The Alabama Catalog*

Mobile's Waterfront, p. 156, *Harper's Weekly* drawing, March 1864

Home of a Working Family in Mobile, p. 162, Gamble, *The Alabama Catalog*

Gustavus Horton, p. 167, *Alabama Portraits Prior to 1870*

Members of the Creole Community, p. 168, Adapted from a photograph in the Chastang collection at the University of South Alabama Archives

Alexander Beaufort Meek, p. 178, *Alabama Portraits Prior to 1870*

Southwestern Legislators: Votes on the Free Public School Act, p. 180, Alabama General Assembly, *House Journal*, 4th biennial sess., 1853-1854 (Montgomery: Brittan and Blue, 1854) and Alabama General Assembly, *Senate Journal*, 4th biennial sess., 1853-1854 (Montgomery: Brittan and Blue, 1854)

William F. Perry, at Age 70, p. 190, Alabama Department of Archives and History

INDEX